The Rise and Fall of Dodgertown

UNIVERSITY PRESS OF FLORIDA

Florida A&M University, Tallahassee
Florida Atlantic University, Boca Raton
Florida Gulf Coast University, Ft. Myers
Florida International University, Miami
Florida State University, Tallahassee
New College of Florida, Sarasota
University of Central Florida, Orlando
University of Florida, Gainesville
University of North Florida, Jacksonville
University of South Florida, Tampa
University of West Florida, Pensacola

University Press of Florida

Gainesville ◆ Tallahassee ◆ Tampa ◆ Boca Raton

Pensacola ◆ Orlando ◆ Miami ◆ Jacksonville ◆ Ft. Myers ◆ Sarasota

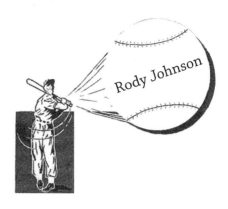

Rody Johnson

The Rise and Fall of

Dodgertown

To Johnny Walker
With best wish

[signature]

60 Years of Baseball in Vero Beach

Dodger-Male

3/11/08

13 12 11 10 09 08   6 5 4 3 2 1

Library of Congress Cataloging-in-Publication Data
Johnson, Rody.
The rise and fall of Dodgertown : 60 years of baseball in Vero Beach
/ Rody Johnson.
p. cm.
Includes bibliographical references and index.
ISBN 978-0-8130-3194-1 (alk. paper)
1. Holman Stadium (Vero Beach, Fla.)—History. 2. Brooklyn
Dodgers (Baseball team)—History. 3. Los Angeles Dodgers (Baseball
team)—History. 4. Spring training (Baseball)—Florida—Vero
Beach—History. I. Title.
GV416.V37J65 2008
796.357'640975928—dc22   2007027539

The University Press of Florida is the scholarly publishing agency
for the State University System of Florida, comprising Florida
A&M University, Florida Atlantic University, Florida Gulf Coast
University, Florida International University, Florida State
University, New College of Florida, University of Central Florida,
University of Florida, University of North Florida, University of
South Florida, and University of West Florida.

University Press of Florida
15 Northwest 15th Street
Gainesville, FL 32611-2079
http://www.upf.com

To Aunt Lil (Lillian Avis Harnsberger)

who gave me my love for baseball

Contents

Preface and Acknowledgments

I walked into Holman Stadium at Dodgertown in my hometown of Vero Beach, Florida, and sat down in the shade of the press box.

Lined up along third base in white and blue Dodger uniforms was the past: Duke Snider, Carl Erskine, Ralph Branca, and Clem Labine from the 1950s; Jeff Torborg and Maury Wills from the 1960s; and Tommy John, Steve Yeager, Reggie Smith, and Rick Monday from the 1970s.

The familiar voice of Dick Crago, Holman Stadium public address announcer since the '60s, introduced the old players. Each one stepped forward and tipped his hat to a smattering of applause from a thousand fans scattered around the stadium. This was the opening ceremony for a game between the Dodger greats and the fantasy camp players, a collection of men and a few women who come to Dodgertown from all over the United States to participate in the Dodger tradition.

The temperature was in the seventies; a few clouds dotted the sky. The American flag in center field rippled from a light easterly breeze. Though it was mid-February, this marked for me the beginning of the baseball season. In two weeks the big team would be here.

The stadium was cozy. The players sat in dugouts exposed to sun and fans. A grassy berm served as an outfield wall. On overflow days, people sit there on blankets. My wife, Katharine, said coming here was like going to a picnic in a park—the flowers, the royal palms, and the lake behind the stands. A visiting friend, seeing the players so close and the smallness of the stadium, compared the experience to going to a Little League game.

My Aunt Lil, a great fan, willed me her seats in section 17 for the exhibition games, five rows up from the Dodger bench and across the aisle from where the Dodger brass sits.

The Dodgers came to Vero in 1948, and I have watched them almost every spring since. The "Boys of Summer" Reese, Robinson, Snider, Campanella, Furillo, and Hodges—the team that would beat the Yankees in the 1955 World Series, came together here.

I loved this place called Dodgertown, as do my children. And now I bring my grandchildren here as well.

But things had changed in recent years. Beyond right field sat a two-story building where pine trees once stood. The building houses the offices for the Dodger management and the clubhouse for the major league players. It's an attractive building, but a reminder of what had happened to Dodger baseball.

The O'Malley paternalistic era ended with the sale to Rupert Murdoch and his Fox organization; corporate America took over. Dodgertown no longer belonged to the team. Using the threat of leaving Vero and moving to Arizona, Fox put Indian River County and the City of Vero Beach in a position where they had little choice but to buy the facility and lease it back to the team for nothing. But this was not the first time the love affair between the Dodgers and Vero Beach had been tested. In earlier days, availability of apartments created tensions, integration brought stresses, and the Federal Aviation Administration threatened to throw the Dodgers off airport property.

Indeed, Fox's decisions both on and off the field almost killed my love for the Dodgers, but there was hope. Fox would sell the team. The new owners, Frank and Jamie McCourt, would struggle to bring back stability, but at least they were a return to family ownership.

The Holman Stadium fans rose as former Brooklyn pitcher Carl Erskine played "The Star-Spangled Banner" on his harmonica. The hundred fantasy campers split into teams named for Dodger farm clubs and played one inning each against the old pros. Maury Wills led off and grounded weakly to the second baseman, who lobbed a throw to first. Steve Yeager scored the first run after hitting a single. The 1950 greats did not play. The two old buddies, Snider and Erskine, managed the Las Vegas team from the sidelines.

Between innings, I chatted with the white-haired Erskine, who seemed younger than his seventy-seven years. Growing up, I saw his picture in the papers, listened to Red Barber describing his pitching in the World Series, watched him practice at Dodgertown, read his book, and now here I was talking with him as if he were an old friend. He told me about renting a house in Vero in the '50s that his family shared with the Sniders.

One of the two ladies among the fantasy campers smacked a sharp line drive over Maury Wills' head and ran to first, her ponytail bobbing. Her hit was the highlight of the game.

I left after the third inning. The score had gotten out of hand; the greats were far ahead. I was ready for the spring exhibition season to begin.

At home, I hunted through my shelves for a book. The cover showed the caricature of a bum looking through the cracks in a ball park fence. This book, titled simply *The Dodgers*, covered in words and pictures the story of Brooklyn baseball from the late 1800s to 1948. On the pages were the inked autographs of Branch Rickey, Jackie Robinson, Roy Campanella, Gil Hodges, Duke Snider, and some of the old-timers who appeared in the initial days of Dodgertown, like Philadelphia A's manager Connie Mack, Hall of Famer George Sisler, and Pepper Martin of the 1930s St. Louis Cardinals Gas House Gang. I'd forgotten I had these autographs. This book should be worth a fortune. But then I remembered that I obtained these signatures on scorecards, programs, and random pieces of paper and then, as only a fifteen-year-old would do, meticulously traced the originals into my book. Looking at it again, after so many years, triggered an interest in me to delve into Dodger history.

I have had my own history with the team. I grew up with the Dodgers from the age of fourteen. Branch Rickey helped me pick out a catcher's mitt in my father's sporting goods store. By chance, I followed the Dodgers west. In the summer of 1958, when I married Katharine, a Californian, we sat in the bleachers of the cavernous Los Angeles Coliseum watching the Dodgers play the Chicago Cubs. Three years later, we moved to Orange County and were immersed in the California Space Age culture as the Dodgers began play in their new stadium in Chavez Ravine. By 1964, we were back in Vero Beach, raising our children in the vicinity of Dodgertown. Our youngest son Charlie, at age five, made friends with Dodger outfielder Dusty Baker, a friendship that lasted until Dusty left the Dodgers. On a business assignment and living temporarily in the San Francisco area, we followed the Giants and the Dodgers through a tight campaign in 1978. As a writer, many years later, I was given by the Dodgers a press pass and the opportunity to view spring training, not as a fan but as an insider.

As I thought about it, I realized the Dodgers had played longer in Holman Stadium than anyplace else, even longer than at Ebbets Field in Brooklyn, and, of course, longer than at Chavez Ravine in Los Angeles. Tradition and constancy were important in baseball. Dodgertown provided a tradition, a bridge between Brooklyn and Los Angeles. Yet the constancy had been threatened.

What follows is the unique story of the Brooklyn Dodgers, the Los Angeles Dodgers, the team's relationship with Vero Beach, and how all have changed.

Nancy Gollnick, assistant to Dodgertown vice president Craig Callan, guided me through the Dodgertown files of documents, newspaper clippings, and photographs. One of the finds in those files was a 1982 unpublished manuscript by Joe Hendrickson, a longtime observer of the Dodgers during spring training as the sports editor of the *Pasadena Star-News*. Other people at Dodgertown who helped me were Keith Smith, Louise Bossey, and Vero Beach Dodger secretary Betty Rollins. Lucy Marine, who served Dodgertown in many administrative capacities over the years, made suggestions and recommendations about information contacts.

Pam Cooper, supervisor of the Archive Center and Genealogy Department at the Indian River County Library, provided me opportunity to research old copies of the *Vero Beach Press Journal*, Dodgertown documents, and Vero Beach, Indian River County, and Naval Air Station history. The Indian River County Historical Society's file of Dodgertown photographs was useful.

A special acknowledgment must go to the Schuman family whose ownership of the *Vero Beach Press Journal*, even when it was a weekly, led to the amazing coverage of Dodgertown over the years.

Penny Chandler, executive director of the Indian River County Chamber of Commerce, gave me access to the chamber's files concerning the city's and the county's buyout of Dodgertown.

The Dodgers' public relations office graciously granted me a spring training working media press pass in 2004, 2005, and 2007. Tony Jackson, beat writer for the *L.A. Daily News*, gave me guidance on the protocol for accessing the clubhouse and the manager's office.

Mark Langill, Dodgers publications editor and team historian, read the early manuscript and provided photographs. Belinda Anderson's writing group in Lewisburg, West Virginia, read chapters and made recommendations. Grammarian Dolly Withrow assisted. J. J. Wilson, former professor of English at Sonoma State College, spent many hours reading and offering editing advice. My wife Katharine Johnson, with an artist's eye for detail, made critical and constructive comments. John Byram, editor-in-chief of the University Press of Florida, with patience and understanding, guided me through the final revisions and suggested format changes that strengthened the book. Copy editor Nevil Parker did an extraordinary job in finalizing the manuscript.

And finally my thanks to the people who gave their time to be interviewed. These individuals, including Dick Bird, Craig Callan, Dick Crago, Billy DeLury, Grace Goodermote, Bump Holman, Alma Lee Loy, Bobby McCarthy, Hugh McCrystal, Steve Mulvey, Norris Olson, Joe Sanchez, Helen Barber Stabile, and Milt Thomas—some with the Dodgers, some members of the Vero Beach community—all had special relationships with Dodgertown, which they were willing to share.

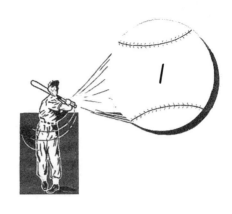

The Late Forties

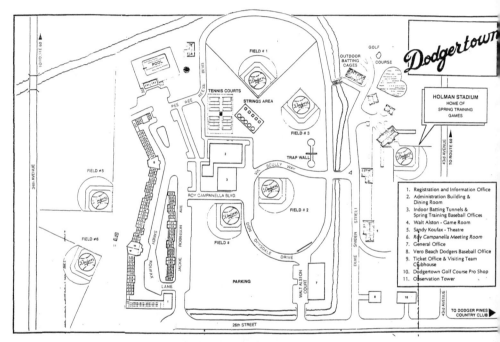

Dodgertown in the 1990s. The original Dodgertown consisted of fields #1, #2, and #3 and the barracks where the administration building (2) and the spring training baseball offices (3) (left center) are shown. The first game at Holman Stadium (right center) was in 1953. Dodgertown Golf Course, alongside Holman Stadium, opened for play in 1966. The villas (stretching from top to bottom left) replaced the barracks in the 1972, and the Dodger Pines Country Club course opened shortly thereafter. Fields #5 and #6 were added in back of the villas in the early 1990s. The new administration building/clubhouse (not shown but located beyond the Holman Stadium right field berm) was built in 2003. As indicated, streets are named for Dodger Hall of Famers. (Courtesy of Los Angeles Dodgers, Vero Beach, Florida.)

Brooklyn Dodgers Select Vero

1945

Rickey and Robinson

A conversation took place in Brooklyn on August 18, 1945, that would impact major league baseball, race relations on a national scale, and the small town of Vero Beach, Florida. Branch Rickey, president of the Brooklyn Dodgers, and Jackie Robinson met in the Dodger offices and had a chat, immortalized in every book written about the two men.

"You were brought here to play for the Brooklyn organization," said Branch Rickey, "to start with our top farm team, the Montreal Royals."

Robinson looked amazed. He thought he had been invited to discuss playing for a Negro team that Rickey was forming.

"Yes, if you can make it," continued Rickey, "you'll have a chance with the Brooklyn Dodgers. We need ballplayers. We've scouted you for weeks. Do you have the guts and what it takes to make it?"

"Mr. Rickey, I'll make it, if I get the opportunity," insisted Robinson.

"Wonderful. You're a real pioneer, and this whole experiment depends on you."[1]

Branch Rickey's momentous decision to desegregate baseball came one year before President Truman desegregated the United States Armed Forces and seven years before the Supreme Court banned racial segregation in the public schools.

A Small Florida Town

Two weeks before Rickey and Robinson met, the Japanese surrendered to end World War II. Like communities all over America, Vero Beach celebrated the victory. The city with its population of 3,600 contained a four-block downtown built during the 1920s Florida boom. Vero was the

Jackie Robinson and Branch Rickey sign a contract that makes Jackie the first black player in major league baseball. (Courtesy of Los Angeles Dodgers, Los Angeles, California.)

county seat for Indian River County, situated on the central east coast of Florida. The county was known for its citrus, the McKee Jungle Gardens, and its motto, "Where the tropics begin." A wooden bridge crossed the mile-wide Indian River and connected Vero to a narrow island and the beach front along the Atlantic Ocean. Citrus groves, cattle land, and marshes spread to the west. The railroad with direct service to New York and Chicago and the Old Dixie Highway (U.S. 1) ran along the edge of downtown. The closest city with any kind of population was West Palm Beach, seventy-five miles to the south. Vero Beach had changed little over the years except for the air base established during the war.[2]

Dive bombers and fighter planes flew overhead, landing and taking off from the Vero Beach Naval Air Station along the north side of town. The airfield had been built through the foresight of Bud Holman, who came

Vero Beach, Florida, as it looked in 1947. Route 60 runs east from the bottom of the frame through the center of town. Indian River and the Atlantic Ocean are visible at the upper left. The Vero Beach Naval Air Base lies to the left, outside the photograph. (Courtesy of Indian River County Historical Society, Vero Beach, Florida.)

to Vero in the 1920s and established an automobile dealership. Holman arranged for Eastern Airlines to stop and refuel on their flights down the Florida Coast. In the 1930s, Eastern began carrying passengers into Vero, making it the smallest city in the United States with regular air service. When the war came, so did the Navy, expanding the airfield to two thousand acres and constructing a training facility for three thousand personnel. Bud Holman, the air base, and Rickey and Robinson would be the main ingredients for bringing the Brooklyn Dodgers to Vero Beach.

1946

Jackie Joins the Dodgers

Jackie Robinson joined the Montreal Royals in spring training with the Brooklyn Dodgers at Daytona Beach. When Jackie and his bride, Rachel, arrived, Branch Rickey was there to greet them. "For me," Rachel said, "Branch Rickey became a familiar source of comfort. . . . When he crouched down by first base in spring training waving his hat and shouting at Jack, 'Be daring, be daring,' my spirit embraced them both with pride."[3]

During Jackie's first spring in Florida, trouble came quickly. In an exhibition game at Deland, a policeman came out on the field and ordered him to leave. "No nigger don't play with white boys," he said. "Get off the field right now, or you're going to jail." Jackie walked off the field as his teammates watched.[4]

The Montreal Royals headed north, attempting to play exhibition games along the way. They found the ball park padlocked in Jacksonville. Local officials canceled games in Savannah and Richmond. Signs on the ball parks said "Whites Only."

Branch Rickey hadn't realized the situation would be that bad. He determined that the Dodgers would have to train out of the country in the future. It would be a while before Rickey discovered the vacant naval air base at Vero Beach.

Jackie Robinson enjoyed a spectacular season with the Montreal Royals. He hit .349 and stole forty bases. The Royals drew a million fans, most coming to see Jackie. But it hadn't been easy. The Baltimore team refused to play against him. The league president told them to take the field or be suspended. They took the field.

1947

A Nasty Season

The next spring the Dodgers and Montreal trained in Havana. Don Newcombe and Roy Campanella, both signed by Branch Rickey, joined Jackie Robinson on the Montreal team. Despite not being in Florida, the three black men lived in a hotel separate from their white teammates and several miles away from the ball park. But Branch Rickey wanted all his players together in one location.

On an exhibition tour in Panama, some of the white players objected to Jackie being on the team. Manager Leo Durocher quelled the rebellion with some strong words: "I don't care if the guy is yellow or black, or if he has stripes like a f'n zebra. I'm the manager of this team and I say he plays. What's more, I say he can make us all rich."[5]

Leo Durocher was soon gone, however. Baseball commissioner Happy Chandler suspended him for some current and past sins, including throwing a towel in an umpire's face, punching a fan, and marrying Hollywood movie star Laraine Day in Mexico before her divorce was final, contrary to the laws of California.[6] Both this Leo business and Jackie Robinson would generate some drama in Vero Beach a year later.

On April 15, 1947, the *New York Times* reported: "Jackie Robinson, 28-year-old infielder, yesterday became the first Negro to achieve major league status in modern times." Branch Rickey had signed Jackie to a major league contract.

When the 1947 season started, things turned nasty. The Phillies came to Ebbets Field and taunted Jackie, knowing that he couldn't fight back. "Hey coon. Hey darkie. You smell. Go pick cotton."[7] The Cardinals threatened not to take the field against the Dodgers. National League president Ford Frick said he would suspend them all. In Cincinnati with insults being screamed, Pee Wee Reese, another southerner, walked over to Jackie and put an arm around his shoulders.[8] Meanwhile, Jackie and the Dodgers played baseball and, despite the distractions, won the National League pennant. Jackie became the Rookie of the Year. The Dodgers drew 1.8 million fans, a new record for Ebbets Field as blacks and whites sat side by side for the first time. In the 1947 World Series, the Yankees beat the Dodgers four games to three.

An Empty Air Base

With the war over, Vero Beach began to boom. Local building permits hit $1.3 million in 1947. Talk spread of a modern bridge to replace the wooden one across the Indian River and of a new shopping center. Dredging began for Vero Isles, the city's first waterfront development.

At the same time, the federal government returned the Vero Beach Naval Air Station to the city with one stipulation: proceeds from any lease or sale of property must be placed in a special fund for the maintenance and development of flight facilities. After some deliberation, the city council leased the airport to Bud Holman to manage. Holman became responsible for the entire facility, including the flight-line operations. He would pay the city a rental fee of one dollar per year plus a percentage of his operating profits.[9] After all, if it hadn't been for Bud Holman, the airport never would have existed in the first place, and there would be no Eastern Airlines service.

Some people thought Holman had shouldered a white elephant. He was responsible for two thousand acres, sixty miles of streets, four runways, and hundreds of buildings. He would have the authority to sublease what he could, but the potential within the Vero Beach area, even with the postwar boom, seemed limited. There had been suggestions of an air college or maybe an old peoples' home.

Then someone mentioned baseball. Major league teams had trained in Florida since the early 1900s. They had farm clubs and lots of players. A team could fill some of those empty barracks at the airport. The quarters weren't fancy, but they had been good enough for Navy fighter pilots. And one team, the Brooklyn Dodgers, didn't seem to have a permanent, spring training home and had twenty-six farm teams and lots of players.

The Dodgers first came to Florida for spring training at Jacksonville in 1907. Until 1941 they trained at Daytona Beach, Clearwater, Miami, and Orlando, with brief interludes in Hot Springs, Arkansas; Augusta, Georgia; and New Orleans. Their longest stay was at Clearwater from 1923 to 1932 and then again from 1936 to 1940. They trained in Havana in 1941 and 1942, spent the war years at Bear Mountain, New York, moved to Daytona in '46 and Havana in '47, and were committed to going to the Dominican Republic in 1948.[10]

The Dodger minor leaguers had trained at Sanford, Florida, and at a naval air station in Pensacola during the two years after the war. The Dodgers were looking for a site for the spring of 1948.

Vero Finds the Dodgers

The best story of how the Dodgers and Vero Beach got together comes from an unpublished manuscript by Joe Hendrickson in the Dodgertown files. As sports editor of the *Pasadena Star-News*, Hendrickson spent many years covering the Dodgers during spring training, so his book is a treasure of firsthand information and Dodgertown tales.

Branch Rickey wanted a site in Florida where all his players could benefit from a baseball college atmosphere. He had seven hundred players under contract. He believed the war would soon end, and, while other teams did little or no recruiting, he signed players. He needed a place where he could bring all these young men together, a place where they would improve their skills to surpass those of other teams' players. But most importantly, he wanted a place where his black players would be comfortable and not have to live in a segregated setting.[11]

Rickey's daughter heard about Vero Beach and said something to her father. Eddie Rickenbacker, president of Eastern Airlines, picked up the information and told Bud Holman, a director of the airline, that Branch Rickey was looking. Holman discussed the situation with soon-to-be-mayor Merrill Barber, who said, "Let's ask Rickey to come here and have a look."[12] During his time as mayor and even later, Merrill Barber would be an important factor in Vero Beach's relationship with the Dodgers. As a young man, Mr. Barber had once managed the city baseball team.

As Bud Holman's son Bump later explained, "My dad didn't know first base from second base, but he got on an Eastern flight out of Vero headed for New York."[13] Bud Holman had an appointment with one of the most famous men in baseball, Branch Rickey.

Rickey came to Vero with an aide, Spencer Harris. According to Bump, this occurred the next day after his father's visit. Rickey and Harris liked what they saw and worked out a preliminary proposal to bring their players to Vero. Both must have been visionaries to see in that abandoned air base a baseball college.

But Rickey wanted to do some further investigation. He sent another aide, Buzzie Bavasi, the young general manager of the Nashua farm club, to look over the situation. He arrived in Vero on November 2, 1947. "When I got off the train," he said, "I took the only cab in town and went to the naval base. There were weeds all over the place. The barracks looked awful from the outside, but they were better when I saw them from the inside. I recommended that we take it."[14] The Dodgers had looked at Daytona Beach, Sanford, Pensacola, and even at El Centro in California, but decided Vero was the best site. Bavasi was supposed to make a final check and see facilities at Fort Pierce and Stuart, but Holman wouldn't let him get away. He invited Bavasi to a "stag" party at the Holman ranch, thirty miles west of town on Blue Cypress Lake. "The other places," said Bavasi, "were trying to sell us something. Vero Beach was trying to give us something."[15]

The Brooklyn Dodgers and the City of Vero Beach quietly reached an agreement. The baseball team would pay one dollar a year to lease the necessary facilities plus donate the gate receipts from one exhibition game to the city's airport fund. In addition, the team would upgrade the buildings they needed and prepare playing fields for the farm teams. The major league club was already set to train in the Dominican Republic in the spring of 1948, but they would play two games against the Montreal farm team in Vero.

Despite Bud Holman's flying off to New York and the Dodger brass' coming to town to inspect and negotiate, nothing appeared in the local paper. How could all this activity occur in a small town like Vero without everyone knowing about it? John Schuman, owner and publisher of the weekly *Vero Beach Press Journal*, may have suppressed the news until the two sides reached a final agreement.

What no one knew at the time was that major league baseball would become a major factor in the Vero Beach economy. The community reacted with surprise when they read the *Press Journal's* headline on December 12, 1947: "Brooklyn Dodgers Select Vero For Spring Training."

2

The Future of the
Brooklyn Baseball Team Is Here

1948

Call It Dodgertown

After the announcement that the Dodgers were coming, the team and Bud Holman had less than two months to turn the run-down Vero Beach Naval Air Station into a baseball facility. Four hundred and fifty ballplayers would arrive in February. Branch Rickey appointed Spencer Harris, an official in the minor league organization, camp director. Ebbets Field groundskeeper, Eddie Durham, arrived to oversee the development of the playing fields.

The two officers' quarters—wood-framed, two-story buildings sitting on concrete blocks—had been painted. A central building between the officers' quarters was modified to include offices, a dining room, and recreation facilities. An expedition went to Banana River Air Station at Cape Canaveral to collect surplus furniture. Groundskeeper Durham built two practice fields in back of the dormitories. He constructed a field with bleachers, named Ebbets Field #2, and another practice field in vacant lots behind the Eastern Airlines passenger terminal, the former Navy control tower. Durham brought in a load of Georgia red clay to mix with the Florida sand to improve the consistency of the infields. Almost overnight, a baseball college or, perhaps more accurately, a baseball factory appeared among the orange trees and pines. One of the New York sportswriters suggested calling the place Dodgertown, and the name stuck.

Behind the old two-story Navy barracks, baseball fields, batting cages, practice pitching mounds, and sliding pits appeared. Baseball players were everywhere. Branch Rickey, in his straw hat and bow tie, stood on

Work is in progress on the baseball fields behind the old Navy barracks as Dodgertown begins to take shape. (Courtesy of Indian River County Historical Society, Vero Beach, Florida.)

an elevated platform, watching his minor league charges perform. Players hit balls from the batting machines, threw at the pitching targets made of string, learned the art of base running in the sliding pits, and took infield practice on the diamonds. Signs on the roads at Dodgertown read Flatbush Avenue, Rickey Boulevard, and Durocher Trail. Leo, his one-year suspension over, again managed the Dodgers. Fans sat on bleachers watching the activity. The crack of bats, the voices of the coaches, the chatter of the infielders swept across the fields, all under a sunny, blue sky. The air smelled of freshly cut grass from the perfectly manicured infields and of orange blossoms from the nearby citrus trees. This was heaven. The atmosphere of that time, over fifty years ago, still exists there today.

All these activities proceeded according to some master schedule. The faculty, led by Branch Rickey, included his son, Branch Rickey Jr. (known as "the Twig"); Burt Shotton (interim manager during Durocher's suspension); Hall of Fame member, George Sisler; Pepper Martin, formerly of the Cardinal Gas House Gang; and coaches Fresco Thompson, Al Campanis, and Walt Alston, among others. (Thompson, Alston, and Campanis would assume more important roles with the team in later years.) It was easy to recognize the coaches. Carrying clipboards, they wore satin uniforms left over from the early days of night baseball at Ebbets Field. They evaluated two hundred pitchers, forty shortstops, and countless others for every position. Each player wore a number and a specifically colored uniform, indicating his level of play.

Branch Rickey started the morning by giving an hour's lecture in the base's old auditorium. He expected the players to take notes. Mr. Rickey

Branch Rickey inspects the form of one of his pitchers. Vero photographer Wally Skisim shoots the picture, with the barracks in the background. (Photograph by author.)

talked about achieving perfection, moving to the majors faster, making the dream come true sooner.

> We must take pains in order to bring about perfection. One of the purposes of this camp—and it's really a school—is to bring you along as rapidly as possible. . . . The average major leaguer was in the minors three to four years. We are trying to make your dream come true earlier. We are developing a system that will bring every hidden player potential to the surface. . . . We will do our best, but what is your contribution? It is you who must make the main effort. The future of the Brooklyn baseball team is here.[1]

After Mr. Rickey's talks, Al Campanis led the players in calisthenics behind the barracks on field #2.

Outfielders Duke Snider and Pete Reiser were in camp, although the big team was still in the Dominican Republic. Duke was there to work on

Rookie outfielder Duke Snider waits for his turn in the batting cage. (Photograph by author.)

his hitting, Pete presumably to work out at first base. But the real reason revolved around Pete's wife joining him in the Dominican Republic, contrary to team policy. The easy solution was to send him and his wife back to Vero.[2] In their Dodger-gray road uniforms, the two major leaguers stood out from the mass of minor leaguers.

The farm teams played exhibition games at Ebbets Field #2. Low wooden bleachers stretched down the first and third base lines. There was no outfield fence, just open space. In the afternoons, the Fort Worth Cats played the Yankees' farm teams, the Kansas City Blues, or the Memphis Chicks. The Montreal team was still in the Dominican Republic, training with the Dodgers.

Sportswriters flocked to Dodgertown. Tom Meany, a New York writer announced, "Mass production and the human assembly line have come to baseball."[3] Jimmy Powers wrote in the *New York Daily News*: "Vero Beach is much farther north than Miami, as a result too decent, and too quiet for the hoodlum element to bother with. Its streets are clean. Its citizens are highly respectable. It has great civic spirit. There is no gambling. No corrupt police or county officers."[4]

A *Life* magazine cover photograph showed the upturned faces of a mass of Dodger rookies. Inside, a four-page spread pictured the players at work, overseen by "the parsimonious panjandrum" as the magazine tagged Branch Rickey.[5] Vero Beach was overwhelmed by the exposure.

Boy Scout Rules

While the production line at Dodgertown ran smoothly, the living facilities lacked some amenities. Danny Ozark, then a minor league player and later a Dodger coach, Phillies manager, and Vero Beach resident, said, "We slept six in a room in the barracks. It was a lot like the army."[6]

All players at Dodgertown were required to observe regulations, posted on the barracks walls, that would make a boy scout camp proud. There was, of course, no smoking, no gambling, no drinking of intoxicating liquors, and no horseplay in the showers. In addition, players were admonished to take their cleats off in the building, to have lights out at 11 p.m., to keep their rooms neat, and not to litter. To conserve food, players were told to take all they wanted, but to eat what they took. They were also asked to pick the fruit in the grove across the street, but to leave that on the trees around the buildings for decorative effect. The regulations concluded: "We are the guests of the city of Vero Beach. It is a small city but full of big people. . . . They have shown the extreme in hospitality. . . . Let's continue to make Vero Beach citizens proud of DODGERTOWN and every individual in the Brooklyn organization."[7]

The barrack's paper-thin walls meant that indoor temperatures varied little from those outside, which could range from the forties in mid-February to the eighties in early April. When someone plugged in an electric heater, the circuits blew. The cots were hard. The plumbing leaked. Palmetto bugs, called cockroaches by those uninitiated to Florida living, shared the accommodations. In the players' off hours, though, they enjoyed extensive recreation facilities: shuffleboard, croquet, a jukebox, pinball machines, pool tables, and evening movies. If those weren't sufficient entertainment, they could walk the mile and a half into town to the Florida Theater to see the likes of Lash LaRue in *Pioneer Justice* or Bud Abbott and Lou Costello in *Buck Private Comes Home*.

Like the Navy airmen who came to Vero before them, the Dodger baseball players found themselves in a small town with three restaurants (the only one of distinction being the Rose Garden Tea Room), four bars, a pool hall, a movie theater, a bowling alley, a roller skating rink, and ten churches as listed in the base recreation guide. Navy personnel quickly rechristened the town "Zero Beach."[8] Little had changed five years later when six hundred Dodger personnel arrived to live in quarters built for three hundred officers.

Vero pioneer Waldo Sexton helped spruce up the administration building by donating some of the old furniture he had accumulated from South Florida mansions during the depression. Sexton had arrived in Vero in 1914 from Indiana. He acquired land and planted citrus groves and participated in the development of the Royal Park Golf Course area and the McKee Jungle Gardens. He then built the Driftwood Inn, the Patio restaurant in town, and the Ocean Grill restaurant on the beach.

Mr. Sexton's daughter, Barbara Tripson, told a story about her mother and father inviting Mr. and Mrs. Rickey to dinner at their house west of town. The men talked at one end of the table, the women at the other end.

Mr. Rickey said, "Waldo, you don't give a damn about baseball." Waldo acknowledged that was true. He knew even less about baseball than Bud Holman but was impressed by the number of players and farm clubs training in Vero.

Waldo's wife, Elsabeth, overheard the reference to a farm team. She asked Mr. Rickey, "With all the time your players spend practicing baseball, when do they farm?"[9]

The Big Team Arrives

On March 30, a Pan American clipper landed at the Vero airport, bringing the Dodger team to play their first exhibition game at Dodgertown. The plane almost didn't make it. The four-engine DC-4 experienced engine trouble in flight and turned back to the Dominican Republic. With the team safely back on the ground, the airline announced a delay in getting new equipment. The first Dodger game in Vero with all its hoopla stood in jeopardy. Buzzie Bavasi, in charge of travel arrangements, threatened to have Bud Holman call Eddie Rickenbacker and have Eastern Airlines come down and pick up the team. Pan Am quickly rerouted a plane, and the Dodgers arrived in Vero as planned.[10]

Local citizens and dignitaries greeted the team. The Dodgers came down the gangway and walked toward the terminal, the old Vero Naval Air Station control tower. Movie star Laraine Day, demurely dressed in a knee-length skirt and white high heels, attracted the most attention. Her husband, manager Leo Durocher, followed her.[11]

Four Air Force A-20 attack bombers, piloted by members of the Brooklyn National Guard, flew in to participate in the celebration. The

Mayor Merrill Barber, Branch Rickey, and Florida governor Millard Caldwell await the arrival of the Brooklyn Dodgers. The Vero Beach High School Band is assembled in the background. (Courtesy of Indian River County Historical Society, Vero Beach, Florida.)

Vero Beach Jaycees presented them with loads of oranges to take back home.[12] Dodger director and stockholder Walter O'Malley, his wife Kay, and their young son Peter arrived from Brooklyn on the Dodgers' Beechcraft.

Leo and the Commissioner Make Up

At a reception for dignitaries before the game at the Riomar Club on Vero's beach, Branch Rickey told Florida governor Millard Caldwell that the Dodgers were the "best bet" for the pennant because of the team's speed. Durocher, tongue in cheek, suggested that "best bet" was an inappropriate term. It reflected gambling, and the commissioner wouldn't like that. Rickey had told Durocher earlier in the morning to be "nice" to Commissioner Chandler. Chandler, reflecting on his suspension of Durocher the previous year, had quoted the Bible, saying, "There is more rejoicing over one who has strayed and returned that for the other ninety-nine."[13]

More than five thousand fans attended the first game ever played by a major league team in Vero Beach. Tickets cost $1.50 for box seats (with folding chairs), $1.25 for the bleachers, and fifty cents for children. The *Press Journal* said that it was "probably the biggest day in the history of Vero Beach" and the "largest crowd ever to assemble for any event in this city."[14] In addition, the town was "all a twitter" over Laraine Day.

Mayor Merrill Barber, local attorney Sherman Smith, and Chamber of Commerce president Bill Wodtke arranged the welcoming. WIRA (Wonderful Indian River Area) broadcast the festivities and the game live, sponsored by the Indian River Citrus Bank, Wodtke's Department Store, and Roland Miller Chevrolet. The Vero Beach High School Band in their red and white uniforms tooted vigorously.

Dignitaries addressed the crowd. Baseball commissioner and former Kentucky senator A. B. "Happy" Chandler said, "With the spirit of baseball and the help of God, this country can solve its problems."[15] Spencer Harris, the "mayor" of Dodgertown, praised the people of Vero Beach for their cooperation with the Dodgers. Florida governor Millard Caldwell threw out the first ball. Bud Holman probably stood quietly in the background, knowing that of all the people there, he was most responsible for this event.

With Commissioner Chandler and Leo Durocher in the same group, an air of tension persisted. A few weeks earlier when Leo's suspension expired, Chandler said to Rickey about rehiring him as manager, "Do as you damn well please." And Rickey, much to the chagrin of fellow Dodger directors Walter O'Malley and John Smith, did just that.

It would be Mayor Barber who had a part in making peace between Leo and Happy. "After the ceremonies on the infield," said Barber, "I walked with Chandler to the sidelines. I steered him to third base where Mr. Rickey had Durocher stationed. Chandler and Durocher had to shake hands. I believe Happy said, 'Good luck, Leo,' and Leo replied, 'Thank you, Commissioner.'"[16]

A photo in the *Press Journal* depicted Happy and Leo shaking hands as Mayor Barber and Branch Rickey looked on.[17] Local photographer Wally Skisim shot the picture, which also ran in the *Sporting News*. Wally served as a Navy photographer at the local air base, remained in Vero Beach after the war, married a local girl, and started Skisim's Photo.

Jackie Hits a Home Run

The souvenir scorecard for the first game included half-page ads for many Vero Beach businesses interspersed with pictures of the community. The only full-page ad with "Best Wishes from Fans and Friends of Jackie Robinson" showed a picture of the first baseman. On either side of the picture, residents from the black community of Gifford listed their names.[18]

When the opening festivities ended, the Dodgers took the field with a lineup that included Jackie Robinson, Pete Reiser, and Pee Wee Reese, with Gil Hodges catching and rookie Jack Banta pitching.

With a bleacher capacity of only 1,200, most of the fans stood. The dignitaries sat in box seats, which were actually folding chairs in an area sectioned off by two-by-fours. Local resident Dale Talbert recalled, as a boy, sitting on his bicycle by the bridge at the entrance to the airport watching cars and trucks full of blacks going to the game. The blacks stood in a segregated area around the periphery of the outfield. The *Press Journal* reported: "Jackie Robinson, colored first baseman, got the game underway when he rammed the second pitched ball out into a crowd of colored spectators, standing where the left field wall would ordinarily be, and the hit was chalked up as a homer."[19]

When Pete Reiser also hit a homer into the outfield fans, the umpires had changed the ground rules, and they waved Pistol Pete back to second with a double. In Brooklyn's Ebbets Field, Carl Furillo played in the outfield with a forty-foot wall behind him in right field. In Vero, he could

An overflow crowd jams the bleachers at Ebbets Field #2 for the Brooklyn Dodgers' first game in Vero Beach. (Courtesy of Indian River County Historical Society, Vero Beach, Florida.)

have chased a fly ball across a road and into what would later be the Piper Aircraft plant parking lot.

The Dodgers beat Montreal 5–4. Duke Snider replaced Reiser in center field. Roy Campanella played in his first game in a Dodger uniform, substituting for Hodges as catcher in the late innings. Leo constantly harassed umpire Jesse Collyer, trying to get himself thrown out of the game so he could take his wife, Laraine, to Miami for the evening. But Collyer, who worked at Sing Sing prison in New York State and would be a fixture at Dodgertown for many springs, would have none of it.[20]

Laraine Day, the stunningly lovely movie star, did not like the "suite" in the Dodgertown barracks where she and Leo were housed. She called a cab (still the only one in town) and moved quickly over to the beach to the Windswept Hotel, which had been spruced up since serving as quarters for the Navy WAVES during the war. Leo followed her. Mr. Rickey was not pleased. Buzzie Bavasi, in his own version of the story, joked, "Laraine didn't like the barracks' wire hangers. She wanted wooden ones."[21]

The Dodgers played Montreal again the next day, winning 8–2, and then headed north. Sportswriter Tom Meany wrote: "This pleasant resort town succumbed to the Dodgers in mass."[22]

Branch Rickey said before leaving Dodgertown, "I hope we can return next year with the big team working out too. Maybe we can have a swimming pool."[23] Bud Holman immediately began a drive to get one.

A Bad Deal

During the 1948 season, Branch Rickey brought up Duke Snider and Roy Campanella from the minor leagues and basically established the team that would dominate the National League. However, trouble developed between manager Leo Durocher and Rickey. Durocher resigned and became the manager of the New York Giants. With this troubling situation, the Dodgers finished in third place. Meanwhile, the relationship between the Dodgers and Vero almost fell apart over a real estate arrangement. To accommodate married staff and reporters, the Dodgers wanted to rent apartments on the base near Dodgertown during the coming spring. Local realtor Charles Kuster, who handled the apartments, agreed but then reneged on the deal. Branch Rickey and Spencer Harris flew to Vero but left with no solution. Bud Holman, in his direct manner, asked what the apartments were worth and offered to buy the buildings for $52,000. His action sparked a citizens' committee to arrange temporary housing for the regular apartment dwellers while the Dodgers stayed in town. The crisis ended.[24]

In the spring of 1949, the Brooklyn Dodgers would train not in Havana, not in the Dominican Republic, but at Dodgertown, Vero Beach, Florida.

Branch Rickey's Kingdom by the Sea

1949

The Love Affair Begins

Early in the year, the *Press Journal* reported that with the construction of the causeway across the Indian River about to start, "rapid development of the beach is likely to follow in this most natural beautiful setting and Vero will become one of the largest beach resorts in the state." The article proclaimed the virtues of Dodgertown—"the largest baseball training camp in the world, publicity worth thousands of dollars being received by Vero Beach, plus the beautiful new ($10,000) pool." Also, the pool and other improvements would be paid for from the proceeds of certain exhibition games at no expense to the taxpayers. The Dodgers painted the barracks silver and blue, built a locker room for the team, and added a Teletype room, a dining room, and a lounge for the press.[1]

This year, the team would train at Dodgertown for two weeks and play four games there. They would play the balance of their home exhibition games in Miami, where they could draw bigger crowds.

The sportswriters flocked to Vero for the initial team workouts. The representatives of the ten New York papers stayed at Dodgertown. It wasn't like the previous spring when the big team came for just a couple of days.

Writer Frank Graham described the activity: "Shrill blasts of whistles in the barracks wake the players. By nine the players are at their battle stations, the wives are knitting or gabbing and the children are romping under the trees or at the swimming pool. The pitchers are at the strings; the batters are at the different pitching machines. Branch Rickey sits on a stool back of the batting tees wearing a pork pie hat that usually he wears only on fishing trips. He is watching, commenting, advising, questioning, criticizing, and applauding."[2]

Columnist Dan Parker called Dodgertown "Branch Rickey's kingdom-by-the-sea."[3]

Red Smith wrote about the orders of the day—some four to five pages prepared after the night staff meeting, where the coaches and Mr. Rickey evaluated the performance of each player in camp. Smith heard one wisecracker say that in the middle of a tight ball game at Ebbets Field a whistle was going to blow and the whole team would march to right field and start sliding practice.[4]

The regular New York writers enjoyed their own lounge in the barracks and, later in the evenings, Waldo Sexton's Ocean Grill, which they called the "swingiest spot on the beach."[5]

But Vero's most wonderful resource, its beach, was off limits to the Dodgers. An undertow caught rookie Bobby Morgan and started taking him out to sea. Outfielder Gene Hermanski rescued him.[6] Mr. Rickey decided to take no further chances with the team's investments.

Tommy Lasorda, then a young minor league pitcher and the Dodger manager thirty years later, arrived at Dodgertown for the first time in 1949. He told about the experience in his autobiography, *The Artful Dodger*. It was late at night. Everyone in the barracks had settled in. He was shown a room. He received only one blanket and almost froze to death during his first night in Florida. At six a.m. a whistle blew, and he jumped out of bed, washed, and headed for the cafeteria. As he approached, he heard the low roar of many voices. He entered and looked around, awed at the six hundred men talking over breakfast. When he discovered that two hundred were pitchers, he told Fresco Thompson that he wanted to leave. He didn't have a chance. He wanted to get married and needed a job. Fresco wouldn't let him go.[7]

Tommy Lasorda remembered Mr. Rickey's instructions: "Run after fly balls and not women, avoid alligators, stay sober, work hard, get plenty of rest, and attend church on Sunday."[8]

Fresco Thompson took responsibility for keeping the young players "in line for their own good." He patrolled the barracks to insure that they did not break curfew. He once chased a player up a ladder to the barracks roof where the offender jumped from two stories up and went limping off into the orange groves. No one could be found with a limp the next day.[9]

After a cloud burst one morning, Fresco called off practice for the day because the fields "oozed mud." He was concerned for the safety of the players on such a field. Mr. Rickey arrived just as the sun popped out. He raised hell with Fresco. He didn't want to waste a day. Mr. Rickey took off his shoes, rolled up his pants, grabbed a broom, and with his cigar in his mouth, tried to sweep the water off the infield.[10]

Race Becomes an Issue

The Dodgers came to Vero so that they could train in a contained place like Dodgertown, where the black players could be comfortable despite being in the South. Rachel Robinson, Jackie's wife, did not find it a comfort. When she wanted to have her hair done, she knew that it would have to be in Gifford, the black community to the north of Vero.[11]

Rachel remembered calling a cab to take her there. When it arrived, the taxi driver told her it was a "white cab" and gave her the telephone number for the "colored cab." Rachel and her three-year-old son Jackie Junior sat on the grass in front of the Dodgertown administration building waiting. An empty bus with broken windows pulled up. After realizing that this was the cab, she and Jackie got on board. The bus swung by the swimming pool with the wives of the white players and their children sitting in the sun, enjoying themselves. Little Jackie stuck his head out the window and waved. Rachel would declare later how humiliated she felt.

Jackie Robinson said of Dodgertown, "It was like being confined to a reservation, and it was the only reason we were quartered along with the whites. That too was difficult for Rea (Rachel). Her relationships with the other wives were tense and uncomfortable for her and for them. She didn't know how to relate to them, and they quite clearly did not know how to relate to her."[12] But with time she did make friends with the other Dodger wives. Buzzie Bavasi said of Rachel: "She was one of the most remarkable women I'd ever met. She was straightforward, honest, and beautiful."[13]

Racial incidents in Vero because of the Dodgers were nonexistent as far as the local community knew. But many years later, Helen Barber, daughter of mayor Merrill Barber, talked about some kind of racial incident that had required an emergency meeting of her father, Don Newcombe, Jackie Robinson, Branch Rickey, and, she thought, the local judge and the police chief. A teenager at the time, Barber didn't recall the

Jackie Robinson is ready for practice as the Dodgers train at Dodgertown in 1949. The previous year, he hit the first home run in the first game played by the Dodgers in Vero Beach. (Photograph by author.)

details, just that Don Newcombe had gotten in some kind of trouble.[14] Sports editor Joe Hendrickson filled in particulars.

Don, who had spent the previous season at Montreal, was trying to win a spot on the Dodger pitching staff. The Philadelphia A's came to Vero for an exhibition game. Their catcher, Mike Guerra, a white Cuban, had managed Havana where Newcombe played one winter. At the time, Guerra had questioned Newcombe's ability and sent him home. Newcombe had always felt Guerra's decision was racially motivated: "When I saw him show up in Vero Beach, I blew my cool. I yelled at him and we started a fight. This riled some fans who thought a black man was overstepping his rights. I was accused of attacking a white man."

Branch Rickey, attempting to quell any further trouble, called a five a.m. meeting at his house at Dodgertown. Present were Merrill Barber,

Rickey, Buzzie Bavasi, Fresco Thompson, and four black players, Don Newcombe, Jackie Robinson, Roy Campanella, and Sam Jethroe who later played with the Braves. Rickey opened the meeting by saying, "Mayor Barber, I wish to discuss the incident which took place during yesterday's game. The blacks have a great future in baseball. However, had this incident caused a riot, we would have suffered a serious setback." Don Newcombe admitted he had lost his temper.

Trying to make sense of things for his buddy, Roy Campanella added, "Newk, if you want to go back to New Jersey and run an elevator that's up to you. Campy likes it here in Vero Beach, being a member of the Brooklyn Dodgers. I'm going along with the way the people in the South want us to do." Jackie Robinson added, "Mr. Rickey and Mr. Barber, we want you to know you'll have no more trouble." Newcombe promised to control his temper.[15]

In 1949, Jackie, with Branch Rickey's encouragement, began to show his competitiveness and started asserting himself on the field. It began at Dodgertown during an intrasquad game. The two teams were ribbing each other. Jackie got a single and hooted at minor league pitcher Chris Van Cuyk. The next time up, Van Cuyk brushed him back with a couple of pitches. Jackie got mad and was ready to go after Van Cuyk. It ended well. They shook hands and admitted that they had lost their heads.[16]

Mayor Barber had Dodger concerns other than racial ones. The City of Miami had built a new baseball stadium and wanted the Dodger big team to train there the next spring. The Dodgers had already scheduled some games in Miami. The mayor wrote a letter to *Miami Herald* columnist Jimmy Burns stating, "You fellows in Miami might as well forget about getting the Dodgers to train in your city. But we will consider it all right if the Dodgers wish to play weekend games for you."[17]

Rickey had brought the Dodgers to Vero so they could all live together in one location, but that didn't happen in Miami. The white players stayed at the "white" McAllister Hotel just off Biscayne Boulevard, while the black players stayed at the "colored" Lord Calvert. They didn't mind as it was a quality hotel that catered to Negro entertainers, but they were segregated from their teammates, which defeated Rickey's purpose.

During the spring of 1949, the Dodgers played a major league opponent in Vero Beach for the first time. The Philadelphia Athletics came up from West Palm Beach for a Sunday afternoon game at Ebbets Field #2. Jackie Robinson hit ball after ball into the black section down left field during batting practice. A crowd of 3,500 fans overflowed the bleachers and stood along the foul lines and around the outfield.

Rex Barney pitched for the Dodgers. He had led the team in wins the previous season and thrown a no-hitter. Renowned for his fastball and his wildness, he did not disappoint. He uncorked a pitch that hit home plate and bounced over the screen and out of the ball park. Dick Fowler, also with a no-hitter to his credit, pitched for the Athletics. Both Barney and Fowler went nine innings, a stint unheard of in today's games. The A's scored two runs in the ninth to win 3–1. Barney wild pitched one of the runs home.

As the Dodgers completed their spring training, the Associated Press predicted the team would finish first in the National League: "The Dodgers appear to have everything, including the exuberance of youth and platoons of reserves. They are all coming out of the same mill at Vero Beach, so may be expected to bat alike, throw alike, run alike, and think alike, but they will all be deluxe models."[18] To train these "deluxe models" and process a multitude of minor leaguers clamoring for major league jobs at Dodgertown, the cost totaled $275,000 a year.[19]

During spring training, the Dodgers made a move that showed they had great respect for Bud Holman and for Vero Beach. Team president Branch Rickey and the other owners elected Mr. Holman to the team's board of directors.

Whirlwinds

Whirlwinds struck both Vero Beach and the Dodgers in 1949. In August, a hurricane hit the Florida Coast bringing winds of 120 miles per hour to Vero. The flimsy barracks at Dodgertown survived, as did most of the structures in the county.

The Associated Press had correctly predicted the Dodger's success in the National League. Manager Burt Shotton led the team to the pennant by beating out the Cardinals one game. Jackie Robinson, in this his third season, became the National League Most Valuable Player and Don Newcombe, the Rookie of the Year. But a Yankee whirlwind struck in the World Series as the Bronx Bombers beat the Dodgers again. In Brooklyn they said, "Wait till next year," a sentiment echoed in Vero Beach where the community looked forward to another exciting Dodger spring.

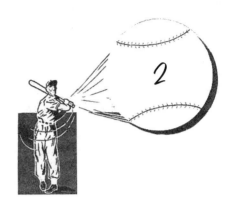

2

The Fifties

Dodger players with Walter O'Malley (right center), the stewardess, and Bud Holman about to board the DC-3 that Holman won in a crap game at an Eastern Airlines picnic. (Courtesy of Indian River County Historical Society, Vero Beach, Florida.)

4

Call Me Walter

1950

Notes from the Bull Pen

The most exciting decade in Dodger history, the 1950s, began quietly at Dodgertown. The Vero Beach City Council authorized improvements at Ebbets Field #2, including new box seats and moving a building from elsewhere on the base to provide more rest rooms, a concession stand, a new press box, and radio quarters. The city covered the $2,000 cost with receipts from two exhibition games, and the Dodgers provided the paint free of charge.[1]

Bud Holman presented Branch Rickey with a DC-3, two-engine, thirty-passenger plane. Rickey traveled a lot, inspecting players in his far-flung minor league system. With a plane this size, he could sleep while he traveled. Son Bump Holman told the story. His dad went down to Miami for an Eastern Airlines mechanics' picnic. "Dad and Mr. Rickenbacker got into a crap game with the stakes double or nothing for the plane. Dad said that's the way the Dodgers acquired the plane, although I am sure some money was involved."[2]

Bump, at eighteen, hung around the Vero airport, learned to fly, and at times flew copilot for the Dodgers' small Beechcraft. With the arrival of the DC-3, he flew as copilot and three years later, when he graduated from college, became chief pilot. He transported Dodger farm teams at St. Paul and Fort Worth to their away games, the first time in baseball that clubs had flown their teams in their own plane.[3]

In his *Press Journal* column "Bull Pen," local reporter Bob Curzon tracked Dodger doings. Curzon described Spencer Harris, the director, or mayor, of Dodgertown as a human dynamo: "Harris has a winning personality. He calls all workers by their first name. He has decided to make Vero Beach his family's permanent home, because he liked the friendship of local people, he became one of us." Curzon provided human interest tidbits on the players and their media coverage. Pee Wee Reese shot in the low 70s at the Royal Park Golf Course (now the Vero Beach Country Club). Preacher Roe fished with local dentist Dr. Bill Eubanks. (In fact, Roe won the Indian River County fishing tournament with a seven-pound black bass.) Paramount Pictures took shots for the new movie about Jackie Robinson. Dodger fan and entertainer Arthur Godfrey gave Vero Beach a plug on his national radio broadcast.[4]

Entertainment at Dodgertown was limited. Pitcher Carl Erskine remembered the evening activity around the Ping-Pong table, the pool table, and the jukebox at Dodgertown: "Fortunately we had a true showman among us, minor league first baseman Chuck Connors. Chuck would entertain us nightly with card tricks, poems, jokes or debates."[5] He specialized in a rendition of "Casey at the Bat." He occasionally gave performances at the old base auditorium, and often local citizens were invited to attend.

Broadcaster Vin Scully's most vivid memory of Dodgertown involved Connors. "I noticed excitement in the lobby one day," said Scully. "Everyone was gathered in a circle. There was loud shouting and cheering. I squeezed through to see what was happening. There on the floor was Chuck Connors wrist wrestling with Branch Rickey, Jr."[6]

Connors was a hard-hitting first baseman at Montreal, but was never going to replace Gil Hodges at first base. He eventually found fame in Hollywood as "the Rifleman" on TV. Tommy Lasorda, who played at Montreal with him, said, "Chuck was the greatest first baseman to ever become a TV star."[7]

Pitcher Rex Barney, after a poor 1949 season, continued at Dodgertown to have problems with wildness. *The Sporting News* did an extensive article on Barney, calling him "A Rickey Riddle Since '43." As Rex later said, "The harder I tried, the more I screwed up." Coach Clyde Sukeforth explained, "It's in his head. It can't be anyplace else." Rickey worked and worked with his player at the Dodgertown pitching strings—what Rex called "Mr. Rickey's famous invention for the improvement of my control." The strings, tied between two posts to represent the strike zone, turned out to be a torture device. Barney resorted to weeping, and Rickey sent him to the Menninger Clinic. The psychiatrist diagnosed Rex as frustrated. He needed to relax. "Big help," said Barney.[8] At twenty-six, his major league career was over.

O'Malley and Rickey

Like Barney's, the Dodgers' season ended in frustration. The team lost the championship on the last day to the Philadelphia Phillies' Whiz Kids.

Branch Rickey was disappointed. With his contract as president expiring that year, Rickey wanted another pennant and a new contract. Walter O'Malley had other ideas. Perhaps, it was an ego thing with O'Malley. Rickey received all the credit for the Dodgers' success. From O'Malley's standpoint, the decision to bring Jackie Robinson on the team may have been initiated by Rickey, but he and the rest of the board approved it. Ebbets Field attendance was down. Rickey had a poor relationship with the press and didn't seem to care. Rickey was spending $250,000 a year on Dodgertown. And because the Dodgers missed the World Series in 1950, O'Malley felt it cost the club a million dollars.[9]

As author Steve Delshon put it, the two men "simply hated each other": "Rickey didn't drink, had an enormous ego and endlessly quoted Scripture. O'Malley loved Irish whiskey, had an enormous ego and privately called Rickey that 'psalm singing fake.'"[10]

In the four years since the war, the team had appeared twice in the World Series, had made money on the player development system (which included Dodgertown), and, what's more, had paid a dividend, a rarity for a baseball team. Despite O'Malley's displeasure, Branch Rickey managed a profitable franchise, perhaps the most profitable in baseball. Plus he built a team that became the most powerful in the National League.

But O'Malley, controlling the ball club's finances, was not content. He squabbled with Rickey over his buying World Series rings for the players and over which beer company should sponsor the team. Dodgertown's expenses were an ongoing irritant. O'Malley wanted Rickey out and sought the support of fellow owners, John Smith and Jim Mulvey. Rickey told his daughter, "He's going to force me out. I am doomed."[11]

A Chaotic Ownership

Since its birth in the 1890s, the Brooklyn Baseball Club had experienced several periods of chaos despite the longevity of some of its owners. Steve Mulvey, a Vero Beach resident and owner of the Quail Valley Golf and River Club, offered some of the details of that ownership. Steve is the grandson of Jim Mulvey and the great grandson of Steve McKeever.

The McKeever brothers, Steve and Ed, joined Charles Ebbets, principal owner of the club from 1900, in financing the construction of Ebbets Field, which opened in 1912.[12] The brothers had made their money picking up dead horses in Brooklyn, as the story goes, and then by going into real estate.

On opening day 1925, Charles Ebbets died. Ed McKeever caught pneumonia at Ebbets' funeral and died a week later. This left Steve McKeever and the Ebbets heirs as owners, an unhappy arrangement.[13]

The team won pennants in 1899, 1900, 1916, and 1920 under Charles Ebbets, but its performance during the "daffy" days of the '20s and '30s under the McKeevers and the Ebbets heirs established its chaotic reputation. National League president Ford Frick insisted the owners hire Larry McPhail, the innovative but volatile general manager of the Cincinnati Reds, to improve the management of the team.

Steve McKeever died in 1940, and his son-in-law, Jim Mulvey, took over the McKeever interests. As movie tycoon Samuel Goldwyn's right-hand man, Jim also ran Goldwyn's New York operations.[14] Jim and his wife, Dearie, would become regulars at Dodgertown.

In 1941, the Brooklyn Trust, concerned about Dodger finances, placed lawyer Walter O'Malley on the team's board of directors. In that same year, McPhail put the Dodgers in the World Series, though they lost to the Yankees. McPhail then left the team to join the war effort. Branch Rickey, longtime general manager of the Cardinals, replaced him.[15]

Two years later, the Ebbets heirs sold their half interest in the club, splitting the ownership equally among Jim Mulvey, the McKeever heir; Branch Rickey, the club president; Walter O'Malley, the lawyer; and John Smith, who purchased an interest at that time. Smith ran the Pfizer chemical company that made penicillin for the war effort. The Brooklyn Trust lent Rickey and O'Malley each $300,000 to buy their shares.[16]

In July 1950, John Smith died, leaving his wife and the Brooklyn Trust as cotrustees of his estate. As a protégé of the bank, O'Malley now voted Mrs. Smith's stock. That gave him 50 percent control, with Rickey and Mulvey each having 25 percent.[17]

With Rickey's contract as president expiring at the end of 1950, O'Malley offered to buy his interest for the original $300,000. Rickey refused and found a buyer, real estate developer William Zeckendorf, who was willing to pay him $1.25 million for an interest in the Dodgers. This forced an incensed O'Malley to match Zeckendorf's offer. Baseball writer Roger Kahn noted that O'Malley had been out manipulated.[18] But, as it turned out, he obtained Rickey's shares for a reasonable price.

At age sixty-eight, Branch Rickey left Brooklyn to become general manager of the Pittsburgh Pirates. O'Malley, now president of the Dodgers, issued a directive that anyone in the Dodger office who mentioned Branch Rickey's name would be fined a dollar.[19]

Vero Beach was shocked. The community did not know O'Malley. Branch Rickey had made the Dodgers what they were. He *was* the Dodgers. With the exception of Pee Wee Reese, who went back to the McPhail era, Mr. Rickey's tenure was longest: he had acquired and developed every player on the team. In the five seasons since the war, the Dodgers had finished first twice, second twice (and then, never more than two games back), and third the year Durocher left at midseason. Branch Rickey, with Jackie Robinson, had integrated baseball. But most important to the community, Mr. Rickey had brought the Dodgers to Vero Beach, developed Dodgertown, and created a lot of Dodger fans locally.

1951

O'Malley Cleanses the Dodgers

Dodgertown did not seem the same without Branch Rickey. It had been his place, but now it belonged to Walter O'Malley.

And who was this Walter O'Malley anyway? Raised in New York City, he had received an engineering degree from the University of Pennsylvania and then gone on to Columbia and Fordham to earn a law degree. He married Kay Hanson, the pretty girl next door. The O'Malleys and the Hansons were neighbors in both Brooklyn and in their summer homes in Amityville, Long Island. In college, Kay was diagnosed with cancer. She had surgery, which replaced her larynx with a voice box, allowing her to talk only in a whisper. She became a beloved figure at Dodgertown.[20]

As a lawyer in New York during the depression of the 1930s, Walter O'Malley established a reputation for successfully collecting bad debts for banks. The Brooklyn Trust assigned him to address the Dodgers' debt that the bank had carried for years. O'Malley was a finance man, not a baseball man. How could he replace Branch Rickey?[21]

Walter O'Malley took immediate steps to cleanse the Dodgers of the Rickey influence. He appointed Buzzie Bavasi vice president of major league operations. Bavasi had worked himself up through the Dodger minor league system, starting at the Class D level prior to the Rickey era. He had Roy Campanella and Don Newcombe on his team at Class B

Nashua and challenged an opposing general manager to a fight for referring to them as "those two Niggers." All twenty-one players on his 1948
Montreal Royals, including Snider, Erskine, and Newcombe, advanced to
the major leagues.[22] Buzzie Bavasi, with his jowls and receding hairline,
tended to play the father role with his players.[23]

O'Malley fired Rickey's old friend, Burt Shotton, and hired Chuck
Dressen as manager. A small, feisty fellow, Dressen had been a Dodger
coach during the Leo Durocher days and then a Yankee coach. Dressen
was shrewd. "There are tricks to this game," he said. "Ya can't just worry
about the next play. Ya gotta worry about two plays or three."[24]

And it was time to quell the anti-Rickey, anti-Dodger sentiments
coming out of the New York press, particularly the *Daily News*, which
frequently referred to Rickey as "El Cheapo" for his dealings with his
players.[25] Bavasi and O'Malley would work on this at Dodgertown by
entertaining reporters.

O'Malley had always criticized Rickey for the money spent on Dodgertown. Buzzie Bavasi convinced O'Malley that Dodgertown was worth it,
that the extensive instruction got players to the majors faster, and that
they could be showcased at the camp and sold to other teams. O'Malley
told Bavasi to "sell enough ball players each year to pay for the operation
of Dodgertown in Vero Beach, Florida."[26]

Rags to Riches

Dodgertown immediately underwent changes. Workers spruced up the
place, painted the barracks, and added siding to make them more comfortable. Despite improvements to the barracks, when a cold front arrived in late February, it chilled the quarters. The players and writers complained. Tired of it all, new manager Chuck Dressen drove to Miami and
bought a quantity of electric, plug-in heaters. But the next day the front
passed and the temperature rose back to its normal eighty degrees.[27]

Under O'Malley, the sparse, military base atmosphere of Dodgertown
disappeared. *Sporting News* headlined, "Bums go from Rags to Riches
at Camp." On arriving at Dodgertown, Duke Snider exclaimed, "What
class—white linen and country club seating in the dining room." The
Dodger brass, the major league players, and the press could order from a
menu. Liquor was served in the Dodger pressroom, which had the air of
a tropical bar rather than a work area. Thirty-year Dodger employee and
jack-of-all-trades Babe Hamberger managed the "saloon," greeting and
taking care of the press and visiting dignitaries. He was called "Billing-

sly" after the owner of the Stork Club in New York. Writer Joe King said the saloon "transformed night life in Dodgertown for the press from the stillness of death in 1950 into the flamboyant gaiety of spring."[28]

According to Joe Hendrickson, O'Malley "wanted everyone to feel light and breezy in camp, especially during the poker games for writers and top Dodger personnel plus invited friends."[29] One poker player, who might not have played with O'Malley but who was close to the writers, was Cowboy Rogers. In the days long before laptop computers and modems, Cowboy, as telegraph operator, transmitted the writers' stories to their newspapers. Hendrickson said that Cowboy was "one of the best senders ever to touch a finger to the 'bug' (telegraph key)." At the poker table, though, he couldn't fold a hand and at times lost big.

With the freer atmosphere and his "Call me Walter" approach, O'Malley was establishing himself as the dominant figure at Dodgertown in place of Branch Rickey.

On a more wholesome note, the *Press Journal* reported that the players and camp personnel drank an average of eighty-six gallons of orange juice every day.[30] There was no record of how much whiskey was consumed by the press at Dodgertown.

Writer Jack Lang stated, "Yes, Dodgertown enlivened considerably when O'Malley took over. Every night before dinner there was a cocktail party hosted by Walter and his wife, Kay, in the pressroom. When dinner was over, there was more fun. In addition to poker, the juke box would provide the music for dancing." After Lang switched to covering other teams, he lamented, "Spring Training never was the same after my Vero Beach experience. . . . There it was a family."[31]

When the big leaguers left to head north, feeding operations changed to cafeteria style for the minor leaguers. But right with them in line, carrying their metal trays, were Walter and Kay O'Malley. The O'Malleys' meeting and chatting with the players and staff fostered a unique family feeling that strengthened the organization.[32]

However, there was some concern in Vero about the growing number of blacks on the team. To Buzzie Bavasi the mayor expressed worry "about our young women." Bavasi sent traveling secretary Lee Scott down to Gulfstream Park in Miami to get $20,000 changed into two-dollar bills. Mr. and Mrs. O'Malley, Mr. and Mrs. Bavasi, and Mr. and Mrs. Fresco Thompson, as the story goes, stayed up one night and stamped Brooklyn Dodgers on each bill. O'Malley closed the Dodgertown cafeteria for the weekend and gave the players the bills to eat out in the community.

According to Bavasi, Vero's mayor called Buzzie back shortly thereafter, saying, "I get your point."[33]

Walter O'Malley's changes at Dodgertown may have done great things for press relations but did little for team performance. The 1951 Dodgers blew a thirteen-game lead over the Giants to end the season in a tie. Bobby Thomson's famous home run off Ralph Branca in the playoffs kept the Dodgers out of the World Series for the second year in a row.

Grace and the Boys of Summer

1952

Fun and Grief

In the spring of 1952, rookie sportswriter Roger Kahn arrived at Dodgertown to cover the Dodgers for the *New York Herald Tribune*. He would report on the Dodgers for the next two seasons before leaving the paper and becoming a magazine writer. Twenty years later, he wrote a book about growing up in Brooklyn, covering the team, and about the lives after baseball of the Dodgers of the 1950s. He immortalized these men, forever after known as the Boys of Summer.

Grace Shilling Goodermote also arrived at Dodgertown that spring. Fifty-one years later, Grace appeared at a talk on Dodgertown given by Dodger vice president Craig Callan to the Indian River Historical Society. Grace said that she had been the secretary to the directors of Dodgertown, Spencer Harris and later Edgar Allen, from 1952 to 1955. In retirement, she returned to Vero Beach to live because of her fond memories of the town.[1]

In the spring of 1952, Grace, a twenty-two-year-old upstate New Yorker, went on vacation to Miami. Thumbing through the *Miami Herald*, she saw an ad for a secretary for Dodgertown. She loved baseball. She called Spencer Harris, and he asked her to come to Vero for an interview. She flew up on Eastern Airlines and stayed in the old Del Mar Hotel downtown. Spencer Harris offered her the job.

Each year, Grace arrived at Dodgertown in early January and worked till the camp closed in May after cleanup and inventory. She lived in the barracks. She loved the oranges on the trees lining the walkway to the administration building. On cold mornings, the groundskeeper would slip an electric heater into her room. She remembers the "beautiful lobby with the nickelodeon and gorgeous furniture and the juke box playing 'Oh Wheel of Fortune.'" She didn't get to the beach or downtown very much. It was more fun to stay at Dodgertown and talk to the players. She knew the "major players" pretty well and had a "liking for some of them," particularly George Shuba, a utility outfielder best known for hitting a home run in the 1953 World Series. Everyone was friendly, and the girls, some who came down from the Brooklyn office, had a good time with the players. Of course, they were "off limits." The players had a curfew, and their rooms were checked.

Occasionally, there were problems. The office typically assigned four players to a room, and touchy situations could ensue if one happened to be black. Some of the white boys simply left camp. Black singer Nat King Cole, on a Florida tour, had difficulty finding a place to stay. The Dodgers invited him to spend the night at Dodgertown, and Grace remembered him sitting at the piano in the lobby, playing and singing.

The O'Malleys, the Mulveys, and their friends stayed in the barracks. Grace did typing for Mr. O'Malley, which made her nervous, but "he was a very down-to-earth man." Grace thought the "O'Malleys were very, very lovely people. You never knew they had a penny."

The O'Malleys' St. Patrick's Day parties were particular fun. Grace kept in her Dodger scrapbook the invitation for the initial affair:

THE O'MALLEY OF COUNTY MAYO AND THE BROOKLYN DODGERS PROCLAIM A BREAK-FAST OCCASION AT 6:00 P.M. WEDNESDAY THE 17TH OF MARCH AT THE TARA HALL, MCKEE JUNGLE GAR-DENS, VERO BEACH. THE FESTIVITIES WILL TERMINATE WITH THE MID-NIGHT. PRIOR THERE TO, COMAHAILLES, A SPOT OF DEW FROM THE HEATHER, AND SUBSTANCE.

The gathering took place in the Hall of Giants around a thirty-five-foot mahogany table.[2] An elephant and an ostrich were painted green for the occasion. The entertainment included a chimpanzee, Walter O'Malley, and Fresco Thompson, all of them quick wits.

The newspaper photographers liked to use Grace as a model. Once she posed with a Dodger who gained more fame as a manager than a player. The tag line read: "The lovely lady, getting a batting lesson from outfielder Dick Williams is the Dodgers' leading 'pinch—hitter.' Grace, who is Edgar Allen's secretary, has been 'pinch hitting' as secretary to Walter O'Malley, Buzzie Bavasi, Fresco Thompson, and [team publicist] Frank Graham, Jr."[3]

Dodgertown secretary Grace Shilling Goodermote visits with first baseman Gil Hodges. (Courtesy of Grace Goodermote, Vero Beach, Florida.)

Vero Beach and Dodgertown continued to receive national publicity. A visiting writer described the new steel and concrete Merrill Barber Bridge, "replacing the rickety, 1920 wooden bridge and connecting the business and beach sections of this picturesquely situated city of 5,000 year-round residents." He also noted the heavily wooded areas adjacent to the beaches and the beach park (Humiston) with its picnic pavilions roofed with palm fronds. He liked the rates at the motor courts and the $2.50 green fees at the Royal Park Golf Course. He stated that a New York travel agent offered for the 1952 spring season in Vero a nine-day vacation package at a price of only $169. It included transportation, accommodations, meals and admissions to all Dodger exhibition games.[4]

In that same spring of 1952, the year after he gave up the home run to Bobby Thomson, Ralph Branca slipped on the waxed floor of the Dodgertown lobby and fell on a coke bottle. He cut himself and damaged his pelvis.[5] Branca's career essentially ended in his ninth year with the Dodgers; he was twenty-six. Over the winter, he had married Ann Mulvey, daughter of Dodger director Jim Mulvey and granddaughter of Ed McKeever.

Ralph Branca and his "fame" became a fixture at the Dodger adult camps at Dodgertown in later years.

O'Malley Builds His First Ball Park

Walter O'Malley wanted a long-term lease with the City of Vero Beach to replace the short-term agreement that expired in 1953. He had something big in mind. "We want to spend $150,000 on improvements at the training base," he said. "We like Vero Beach. If Vero Beach wants us, we are prepared to stay."[6] He further asserted his "faith in the future growth of Vero Beach" and that the area would soon "be in a position to support a larger exhibition schedule." "If a large number of fans turn out and indicate they want to see big league ball, they will get it," he said.[7]

The Vero Beach City Council happily agreed to a twenty-one-year lease with an option that would keep the Dodgers in the community until 1994. The *Sporting News* reported that O'Malley reached into his wallet and "peeled off $21 in cash and handed it to a city official" to cover the basic lease.[8] The Dodgers paid off the $3,000 swimming pool debt and agreed to have the big team train in Vero for at least fifteen days each spring and play a set number of exhibition games at Dodgertown. The Dodgers would continue to donate the proceeds of one game to the airport development fund.

Furthermore, O'Malley announced that he would build the "finest baseball stadium in the state" to replace Ebbets Field #2. O'Malley with Emil Praeger, a consulting engineer for both the United Nations complex and the White House renovation, created an innovative ball park design with the stadium built on a rectangular berm of fill dug from an adjoining lake. Seats were to be constructed on two sides of the berm; the other two sides would be the outfield walls. The designers' intent was to create a low-maintenance stadium with unobstructed views, which fit well with the natural surroundings. It would be an intimate ball park, bringing the fans and the players close together. The stadium was a "tryout" for a fifty thousand–seat ball park that O'Malley had in mind for Brooklyn. He believed that Ebbets Field—its age, size, lack of parking, and deteriorat-

Holman Stadium ready for its opening game. (Courtesy of Indian River County Historical Society, Vero Beach, Florida.)

ing neighborhood—was no longer a satisfactory place to play baseball. Through designing and building this prototype at Dodgertown, O'Malley would learn on a small scale about stadium-building processes, potential mistakes and budget problems, and construction schedules.[9]

In July 1952, construction began on the stadium at Dodgertown, which was completed in time for the beginning of spring training in 1953 at an approximate cost of $100,000.[10]

O'Malley acquired two thousand portable seats from the Polo Grounds, paying New York Giants president Horace Stoneham one dollar apiece. Mrs. Mary Louise Smith donated fifty royal palms to be planted on the berm around the outfield in memory of her husband, John Smith, the former Dodger partner and board member.

This 4,200-seat ball park in Vero also became in several ways the prototype for the stadium O'Malley would build in Los Angeles nine years later.[11]

With a long-term lease in hand and construction of a stadium under way, Walter O'Malley wasn't through with his plans for Dodgertown. He proposed to the Chicago Cubs that they come to Vero and share the camp (and its cost) with the Dodgers. The Cubs declined and moved from Catalina Island off California to Mesa, Arizona.[12]

1953

Holman Stadium and a Record Season

When Walter O'Malley arrived in Vero eager to check out his new stadium, *Press Journal* publisher John Schuman wrote, "It was almost the homecoming of a local son."[13] Three hundred and fifty people greeted the arrival of the team, when it pulled into the Vero train station. City councilmen Lou Berger, Ton Trent, and Jimmy Barrett were there. So was Bud Holman. This man, O'Malley, was endearing himself to the community.

Bud Emlet probably met the train as well. He owned a restaurant in Vero that O'Malley enjoyed, and they became friends. O'Malley would go into Emlet's and ask for the "north end of a south bound snapper," wanting the tailpiece with no bones. He liked the snapper broiled, a side dish of turnip greens, and pecan pie for dessert. He called Emlet one day and asked about renting the place after hours for twenty-five people coming down from New York. O'Malley would bring the steaks and cook them himself. Bud Emlet said that was fine: "We had just painted our kitchen so the place was spic and span for them. When Walter arrived, he said he was going to show us how to cook. Yes, he cooked all right. The broiler got red hot and the steaks caught fire. The whole place was smoked up. But nothing could smoke out our beautiful friendship." Bud remembered Walter O'Malley as "doing anything to win a $2 golf bet" but, on the other hand, picking up the bill for eighty people to have a couple of days in the Bahamas.[14]

The *Press Journal*'s Bob Curzon reported that "Dodgertown, the nationally famous baseball 'city'" had lost its "mayor." Spencer Harris, who had had held the position since the Dodgers' arrival in 1948, resigned in 1953 to become the general manager of the Fort Worth farm team. Harris had "realized that the community was important" and had made

Vero Beach his home. "He became one of us," wrote Curzon.[15] Edgar Allen, former president of the Mobile Bears, a Dodger farm affiliate that trained in Vero, became the new "mayor."

On March 11, 1953, an overflow crowd of 5,532 dedicated Holman Stadium. The sun sparkled on the royal palms lining the outfield as Merrill Barber, now a state senator, emceed the event. Baseball commissioner Ford Frick, National League president Warren Giles, and American League president William Harridge attended.

At home plate, Walter O'Malley, with Bud Holman at his side, unveiled a plaque:

THE BROOKLYN DODGERS DEDICATE HOLMAN STADIUM TO HONOR
BUD HOLMAN OF THE FRIENDLY CITY OF VERO BEACH,
WALTER F. O'MALLEY, PRESIDENT,
EMIL H. PRAEGER, C.C., DESIGNER, 1953

Holman responded briefly. The color guard from Felix Poppel Post of the American Legion raised the flag, and the high school band played "The Star-Spangled Banner."

Observing the ball park with its earthen outfield fence from the press box, author Roger Kahn credited Praeger and O'Malley for "conceiv[ing] an innovative organic Florida field": "The little field was a beauty."[16]

At the dedication of Holman Stadium, Walter O'Malley congratulates Bud Holman, the man who brought the Dodgers to Vero Beach. (Courtesy of Indian River County Historical Society, Vero Beach, Florida.)

The Dodger lineup included Don Thompson (a utility outfielder) leading off, followed by Reese, Snider, Robinson, Campanella, Hodges, Furillo, Cox, and pitcher Carl Erskine. Late in the game, Jim Gilliam substituted for Robinson. Duke Snider drove in two runs, and Erskine became the winning pitcher as the Dodgers beat the Philadelphia Athletics 4–2.

The commissioner, the two league presidents, O'Malley, and Braves' owner, Lou Perini, all members of baseball's executive committee, missed the game. They excused themselves after the dedication to privately discuss moving the Braves from Boston to Milwaukee, the first such move in the modern era of baseball and, like Holman Stadium, a precedent for what would happen in Los Angeles.[17]

The Dodgers played the Braves as well as the Philadelphia A's, the Washington Senators, and the Montreal farm team in Holman Stadium that spring.

The game with the Senators caused a stir, as former Vero Beach High School football player Chuck Stobbs was to pitch for the visitors. Chuck's father had been the athletic director at the Naval Air Station in 1943. Stobbs, a fourteen-year-old freshman, starred as a runner and a passer for the high school. Walter O'Malley invited Chuck's football teammates and his coach, Harold Mossey, to be guests of the Dodgers for the game.[18] Unfortunately, Chuck did not pitch because of a sore arm but came with the team and greeted his many Vero Beach friends. Chuck won 107 games in a fifteen-year major league career. He has returned to Vero occasionally for high school reunions.

A new pitcher arrived at Dodgertown. The Dodgers acquired Russ Meyer to strengthen their staff. Jackie Robinson and Russ Meyer, as competitors, didn't like each other. When Meyer played for the Phillies, Jackie got caught in a rundown between third and home. Five Phillies, including Meyer, tried to tag him. Jackie dodged them all and scored. In frustration, Meyer tackled him after he crossed home plate. When Meyer walked into the clubhouse at Dodgertown at the beginning of spring training, Jackie approached him and said, "We've been fighting one another. Now let's fight them together." Meyer said, "Okay pal, you've made things a lot easier for me."[19]

A huge photograph hangs in the Dodgertown Conference Center, showing Jackie between third and home, being chased by the five Phillies.

As they had done in '52, the '53 Dodgers won the National League pennant, setting a team record with 105 wins. But in both years the Boys of

Summer lost to the Yankees in the World Series. Walter O'Malley had to be pleased with the Dodger's financial performance, however. The team made a profit of $2 million, while having the highest payroll in the major leagues. O'Malley's favorite saying was, "In Brooklyn, you're either first or bankrupt."[20] After all of O'Malley's fuming and fussing, his $1 million buyout of Branch Rickey three years earlier looked pretty good. And the expense of Dodgertown that O'Malley had once opposed was a dead issue.

Who Is Walter Alston?

Manager Chuck Dressen, with two successive World Series appearances, felt that he deserved a three-year contract and approached O'Malley. This didn't sit well with the boss. O'Malley reacted. He needed to get rid of his manager, who was too cocky and received more publicity than he deserved.[21] Jackie Robinson would later say that Chuck Dressen was the best manger he ever played for. Duke Snider agreed: "Chuck was the smartest manager of them all."[22]

Buzzie Bavasi recommended that Walter Alston replace Dressen. Bavasi and Alston had first worked together at Nashua in 1946. Alston, a career minor league manager, enjoyed great success at St. Paul and Montreal. A bland Midwesterner, he seemed more at home on his Ohio farm than as a high-profile figure in New York. He was competent and, certainly, wouldn't steal anyone's thunder. The headline in the *New York Daily News* read: "Alston (Who He?) To Manage Dodgers."[23]

Anyone who had hung around Dodgertown over the years knew Alston. But he seemed an unusual choice. Would he fit in with the Boys of Summer?

6

Champions of the World

1954

A Tough Spot

Later in his career, Walter Alston remembered his thoughts as he headed south for his first year as the Dodger manager: "Each year my wife, Lela, and I drove to Vero Beach from our home in Darrtown, Ohio. But 1954 was special. I was manager now, not a minor-league skipper. When February came, I couldn't wait until it was time to start spring training. I would think of the smells and sights of the clubhouse, the reunions with the other coaches I had been working with for years. I would wonder about the new players. I would be anxious to see which kids were ready to move up. It was exciting to speculate who would be the next discovery."[1]

But Walter Alston started off the spring with an unfortunate remark. "Every man on this ball club will have to fight for his job," he told the assembled team at Dodgertown. Jackie Robinson, who would never quite relate to his new boss, remembered thinking, "I don't know what the hell that man is trying to do. Upset us all?"[2]

Walter Alston was no Durocher or Dressen. He married at eighteen and taught school in the off-season. His career in the major leagues amounted to one at bat. But he was no stranger. Many on the big team had played for him as they came up through the minor leagues. He managed all the black players except Robinson. In fact, when Campanella played for him at Nashua and Alston was thrown out of a game, he told Campy to manage the team for him.[3]

Campy said of Alston, "It was a tough spot for any manager, let alone a fellow who had never managed or even coached in the major leagues before."[4] The talk had been that if Alston didn't win a pennant that first year he wouldn't be back the next. He didn't win; the team finished second behind the Giants. But he was right back at Dodgertown the next spring and would stay on as team manager for twenty-three years. He also became a member of the Baseball Hall of Fame.

Two Losses

Another future Hall of Famer arrived at Dodgertown that spring. Roberto Clemente was an unknown, and the Dodger brass wanted to keep it that way. This young Puerto Rican outfielder was one of the five hundred players in training. He had been paid a $10,000 bonus to sign a contract and, according to major league rules, had to be carried on the Dodger big league roster. If not, other teams could draft him. But the Dodgers were well stocked and didn't think he was needed on the varsity at that time. Clemente was assigned to Montreal and would play only intermittently so that his talent would not attract attention. "Our efforts were for naught," said Buzzie Bavasi. "Branch Rickey was running the Pirates then. . . . They knew what was happening. . . . The Pirates drafted Clemente. We lost one of the game's greatest players, a man who had 3,000 hits in a very distinguished career." Imagine an outfield of Snider, Furillo, and Clemente.[5]

Rex Barney was another loss. He came to Vero Beach in 1954, not to play baseball, but to start a new life. At twenty-nine, if he could have controlled his fastball, he would have been at his peak and one of the dominant Dodger pitchers of the era with Roe, Erskine, and Newcombe. Instead, he sold cars and worked part time at Vero's radio station WTTB. His wife, Carol, sang at the Ocean Grill and other spots locally. When Rex left Vero, the couple divorced. Carol remarried, continued singing with her new husband, and was known locally as Carol Moss.[6] People in Vero Beach didn't know what had happened to Rex Barney. Fifty years later, his obituary in the *New York Times* indicated that he had ended up in Baltimore, broadcasting Oriole games and later becoming the popular public address announcer at Camden Yards.

Boys and Girls

In what became Walter O'Malley's first attempt to diversify and gain income from his Vero baseball operation, he started the Dodgertown Camp for Boys in 1954. "It seemed a shame to leave those beautiful quarters unoccupied, the playing fields idle, the swimming pool empty until the next spring," said O'Malley.[7] In his typical fashion, he researched the best sports camps in the country, looking for a model to follow. He hired former New York University track star Les McMitchell to run the camp.

Two hundred boys, ages twelve to sixteen, from all over the country attended during the months of July and August. The cost was $500 per camper. Using the Dodgertown facilities and living in the barracks where the players resided in the spring, the boys enjoyed a variety of sports including baseball, swimming, tennis, fishing, basketball, and shuffleboard. A message on the wall of one of the recreation rooms said, "George Washington didn't sleep here, but Pee Wee Reese, Duke Snider, Carl Erskine, and other Dodgers did." The fifty counselors included sixteen-year-old Peter O'Malley, getting his first experience working in the Dodger organization. Walter O'Malley visited regularly and enjoyed a swim in the ocean with the campers.[8] A sign at Brooklyn's Ebbets Field on the wall in front of the left field stands said:

SEND YOUR BOY TO DODGERTOWN CAMP—

VERO BEACH, FLORIDA

FOR THE SUMMER OF *HIS* LIFE

By 1957, the camp had received five thousand inquiries for the two hundred spots. But in the 1960s, attendance declined, perhaps due to the social changes the country was experiencing. The camp did provide a training ground for Peter O'Malley who advanced from counselor to camp supervisor before it closed. His sister Terry worked at the camp as a secretary when she was in college.

Terry O'Malley Seidler shared with writer Joe Hendrickson her wonderful memories of her teenage years at Dodgertown. She described the pool as the center of activity. The kids swam and dove, tried not to get too sunburned and not to forget the homework lessons they were supposed to do. She enjoyed meeting the players, their families, and all the other people at Dodgertown, who came from all over the country and even faraway places like Montreal, the Dominican Republic, Cuba, and Haiti.

She particularly liked Fresco Thompson, who she described as "a lovable former ballplayer with a famous sense of humor." His daughter Ann was her best friend. They went to different schools in New York but looked forward to getting together for "those special weeks at Dodgertown." The girls were the "official scoreboard operators" at Ebbets Field #2 and had to "stand on their toes to hook the numbers on the nails." As they got older and learned to keep their "mouths closed and ears open," they listened in on staff meetings. They helped with filing in the minor league office when things were busy. They kept "mental files" on the "most handsome" younger players.

"During a double date with two of these rookies," said Terry, "our borrowed car had engine trouble and we were late returning to camp. The boys had to climb in a second-story window to avoid being caught for being out after curfew. Unfortunately, a dangling screen gave them away and at the ball game the next day, Fresco announced them in the batting order over the PA system as "Twinkle Toes" Devlin and "Mountain Goat" Bartz. Terry said, "It was hard to tell who was the most embarrassed—the ballplayers or the scoreboard workers."[9]

Red Departs

After an off year, there was concern at Dodgertown about the team. Had they peaked in 1952 and 1953? With questions about Alston, could the aging Boys of Summer bounce back? Would there be any more trips to the World Series?

Gone also at the end of the '54 season was legendary broadcaster Red Barber, the southern voice that the Brooklyn community had loved for sixteen years. The Redhead and O'Malley had a salary dispute. This dispute, according to Harold Parrott, was all by O'Malley's design. Vin Scully had joined the Dodger broadcast team fresh out of Fordham in 1950. When he arrived at Dodgertown that year, he said, "They didn't know what to do with me. So I slept on a cot in a little room off the main lobby."[10] At twenty-six, he had been trained by Red Barber, proven his ability, and made far less money than his mentor.

For O'Malley letting Barber go was a business decision. Red Barber saw things differently: "O'Malley wanted to cut me down. He tried to do it subtly. O'Malley is a devious man, about the most devious man I ever met."[11] Red Barber went to the Yankees. Fortunately for O'Malley, Scully became an instant success.

In his later years, Red Barber remembered Dodgertown fondly, especially the things that made it special: "My first recollection is Mr. Rickey. He was so vocal and informative. Rickey knew so much about the game. I learned from him. . . . Everybody and everything was right there before your eyes. It was so much a big family. When you moved about that camp, you knew you were in the heart of baseball. Mr. Rickey had such an atmosphere in mind when he picked Vero Beach. He sought an environment adaptable for the birth of his convictions that black players were to become an important part of baseball."[12]

1955

Concern and Optimism

The Dodger DC-3, with Bump Holman at the controls, taxied up to the old Naval Air Station control building. The cabin door opened and Mr. and Mrs. Walter O'Malley descended. Next came Dodger vice president Fresco Thompson wearing an overcoat and wrapped in a blanket to mock the cool Florida day. He remarked that at least there was no smog, perhaps foretelling the Dodgers' California future. Head winds had delayed the plane in flight from New York, but a hundred friends and fans waited patiently. In a traditional Florida-style, bathing-beauty greeting, Ellen Catron and Julie Conkling, local Vero Beach High School students, shivering in swimsuits, posed for pictures with the arrivals.[13] The 1955 Dodgers would follow in a few days.

With the Dodgers in camp, an editorial in the *Press Journal* gushed: "The Dodgers and Vero Beach have become synonymous. . . . Friendships are again being renewed. . . . the players really like the community and the fine people that live here. . . . As President Walter O'Malley said on his arrival, 'This is like coming home. In fact Vero Beach is our second home.' . . . With the official approval by the CAA (Civil Aeronautics Administration) the Dodgers family and the citizens of this community may look forward to many years of friendly relations."[14] Little did Mr. O'Malley know the problems the CAA, soon to be called the FAA (Federal Aviation Administration), would cause in future years.

Things were not quite as jolly as the local paper portrayed. The team was coming off a season in which the hated Giants under Leo Durocher took away their National League Championship and then won the World Series. Walter Alston, in his first year as manager, faced severe criticism and had not yet been offered a contract for the season. Carl Furillo, Jackie Robinson, Roy Campanella, and Pee Wee Reese were now in their thirties and considered past their peak. Feisty Don Zimmer thought he was going to replace Pee Wee. With Junior Gilliam established at second base, Sandy Amoros in left field, and Don Hoak a candidate at third, the question hanging over Dodgertown was again where Jackie would play.

General Manager Bavasi solved the manager problem. As Alston explained, "Buzzie Bavasi handed me a contract which I signed after practice one day. . . . We had forgotten about it and decided to get the detail over with."[15]

In an incident at Dodgertown, Walter Alston showed that he had taken charge. Don Newcombe refused to pitch batting practice for no apparent reason. Alston, in front of the whole team, ordered him to leave the field. He did. Campanella chased his six-foot-four, 240-pound roommate into the clubhouse. "Don't you take that uniform off," shouted Campanella. "You never take that uniform off. You make them tear it off." Campanella convinced Newcombe to go back on the field.[16]

Roy Campanella spoke optimistically about the 1955 season. On the first day of workouts he declared himself "O.K." after the problems with his hands that he had endured the previous year. He said, "We're going to run away with this thing."[17] Few people believed him. But the pitching was deep with Don Newcombe, Carl Erskine, Johnny Podres, Billy Loes, Russ Meyer, Clem Labine, Roger Craig, Ed Roebuck, and Karl Spooner.

Three Young Pitchers

Spooner, a rookie phenomenon, joined the Dodgers late in '54 and pitched two consecutive shutouts, striking out a combined twenty-seven batters. Karl Spooner said, "I figured the next year I was going to set the world on fire. And I hurt my arm in spring training."[18] At Dodgertown, Spooner rushed to warm up for an exhibition game, blew his arm, and his baseball career. He pitched sporadically for the Dodgers in '55.

Karl Spooner, like Rex Barney, moved to Vero Beach. He had no profession, and his World Series check was long ago spent. He refinished floors, tended bar, and built roof trusses. He worked as a counselor at the Dodgertown boys' camp. Karl became a packinghouse manager for local citrusman, Jerre Haffield. A rabid fan since the arrival of the Dodgers in Vero, Haffield had flown to New York to see the Dodgers and, by chance, saw Spooner pitch his first major league game.[19]

In 1955, Dodgertown received two teenage pitchers, who would become Dodger legends—eighteen-year-old Don Drysdale and nineteen-year-old Sandy Koufax. Drysdale remembered the experience for Joe Hendrickson: "I had never been out of California before. I got into a Constellation in Los Angeles and headed for Florida, naturally very excited. The flight took all day and all night with three stops before I got to Vero. I arrived at eight in the morning and was in uniform by nine." Of field

#1, Drysdale recalled, "that was where pitchers were sent to run in the outfield to get in shape. I spent many a suffering moment there. . . . And those barracks. Voices carried so well there one could carry on a conversation with someone three or four rooms down the hall." For Drysdale, "Vero Beach provided . . . young hopefuls the chance to live with the proven players and absorb their knowledge."[20]

Duke Snider helped Drysdale out. Don, pitching batting practice and showing off, threw high fast ones in close to Jim Gilliam and Pee Wee Reese. Duke got up and asked Drysdale to give him a change up. Snider lined it back at the young pitcher, who turned and got plunked in the back, fell down, and cut himself in the leg with his spikes. He limped off the field. Don Drysdale needed to improve his temperament more than his pitching. Duke Snider applied the first lesson.[21]

Raised in Brooklyn, Sandy Koufax played basketball in high school but also participated in sandlot baseball. He received a basketball scholarship to the University of Cincinnati and in the spring of 1954 was a walk-on for the baseball team. There, he got some major league attention for his fastball. Back in Brooklyn for the summer, playing in a local league, he received more attention. Dodger scout Al Campanis signed him. "I was concerned when Sandy first came to [Dodgertown] because . . . he was ballyhooing his potential," said Campanis. "Bavasi was calling him the 'Wild Man.' I felt much better one day when Sandy went into an exhibition game and pitched two innings, striking out five of the six men to face him."[22]

Koufax felt good after his performance. But as a bonus player he would sit on the Dodger bench most of the coming season, pitching just enough to win two games and lose two. While Koufax sat, Don Drysdale gained experience pitching for Montreal.

Local Interest

Meantime, as reported by the *Press Journal*, Dodgertown was busy. Walter O'Malley, the amateur horticulturalist, proudly showed Dodgertown visitors his orchids. Mrs. Walter Alston and Mrs. Bobby Morgan, the coach's wife, were a steady golfing twosome at the Royal Park Golf Course. Billy DeLury, down from the Brooklyn office, was running the Dodgertown Post Office for the six hundred players, coaches, and staff. He was handling the hundreds of fan letters coming from all over the country requesting player pictures and autographs. Mrs. Ralph Branca visited her parents, Mr. and Mrs. Jim Mulvey, who as part owners of the

Dodgers were staying at Dodgertown. But Mrs. Branca's husband was not there. He was in training with the Minneapolis Millers, a Giant farm team, attempting a comeback. There were forty-seven children of players, coaches, and sportswriters in camp.[23]

Walter O'Malley invited Vero Beach pioneer Waldo Sexton out to watch practice. Waldo wrote a letter to Zora Neale Hurston, the best-known, African American woman writer of the time. She lived in nearby Fort Pierce. "When I saw those fine colored boys out there making a good showing," he wrote, "I thought about you and thought there might be a possibility of your writing an article about them." Whether Zora ever wrote such an article is unclear.[24]

The Dodgers spent nine days at Dodgertown before moving to Miami to begin their exhibition schedule in Miami Stadium. They returned to Vero for games with the Orioles, the Yankees, and the now Kansas City Athletics.[25]

The Yankees maintained their jinx over the Dodgers, winning 19–8 before a Holman Stadium crowd of 3,727. Mel Allen and former Dodger broadcaster Red Barber called the game for the Yankees. Vin Scully sat within earshot broadcasting the game for the Dodgers. Mel Allen said after viewing the stadium, "Man, they sure have a beautiful plant here."[26]

One of the sportswriters asked Walter O'Malley why the Dodgers had played only three games in Vero. He explained that the major league games must first average five thousand spectators before that would be feasible. "We realize that the city is small," said O'Malley, "but we know it is growing and that the day will come when we can expect crowds of this size."[27] Vero's population was 6,500 then. It would be 1980, when the city's population reached 17,000, before the Dodgers began playing a full spring schedule of thirteen to fifteen games in Holman Stadium.

The Holman Stadium game between the Dodgertown All-Stars and the Dodgers generated some local interest. "Vero Beach's own" Bill Letchworth pitched for the All-Stars, a group of top minor leaguers. He was working out with the Fort Worth farm team. He grew up in Indian River County, pitched for Auburn University, and spent two years in the Detroit Tigers minor league organization. Koufax and Drysdale pitched for the Dodgers, a team composed mostly of rookies. Bill Letchworth never made the majors, and he didn't need to. He already owned the Oldsmobile dealership in town. He could claim, however, that he pitched against two future Hall of Famers.[28]

Per the Dodgers' lease with the City of Vero Beach, the proceeds of the All-Star game, a grand sum of $419, went to the airport maintenance fund. The FAA would later complain that such paltry sums were inappropriate. Meanwhile, Fort Myers invested $100,000 in a stadium to attract the Pittsburgh Pirates for spring training. The City of Miami was considering spending $800,000 to buy Miami Stadium in hopes that the Dodgers would play more games there. At the same time, Vero Beach had invested nothing to gain one of the most popular and well-known teams in the country.[29]

A Historic Season

The Dodgers jumped to a quick start and went on to win the 1955 National League Championship easily. They would again meet the Yankees in the World Series, the team they had yet to beat in five tries.

Grace Shilling Goodermote, who in her job as secretary at Dodgertown had encountered the Boys of Summer every day for four springs, missed what was for the Dodgers the World Series of all World Series. Grace, the lover of baseball, had another love: she was busy planning her wedding, which took place shortly after the games.

Grace nonetheless came by a 1955 World Series program, which reviews Dodger history, depicts the marvelous season, and introduces the players and the management. Near its end, the program features pictures of the Yankees, including Mickey Mantle, Yogi Berra, Whitey Ford, and manager Casey Stengel. But the most interesting item, looking at the program from the perspective of time, is its introduction by Walter O'Malley. The intro began, "This is the Dodgers' year," and ended, "Let us hope the World Series of 1958 is played in baseball's finest stadium—right here in Brooklyn." O'Malley was working to acquire a site in Brooklyn to build a new stadium. In 1958, though, the Dodgers would neither play in the World Series nor be in Brooklyn.

A twenty-four-man delegation, led by Bud Holman, flew out of Vero Beach on Eastern Airlines en route to New York for the World Series. Vero's two drugstores installed television sets so that anyone downtown could stop in and see the action.

The Dodgers lost the first two games, and it looked like another typical Yankee year. But the team fought back and tied the Series at three wins apiece. In the deciding game, pitcher Johnny Podres fought off the Yankees inning by inning for a 2–0 Dodger win. Dodger broadcaster Vin Scully, holding back tears, managed to say calmly, "Ladies and Gentlemen, the Brooklyn Dodgers are the Champions of the World." Walter

O'Malley joyously kissed his wife, his daughter, and the other guests in his box, Mrs. Douglas McArthur and Brooklyn borough president John Cashmore.[30]

Brooklyn went wild. Car horns, church bells, factory whistles all rang out across the borough. In downtown Vero there was hollering and shouting from the people crowded around the TV sets at the McClure's and Osceola drugstores. "Wait till next year" was this year!

That evening, Borough President Cashmore issued an official statement ordering a survey for a new Dodger Stadium. "They must never leave Brooklyn," he said.[31]

Grace, the newlywed, received a letter on new Dodger stationary with a team picture and "Brooklyn's First World Champs" emblazoned in large, red print. The note read: "Dear Grace, You were swell to take the trouble to wire and I appreciate it, Walter O'Malley."

A *Press Journal* headline declared: "It'll Be World Champion Dodgers in Dodgertown Come Next Spring."[32]

The line "'55 World Champs" was added to the "Winter Home of the Brooklyn Dodgers" sign on U.S. 1 at the entrance to downtown Vero.

A sign in downtown Vero Beach commemorates the Dodgers' World Series win over the Yankees. (Courtesy of Indian River Historical Society, Vero Beach, Florida.)

So We're Going

1956

Back in the Doldrums

Vero Beach greeted the '55 World Champions "back home" with a welcoming reception at Holman Stadium attended by 1,500 local citizens. Walter O'Malley was "more than pleased with the turnout" and said that with this size crowd it "might pay to put a Class D ball club in Vero Beach."[1] It would be 1980 before minor league baseball came to Vero.

Rookie pitcher Don Drysdale made the big team in 1956. At nineteen, he became the youngest pitcher in the major leagues. World Series hero Johnny Podres had been drafted into the Army, Karl Spooner and Billy Loes had bad arms, and Don Bessent, who had some potential, hurt his arm during the spring. Bessent's injury occurred on the golf course, when he threw his golf club at a snake at the Vero Beach Country Club.[2] Bessent's nickname was "Weasel." Whether he was called that before or after the snake incident isn't clear.

Despite their World Series win, no one expected the Dodgers to repeat in 1956. But with the help of former Giant pitcher Sal Maglie, the team nipped the powerful Milwaukee Braves on the last day of the season for the league championship. The Yankees appeared in the World Series for the eighth time in ten years and Brooklyn for the sixth time in that period.[3] Despite breaking the jinx in '55, the Dodgers fell back into their old ways, losing four games to three.

After the Series loss, an unhappy group of Dodgers traveled to Japan. It was an O'Malley extravaganza, and he had a talk with the team. They were to be goodwill ambassadors, but when they put their Dodger uni-

The Dodger management—Buzzie Bavasi, Walter Alston, Fresco Thompson, and Walter O'Malley—are welcomed back to Vero Beach as World Champions. Bud Holman looks on. (Courtesy of Indian River County Historical Society, Vero Beach, Florida.)

forms on to go out on the field, he said, "I want you to remember Pearl Harbor."[4]

As a result of this "goodwill" trip, O'Malley invited a star Japanese battery—a pitcher named Horichi and a catcher named Fujio—to come to Dodgertown the next spring. Their visit was a prelude to the Tokyo Giants coming to Vero Beach on several occasions beginning in 1961.

That fall, Walter O'Malley announced that real progress was being made on building a new stadium in Brooklyn.[5] In reality he was having trouble. To exert pressure on New York City officials, the Dodgers had played seven "home" games in Jersey City in 1956. To further make his point, Walter O'Malley arranged to sell Ebbets Field to a developer with the stipulation that the Dodgers could play there through 1959.[6]

Something Big Going On

In Vero Beach, Piper Aircraft, manufacturer of the Piper Cub, joined the Dodgers and was a prime tenant at the airport, transferring its engineering and development center from Lock Haven, Pennsylvania. The forty-acre site lay just to the east of Ebbets Field #2. As with the Dodgers, Bud Holman had been instrumental in bringing Piper to the community.

While Vero celebrated its new industry, Brooklyn experienced a miserable year.

Jackie Robinson began the misery by leaving the Dodgers. Walter O'Malley wanted to get rid of him. Robinson was a "Rickey man" and his aggressiveness off the field, particularly his speaking out on racial issues, made O'Malley uncomfortable. As Roger Kahn points out: "Walter liked blacks docile."[7] O'Malley worked out a deal in the winter of 1957 to sell Jackie to the Giants.

But like Branch Rickey, Jackie outmaneuvered O'Malley. Jackie, at thirty-eight, decided to quit baseball and had already accepted a position as a vice president with Chock full o'Nuts, a large New York coffee counter operation with many black employees.[8]

In his autobiography, Jackie stated: "I was one of those uppity niggers in O'Malley's book."[9] Rachel Robinson remarked years later in *Jackie Robinson, An Intimate Portrait*, that Walter O'Malley's son, Peter, supported the Jackie Robinson Foundation in a major way and that she and Peter enjoyed a close friendship. "We have worked to put the tensions between Jack and Peter's father, Walter, behind us," she said.[10]

At Vero Beach on February 21, 1957, an early morning rain delayed twenty-six Dodger pitchers and catchers from beginning their first day of spring training. At noon the players moved onto the practice fields behind the Dodgertown barracks, throwing back and forth, playing pepper games, and running.[11]

Manager Walter Alston's usual after-workout press conference was canceled. Instead, Walter O'Malley, sitting on a table in the Dodgertown pressroom, addressed the writers. He announced that he had traded the Dodgers' Fort Worth franchise to Philip Wrigley, owner of the Chicago Cubs, for his Los Angeles Angels minor league franchise plus its Wrigley Field stadium in Los Angeles. O'Malley had not exactly "traded" the franchises; he paid Wrigley $2 million for the Los Angeles property. But having sold the Montreal and Fort Worth real estate plus Ebbets Field, O'Malley now had sufficient funds to build a stadium in Brooklyn or wherever.[12]

The next day, a front-page article in the *New York Times*, datelined Vero Beach, declared, "Dodgers Buy Los Angeles Club, Stirring Talk of a Shift to Coast." Writer Roscoe McGowen said, "This surprising action may have moved the Brooklyn Dodgers a little closer to becoming the Los Angeles Dodgers."[13] The Dodgers now had the baseball rights to Los Angeles.

On March 5, a delegation of Los Angeles officials arrived in Vero Beach.[14] It was raining again, and the *Press Journal* reported "a few drops of California dew in evidence." The group included Los Angeles mayor Norris Poulson, Los Angeles County supervisor Kenneth Hahn, city councilwoman Rosalind Wyman, and city council president John Gibson. The group posed for a photograph with O'Malley; famous clown Emmett Kelly, who was entertaining fans at Dodgertown that spring; and Dodgers Duke Snider and Roy Campanella.[15]

When the L.A. contingent showed up, Walter Alston suspected "something big" was going on. Roy Campanella observed that "politicians came swarming in on us at Vero Beach. They arrived in camp like conquerors, looking us over the way a guy does a piece of property." The press asked Campy to pose with Mayor Poulson, wearing a Dodger cap that had been rigged up with L.A. on it. "I went along with it but to me it was a big joke," said Campy. "The Dodgers leave Ebbets Field? Maybe. But the Dodgers leave Brooklyn? Never."[16]

Meeting at Holman Ranch

The delegation met with Walter O'Malley, Jim Mulvey, and Bud Holman in the seclusion of Holman's ranch, west of Vero off Route 60. "It was about forty miles from Vero Beach," said Kenneth Hahn, "on a remote road and in a swampland. I do remember that there wasn't even a telephone in this hideaway home of Bud Holman's. It looked like an abandoned Quonset hut base, kind of rough. I didn't stay too long at Vero Beach."[17]

The Holman ranch was situated between a dirt road running to Middleton's Fish Camp and Blue Cypress Lake. The one-story ranch house with a long screened porch across its front stood on an ancient Indian mound. Inside was a huge room with a fireplace at one end. Deer heads and pictures of Walter O'Malley and Bud Holman hung on the wall. One

At Dodgertown, fans commiserate with infielders Pee Wee Reese and Don Zimmer about the possibility of the Dodgers leaving Brooklyn. (Courtesy of Los Angeles Dodgers, Los Angeles, California.)

picture, taken when the Dodger team flew down to Havana on the spur of the moment when the weather was bad in Vero, showed them with a bunch of rowdy Cubans. One of the Cubans was reported to be Castro's brother. Baseball bats with '50s-era names like Ralph Kiner, Andy Seminick, and Enos Slaughter lined the wall of the hallway that led to the sleeping quarters. This ranch house had a history. Bud Holman had entertained General Hap Arnold there in the 1930s, when the Army Air Force conducted an exercise at the Vero airport. Eastern Airlines' Eddie Rickenbacker and Georgia Tech football coach Bobby Dodd visited regularly.[18] For the group from Los Angeles, it must have seemed like the end of the world. The Holman heirs sold the ranch in 2003.

In the meeting at the ranch, the L.A. delegation discussed an area of sparsely settled hills and gullies above downtown Los Angeles, called Chavez Ravine, as a possible site for a stadium. Mayor Poulson called the meeting "a sparring match": "One of our officials promised O'Malley the moon and Walter asked for more. . . . I assured [him] we wanted him desperately but made it clear we would have to come up with a plan that wouldn't get us run out of the city."[19]

According to Hahn, the delegation went back home believing they had O'Malley hooked. O'Malley, on the other hand, made no commitment. He divulged nothing to the press, which included the New York writers in Dodgertown, as well as a contingency from Los Angeles.

Visitors from Brooklyn walked around Dodgertown wearing tee shirts printed with "Keep the Dodgers in Brooklyn." Rumors spread through Vero that Dodgertown would be a ghost town within a year and that California would be the training base for the entire Dodger organization.[20] O'Malley quickly clarified the situation by saying, "Vero Beach is the only city in the United States that doesn't have to worry where the Dodgers might or might not be going."[21]

For three years prior to the Holman ranch meeting, the Los Angeles officials had been looking for a major league team. Councilwoman Rosalind Wyman, elected on a platform of bringing a major league team to Los Angeles, tried to contact O'Malley during the 1955 World Series, but he declined to meet with her.[22] He was too busy trying to work out a deal in Brooklyn.

Kenneth Hahn attended the '56 Series to talk with the Washington Senators about their making a move to Los Angeles. But now O'Malley was looking and sent Hahn a note on a napkin asking him to sign nothing until they could meet.[23]

After the World Series, O'Malley called Hahn. During a stopover on the Dodgers' flight to Japan, O'Malley and Hahn met for a quiet breakfast at the Los Angeles Statler Hotel.[24] While O'Malley was in Japan, one of his underlings completed the sale of Ebbets Field. The next step was the meeting at Bud Holman's ranch.

Deterioration and Obstruction

Walter O'Malley had been dissatisfied with Ebbets Field for years. The walkways stunk of urine. Seats had splinters. The girders were rusty. There were only seven hundred parking places. Despite the 1955 championship, Ebbets Field on average remained half empty. With the area around Ebbets Field deteriorating, the faithful stayed home and watched the Dodgers on TV.[25]

Brooklyn began to lose its generally pleasant neighborhoods. After World War II, the middle class, encouraged by inexpensive land and housing in the suburbs, started moving out to Long Island and New Jersey as lower-income families moved into Brooklyn.

In 1952, the Mulveys left Brooklyn for New York's Westchester County. For years, the McKeevers and the Mulveys had lived side by side on Maple Avenue in Flatbush, not far from Ebbets Field, in old brick homes on ample lots.[26] The O'Malleys already lived out on Long Island.

After the 1953 meeting of baseball's executive council at Dodgertown during the Holman Stadium dedication, the Boston Braves moved to Milwaukee. There, the local government provided the Braves with a new stadium. They drew two million fans, twice the Dodgers' attendance at Ebbets Field. O'Malley worried that the Braves would build a dynasty that would surpass the Dodgers. The prophecy came true, as the Braves quickly became their toughest competitor in the National League.[27]

O'Malley selected designer Emil Praeger to develop plans not only for Holman Stadium in Vero Beach but also for a new stadium for Brooklyn. O'Malley was willing to build the stadium himself, but he needed land. In September of '53, he met for the first time with Robert Moses, the powerful commissioner of public construction in New York City. Moses controlled millions of dollars of federal funds and, with those funds, had more power than the mayor and the borough presidents who presumably ran New York City. Author Michael Shapiro described him as "an overbearing bully . . . with people who disagreed with him," but also as "a lone and powerful voice in defining the public good."[28]

O'Malley wanted a site in the middle of Brooklyn, and Moses had the means to condemn land. In 1954, Brooklyn borough president John Cashmore suggested a centrally located spot, where the Long Island Railroad and New York subways intersected. Moses didn't like the idea. He suggested a more peripheral location. O'Malley considered Moses' suggestion, a rundown, tenement neighborhood, worse than the Ebbets Field area. Cashmore and O'Malley met with Moses about the central Brooklyn site. Moses said it was "futile"; a stadium there would make the location too crowded. In addition, he took the position that federal funds could not be used to benefit a private endeavor such as the Dodgers.[29]

It was then that O'Malley announced the Dodgers would play seven games in Jersey City in 1956 and that he would stay at Ebbets Field only two more years. New York mayor Robert Wagner held a meeting to seek a solution, saying he was "very anxious to keep the Brooklyn Dodgers in New York City."[30] Cashmore proposed a study to look at a sports complex that would include the Dodgers at the central Brooklyn site.

The New York City bureaucracy did little in 1956 to move O'Malley's project forward. In frustration, he began to talk to the Los Angeles people. Buzzie Bavasi recalled a staff meeting with O'Malley at the end of '56 in which everyone was asked what they thought about moving to Los Angeles. O'Malley concluded the meeting by saying, "Everyone wants to stay except for me. So we're going."[31]

As a follow-up to the meeting with the Los Angeles delegation in Vero Beach, Walter O'Malley flew to Los Angeles in May 1957 for a visit with Kenneth Hahn. They took a helicopter tour of the city and flew over Chavez Ravine. O'Malley said to Hahn, "You could build a ball park there."[32]

Meanwhile, O'Malley talked with New York Giants owner Horace Stoneham about moving the Giants to San Francisco. If O'Malley was going to Los Angeles, he needed another team on the West Coast. With attendance declining at the Polo Grounds, Stoneham had already thought about leaving New York.[33] In August, the Giants announced a move to San Francisco where the city would build them a stadium—Candlestick Park.

In New York, the stadium feasibility study had concluded that it would be *possible* to put a baseball stadium in central Brooklyn, but also tremendously expensive. O'Malley ignored the study's financial conclusions, offered to buy land at the site, build a stadium with his own money, and pay taxes on the property. But first the city would have to condemn the land. Public construction commissioner Moses urged the city's legal council not to "give the time of day to Walter O'Malley's latest offer."[34] On September 20, 1957, the New York City Board of Estimates killed any possibility of a deal.

Last Game at Ebbets Field

During the 1957 season, the Dodgers, distracted by talk of moving west, finished third as the Milwaukee Braves won the championship.

The Dodgers played their last game at Ebbets Field on September 24th. With the move to Los Angeles inevitable, only 6,702 fans came to say good-bye as the Dodgers beat the Pirates 2–0. Organist Gladys Gooding rendered farewell dirges. Thus ended Brooklyn's sixty-seven years in the National League and its forty-five years playing at Ebbets Field.

Broadcaster Red Barber reflected on what Ebbets Field had been: "a little small, outmoded, old fashioned. . . . dirty, stinking, old ballpark. But when you went in there, as a fan, it was your ballpark. You were practically playing second base, the stands were so close to the field. Everybody was in touch with everybody else at Ebbets Field."[35]

Meanwhile, the Los Angeles City Council battled over the offer to the Dodgers. The opponents, like those who quashed O'Malley's stadium plans in New York, argued that the city was giving too much away. On October 7, after some tense delays, the city council reached an agreement on a contract with the Dodgers. The county supervisors had already approved the contract unanimously.[36]

The two Los Angeles political bodies succeeded while the New York City Board of Estimates, battling the obstructionist policies of Robert Moses, had failed. The Los Angeles offer stipulated that O'Malley would trade the Wrigley Field property in Los Angeles, which encompassed an entire city block, for three hundred acres at Chavez Ravine. The city owned part of the acreage and would procure the rest. The county would prepare the terrain and build access roads; O'Malley would build the stadium.[37]

On October 8, 1957, a Dodger underling read a terse statement in the Waldorf Astoria's pressroom that concluded: "The stockholders and directors of the Brooklyn Baseball Club have today met and unanimously agreed that necessary steps be taken to draft the Los Angeles territory [from the Pacific Coast League]."[38] O'Malley was not at the Waldorf Astoria to take questions. No parting words were said, no farewell given. The team just left.

On the same day the Dodgers announced their departure from Brooklyn, they issued a statement that the team would have spring training again next year at the Vero Beach camp.[39] But in Vero the community worried about how silly it would seem for a California baseball team to be training in Florida.

8

Los Angeles Dodgers

1958

A New City, A Dispirited Team

"In 1958, we come not as the Brooklyn Dodgers but as the Los Angeles Dodgers," wrote Walter O'Malley in a letter to the community. "The success of our Vero Beach operation is shown in the successful record of the Dodgers over the postwar era. Six pennants, three seconds, and two thirds have resulted since teams returned to full strength after World War II—and most of these springs have been spent right here in your beautiful Indian River County."[1]

And this beautiful area continued to grow, particularly on the island in what is now called Central Beach. New, three-bedroom, two-bath "Beautiful Beach Homes" were priced beginning at $23,900. Dredging began on eighty-five acres of river marsh for the Riomar Bay project.[2] Development on the island had come a long way since 1950, when Billy DeLury first arrived at Dodgertown to run the mailroom. As he remembered it, "Once you crossed the river, it seemed as though you had entered a jungle."[3]

The Dodgers celebrated their tenth anniversary at Vero. Five hundred players were in camp. But even beyond the Los Angeles name change and the players' concern about relocation, another difference existed. Roy Campanella was absent.

On January 28, 1958, Roy Campanella, driving home late at night to Long Island from his Harlem liquor store, skidded on an icy road. The car smashed into a telephone pole and landed on its side. An ambulance rushed Campy to the hospital. The doctors found his neck broken and his spinal cord almost severed. Surgeons operated the next morning. Walter

O'Malley arrived during the long surgery and stayed until it was over.[4] Roy Campanella remained in the hospital for several months.

Manager Walter Alston faced some tough personnel decisions. Besides replacing Campanella, he had to handle a dispirited team soon to move to a new environment. Pee Wee Reese, the captain, wanted to retire, but O'Malley talked him into one more year so the team could retain in Los Angeles as much of the old Dodger flavor as possible. Already in camp were Hodges, Furillo, Snider, and Gilliam. Johnny Roseboro, a rookie in 1957, replaced Campanella. Don Newcombe would be traded early in the season. He had an alcohol problem that surfaced during the 1956 Japan trip. He joined Alcoholics Anonymous, married a "good woman," as Johnny Roseboro said, and whipped his problem.[5] Newcombe returned to the Dodgers in 1971 as director of community relations, helping with a variety of local projects and working with teammates and others with alcohol problems.

Trouble in L.A.

While the Dodgers practiced in Vero, the move to Los Angeles proceeded. Until O'Malley built the Chavez Ravine stadium, the Dodgers would play in the Los Angeles Coliseum despite having to modify a football stadium for baseball.[6] The coliseum's ninety thousand seats consisted of wooden benches that climbed sixty-five rows: So much for the cozy confines of Ebbets Field and Holman Stadium! From Walter Alston's perspective, "Center field seemed like it was in another country."[7]

But then the Chavez Ravine deal suddenly seemed in doubt. "I never anticipated a referendum," O'Malley said. "They never had that in New York. They have initiatives and referendums out here. Very peculiar."[8] In New York, politicians (or a Robert Moses) made the decisions for the people. California's state constitution allowed the people to override the politicians if they wished. With a vote, called Proposition B, set for June on the Chavez Ravine agreement, O'Malley faced a delay in starting construction on the new stadium.

Early indications showed that the populace heavily favored the Chavez Ravine agreement. Confident of a victory, O'Malley and Mayor Poulson took a "hands off" approach to the election.[9]

On opening day, 78,672 fans, including a bevy of Hollywood stars, poured into the Coliseum to set a league attendance record. The Dodgers beat the Giants that day, but went on to play mediocre ball and to lose regularly. Don Drysdale described the situation: "There was complete chaos on the ball club because of our move. . . . We lost the community closeness. . . . Everything was on top of everything in Brooklyn, but in Los Angeles we were in the wide-open spaces."[10]

The Dodgers continued to lose. Attendance dropped. As the June referendum approached, the population began to wonder what kind of team and what kind of deal they were getting. The election, a sure bet at first, began to be in doubt. O'Malley worried. He arranged for some of the Hollywood crowd, led by George Burns, Cary Grant, Groucho Marx, and Jack Benny, to do a TV marathon touting the advantages of having the Dodgers in L.A. Ronald Reagan, then president of the Screen Actors Guild, participated.[11]

On election day, June 3, 1958, as Los Angeles County citizens went to the polls, the Dodgers fell into last place in the National League. The vote was close—52 percent for the Chavez Ravine deal, 48 percent against.[12] Bavasi remarked "If not for Hollywood (and the efforts of people like Cary Grant and Ronald Reagan), we might have lost."[13]

Walter O'Malley had little time to celebrate. Despite the referendum victory, opponents initiated a lawsuit to stop the Chavez Ravine agreement. Hearings began in Los Angeles Superior Court. On July 14, the judge shocked O'Malley, Mayor Poulson, and the other Dodger supporters. He ruled the Chavez Ravine contract invalid, taking the same position as Robert Moses had in New York. The judge stated that "public funds could not be used to obtain property to be transferred to a corporation for the operation of a private business."[14]

Construction at Chavez Ravine remained on hold with the possibility that the suit, during appeal, could be tied up in the courts indefinitely.

The Dodgers finished the 1958 season in seventh place. Buzzie Bavasi called the year an "embarrassment."[15]

Walter O'Malley had to be glad to get his first year in Los Angeles behind him—the Coliseum controversy, the referendum, the law suit, the delay in starting his new stadium, and the team's poor performance.

1959

Walking On Eggshells

The situation turned around with the new year. In early January, the California State Supreme Court overruled the lower court. The contract, it stated, must be viewed as a whole. Some provisions of the contract could benefit the baseball club, as long as "the city receives benefits which serve legitimate purposes." The court believed that the receipt of the Los Angeles Wrigley Field property and the Dodgers' agreement to provide recreation facilities at Chavez Ravine for twenty years were proper benefits to the city.[16]

Construction at Chavez Ravine began.

At Dodgertown, twenty-nine-year-old rookie shortstop Maury Wills joined the big team. He had proven himself by coming up in midseason the previous year. Maury had first arrived in Vero in 1951 as a pitcher assigned to Class D Hornell of the New York State League. As had been the case for others, the number of competitors at his position at Dodgertown overwhelmed him. He asked if he could become a second baseman. His manager agreed after watching him work out. Wills was amazed that the white and black players were mixed together: "Rooming with white players was a grand experience for me."[17] But he yearned to move out of the minor league barracks with six to eight to a room into what he called "the classy side," the major league barracks with two to a room and a bath in between. Maury liked the food, the fishing, and playing his banjo at camp functions. "Enjoyable as it was," said Maury, "after seven weeks in Dodgertown each spring, it was good to see the rest of America."[18]

Years later, Wills wrote: "I played ball twenty-three years and went to Vero Beach with the Dodgers twenty of them. I saw at least three generations of little black kids in Gifford—the father, their sons, and their grandsons—growing up picking oranges. That's the only thing they had a chance to do."[19]

Catcher Johnny Roseboro, who replaced the injured Campanella, did not find spring training in Vero Beach as pleasant as Maury Wills did. For Roseboro, who had grown up in a small Ohio town where there was very little racial prejudice, "Beyond the base there was bigotry, even if there was none on the base." He liked Dodgertown, describing it as "nice looking, surrounded by orange groves, and you could pick all the oranges you wanted." "There," he said, "you were segregated by ability, not color."[20]

Wills, who arrived at Dodgertown a couple of years before Roseboro, described Gifford to him as "the colored town where the niggers went on the town after the day's work was done." To Roseboro, Vero Beach, "the white town, wasn't much better. It was a tiny tourist type town." Over on the beach, as Roseboro observed, there were "some nice hotels and motels, nice restaurants and shops. Blacks weren't welcome there." The city's white taxicab wouldn't carry blacks. The "white guys" got invited to go offshore fishing, not the blacks. "We always felt like we were walking on eggshells when we had to be in that town," said Roseboro.[21] He would come to Vero for fifteen springs.

It took Wills nine years to move into the major league quarters. He finally reached the "classy side" in 1961, but only after he stole fifty bases and became a regular.[22] His friend Johnny Roseboro was already there, having made the move in 1956, after his rookie year.

Campy Returns

In 1959, Roy Campanella returned to Dodgertown. Mr. O'Malley told Campy "that he not only wanted him down there but he needed him." Campy mentored the young catchers: "I was to teach Roseboro in a short time what I had learned in a long time." The Dodger Convair 440 flew Campy in his wheelchair, along with his two attendants, to Vero. Campy remembered pilot Bump Holman and the attendants carrying

Roy Campanella returns to Dodgertown after his injury. He is flanked by Los Angeles city councilwoman Rosalind Wyman, who was active in the Dodgers' move from Brooklyn, and by Walter O'Malley, who is taking Campanella's picture. (Courtesy of Los Angeles Dodgers, Los Angeles, California.)

him down the gangplank at the Vero airport, where welcoming him was what seemed to be "the entire population of Dodgertown! Mr. O'Malley, Buzzie Bavasi, Walter Alston, Pee Wee, Duke, Carl, Gil."[23]

Roy Campanella described his return to Vero: "Rolling over the green grass in my chair to the batting cage where I'd station myself to one side was sure 'going home.' The sights and the smells and the sounds that I'd missed for so long came back to me in one big whiff. The thud of baseballs smacking into glove . . . the sharp crack of the bat against the ball . . . the hard work and the sweat . . . the quiet determination that this had to be a new and better Dodger ball club . . . down there I felt it all through me."[24]

Campanella lived in the Dodgertown infirmary. During exhibition games at Holman Stadium, he sat in his wheelchair at the top of the stands next to the press box. His attendants stood close by to protect him from foul balls. It embarrassed Campy that the paralysis prevented him from writing his name and giving fans autographs. After dinner, he sat out back of the barracks kitchen, "chewing the fat" with whoever came along: the kitchen staff, his teammates, or the minor leaguers. That spot between the main reception hall and the mess hall became known as Campy's Bullpen. A sign commemorates the spot today behind the new Dodgertown quarters. Campy would tell people about the mustache he grew over the winter and the every-spring ritual of Pee Wee Reese shaving it off.

Campy enjoyed eating fish, particularly trout caught by outfielder Carl Furillo in the Indian River.[25] He also loved crab fingers from Sockwell's, a crab-processing house on the river. Chuck Dressen introduced him to this delicacy. Campy liked the crab fingers so much that he had them shipped to his Long Island home. Johnny Roseboro remembered Campy bringing a five-gallon barrel of iced crab fingers to the ball park: "After the game we'd dig into that barrel. We'd sit around licking our fingers, having fun. Lord how he loved to have fun!"[26]

L.A. Wins a World Championship

During that spring of 1959, a front stalled across the Florida peninsula. Rain fell for five straight days in Vero with no sign of a letup. The team, especially after the '58 season, needed practice. Buzzie Bavasi and Walter O'Malley took action. Bump Holman flew the Dodgers to Havana, then picked up the Cincinnati Reds and flew them there. The Reds and Dodgers played each other for the next four days. Writer Bob Hunter reported, "When we arrived in Havana, Castro welcomed us and sat with O'Malley at the games." The group was invited the first night to a fancy casino owned by an American. They were asked back the next night, but as Hunter pointed out, "There wasn't any next night at the casino. The place was closed as Castro had broken off with the United States and American businesses had to leave Cuba."[27]

An unlikely Dodger team that had played so poorly the previous year stayed in the pennant race throughout the summer. At season's end, the Braves and the Dodgers stood tied for the league lead. The Dodgers won the playoff and faced the Chicago White Sox in the World Series. The White Sox were not the Yankees, and the Dodgers won four games to two.

The Dodgers took sixty-five years to win the World Series in Brooklyn and two years in Los Angeles. Buzzie Bavasi said, "It was the worst club to win a World Series. But it's also my favorite club. Those kids won on sheer courage and fortitude. That's really all it was."[28]

Walter O'Malley's risky move to Los Angeles had worked out. The legal battles were over, the Chavez Ravine stadium was under construction, a team attendance record was set, and the Los Angeles Dodgers were World Champions.

But Walter O'Malley, after dealing with political fiascos in New York and Los Angeles, faced another one—in Vero Beach, of all places.

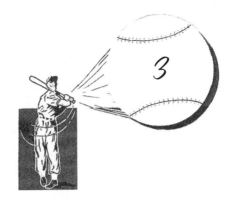

3

The Sixties

Dodgertown as it looked in 1960. The photograph shows the barracks and a game in progress at Holman Stadium, with cars parked on fields #1 and #2. The property was still being leased from the City of Vero Beach. Dodgertown Golf Course and the Dodger Pines Country Club would be added later (upper left). (Courtesy of Indian River County Historical Society, Vero Beach, Florida.)

Dodgers Not Being Booted

1960

Horse Whipping the City

The citizens of Vero Beach turned out in mass to greet the World Champion Los Angeles Dodgers at the airport. Few realized what lay ahead for the city and the Dodgers, politically and on the field. With the New York and Los Angeles political problems behind him, Walter O'Malley now faced a Vero Beach problem. The Federal Aviation Agency wanted to throw both Bud Holman and the Dodgers off the airport property.

It started in January when the owners of Indian River Flying Service, Sig Lynse and Punky Orth, requested space on the Vero Beach Municipal Airport flight line. Operating out of the Hibiscus Airpark, their own airstrip across town, they had just obtained a Cessna dealership and wanted to move their sales operations. Bud Holman said no; he held an exclusive lease for the flight line. Lynse and Orth approached the city directly to no avail, then complained to the FAA.[1]

Investigators from the FAA arrived in Vero in May and voiced a series of concerns. They stated that Bud Holman, to whom the city had leased the airport, was mismanaging the facility and shouldn't have an exclusive right to operate the flight line. In addition, runways were not being maintained, equipment and buildings had disappeared, the city had shortchanged the airport fund $28,000, and the Dodgers and Piper paid too little into the airport development fund. The FAA declared that they had never approved any of the leases and that the Dodger lease, in particular, allowed the team to pay a "mere pittance" for use of the Dodgertown property. The FAA threatened to take the airport back from the city.[2]

City councilman Jack Jennings accused the FAA of "horse whipping" the city.[3] He had been an engineer for the Holman Stadium construction and rented his beach house to Dodger players during the spring. His son Flip remembered Bud Holman and Walter O'Malley coming to the Jennings' house for meetings.

The council panicked and put all airport leases on a month-to-month basis. The news spread to Los Angeles where Dodger publicist Red Patterson read in an area paper that the Dodger lease was being canceled. He called *Press Journal* editor Harry Schultz. Patterson said he was "shocked" and hoped that Harry and "all our friends in Vero Beach will be with us in the fight to stay in Dodgertown." He stated that already cities in Florida, California, Nevada, and Arizona were offering training sites to the Dodgers. The *Press Journal* countered the rumors with a front-page headline: "Dodgers Not Being Booted."[4]

Vero Beach mayor Harry Offutt, the local Ford dealer, stepped into the fray and publicly declared: "I am personally convinced that B. L. Holman's operation has not been in the best interests of the city."[5]

Holman, saying Offutt's statement was "false and known to be false," immediately sued the mayor and city councilman Harry Jones, who shared the mayor's position. Bump Holman would later say that his dad wasn't going "to put up with that s—t" from those "g-ddam politicians."[6]

In August, Lynse and Orth, fed up with lack of action on their flight line request, sued Bud Holman and the City of Vero Beach.

The FAA formally notified the city in November 1960 that the defaults must be cleared up in sixty days or the airport ownership would revert back to the federal government. City attorney L. B. "Buck" Vocelle pegged Bud Holman as the "cause of the default" and declared that the leases were invalid. The pro-Dodger, city council majority of Jack Jennings, citrusman Reed Knight, and jeweler Bob Dubose immediately fired Vocelle. Going out the door, Buck Vocelle reminded them, "Holman is a very powerful individual."[7]

In the December city council election, the pro-Holman majority became a minority as Taylor Simpson replaced Knight and Councilman Jones was reelected. Harry Offutt continued as mayor, and the new majority rehired Vocelle.[8]

Fabulous Frank

Despite the political shenanigans, spring training proceeded as usual. Six-foot-seven-inch Frank Howard became the top attraction at Dodgertown. "Fabulous Frank," the slugging, rookie first baseman, declared to the press that he had come to learn, and if anyone thought they could "drive him off this ball club, he'll know he's been in a fight." At the same time, Brooklyn nostalgia came to Dodgertown. The wrecking ball was demolishing Ebbets Field so that apartments could be built in its place. But the Dodgers saved the box-seat chairs and installed them in Holman Stadium. A picture in the paper showed Bud Holman testing one of the seats.[9]

Skipper Walter Alston expressed optimism about the coming season: "The pennant drive of 1959 started right here in Vero Beach, and we're a little ahead in our conditioning so far."[10] But the 1959 World Champions flopped, finishing fourth. Branch Rickey's Pittsburgh Pirates won the World Series.

The seventh annual Dodgertown boys' camp opened in July with 110 boys from eighteen states attending. Hank Majeski, formerly a player with the Philadelphia Athletics, and Vero resident Karl Spooner coached baseball. Spooner returned to the mound to pitch three scoreless innings in a camper-counselor game. In '61, Peter O'Malley assumed more responsibility, becoming camp supervisor. However, social changes in the 1960s made camping less popular, and the number of participants declined.[11]

1961

Sandy Grows Up

While Vero Beach's situation with the FAA remained in limbo, the Tokyo Giants baseball team arrived at Dodgertown for spring training. Walter O'Malley had invited the team as a follow-up to the Dodger Japan trip of 1956. A welcoming crowd of a thousand greeted the Giants as they flew in on the Dodgers' new DC-6, four-engine plane. As part of the ceremony, Mrs. Jim Mulvey christened the new plane "Dearie," her childhood name. Officials toasted the Giants with orange juice and champagne.[12]

Star player Sadaharu Oh, the "Babe Ruth" of Japanese baseball, said of his experience at Dodgertown: "I saw that a veteran player should work harder. . . . Spring training should not only be physical preparation. It

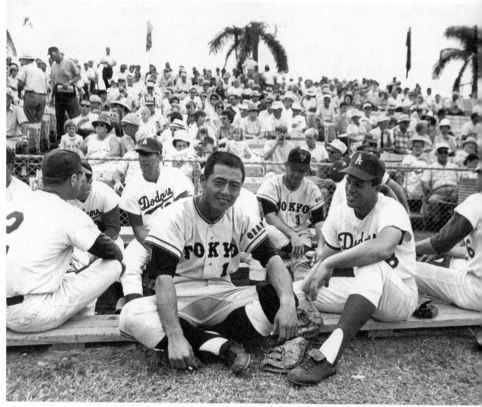

Sadaharu Oh, the "Babe Ruth" of Japanese baseball, chats with Dodger first baseman Wes Parker before a Tokyo Giants–Dodger game at Holman Stadium in 1967. (Courtesy of Los Angeles Dodgers, Los Angeles, California.)

should also be mental readiness. It is obvious that victory comes from team play. This you can gain in a place like Dodgertown. It brings everyone together more."[13]

In the Dodgertown barracks one night, Walter Alston experienced a run-in with Sandy Koufax and Larry Sherry. Alston was reading at 1:30 a.m., when he heard "a lot of giggling and carrying on." He leaped out of bed and opened the door. He saw Sandy and Larry sneaking into their room down the hall. By the time Alston reached their door, it was locked. He banged on the door with his fist. He hit the door again. His 1959 World Series ring split on his finger. "Now I was angry," he recalled. He started to kick in the door. It swung open. There stood Sherry explaining that he and Sandy had gone out to get a hamburger. (At one in the morning in Vero Beach?) The ruckus woke everyone in the barracks, including Mr. and Mrs. O'Malley, who had an apartment below on the first floor.[14] Alston calmed down, had a few words with the boys, and fined them for breaking curfew.

Sandy Koufax encountered other things that spring that changed his career. Over the winter, he realized he didn't enjoy selling lighting fixtures. Baseball was important. He began to accept responsibility for his situation. He hadn't worked hard enough. "Growing up, it's called," he told friends and reporters. He started working out. He arrived in Vero with a new attitude.[15]

In a B-team game with the Twins in Orlando, Sandy was his normal, wild self. His catcher Norm Sherry, brother of Larry, told him, "At this rate, you're gonna be out there all day. Why don't you take something off the ball? Don't even try and strike these next guys out. Just throw it over the plate and let them hit it." Sandy listened, struck out the side, and pitched seven innings of no-hit ball.[16]

In another incident, Norm Sherry, Ed Roebuck, and scout Kenny Myers joined Koufax for a beer in Lennie's Bar. Lennie's was the closest drinking establishment to Dodgertown, but the players had to walk through dark woods and cross Route 60 to get there. Roebuck said, "That bar was the pits," but it was convenient. Myers marked a spot on the bar wall with his cigar. He told Koufax to get up and go through his motion as if throwing at the spot. Myers noticed that Sandy's windup caused him not to see the spot and that he needed to change his motion.[17]

Sandy Koufax, now in his seventh year in the majors, finally arrived. He had an 18–13 record, made the All-Star team, and led the league in strikeouts. Norm Sherry's and Kenny Myers' advice worked. The Dodgers finished in second place.

O'Malley Gets Mad

In Vero, 1961 started well. Piper Aircraft dedicated a $1.5 million manufacturing plant at the Vero Beach airport before a large crowd.[18] Evangelist Billy Graham and entertainer Arthur Godfrey attended. But with the FAA situation affecting both Dodgertown and Piper, the company put further expansion on hold.

Shortly after the Dodgers completed spring training, Billy Graham conducted a Good Friday service before a capacity audience. A choir of four hundred local people accompanied him. He and his family had spent the winter in Vero, renting a house on the ocean.[19]

Meanwhile, the FAA did not initiate formal action but persistently demanded that the city take complete control of the flight line and insisted that the Dodgers pay a $12,000 annual rent. The city council, attempting to appease the FAA, replaced Bud Holman as airport manager, but he continued to hold his exclusive lease.[20]

The pro-FAA majority on the council went even further, voting to sue Bud Holman for "mismanagement."[21] Holman countersued, denying the city's charges and declaring once again that he held a valid lease. With the Holman suit, the Indian River Flying Service's suit, and the City of Vero Beach's suit, it now became Circuit Judge D. C. Smith's responsibility "to try to bring some order out of chaos in the hottest civil and political matter ever to rock the city." [22]

At this point, Walter O'Malley got mad. He telegrammed Mayor Offutt, advised the council "to go fishing and relax," declared the city's position to pay a rent as part of his lease "morally and legally wrong," and asked if the city wanted to challenge the Dodger lease in court.[23] He and his Vero Beach lawyer, judge Lester Merriman, made a presentation to the council. The Dodgers had met all their obligations. This included maintaining their facilities, paying one dollar per year rental to the city, and donating the proceeds of one exhibition game a year to the airport fund. (The most recent game between the Dodgers and the Dodgertown All-Stars—a group of minor leaguers—netted $100.)

O'Malley said that the Dodgers spent $3 million in developing Dodgertown and received in return only $122,000 from exhibition games during their fourteen years in Vero. Other teams paid rent, but they didn't have to pay to build facilities.[24] He asked, in effect, "Do you think the City of Vero Beach has strained itself in any way in spending $19,000 . . . dollars in fourteen years in order to have in its midst the finest, biggest, major league winter training quarters in the U.S.A.?"[25] The city council listened and then asked the FAA to reevaluate their position on the Dodger lease.

In the meantime, other cities invested large sums to keep major league teams training in their communities. At a cost of $750,000, Fort Lauderdale built an eight thousand–seat stadium for the Yankees. Tampa constructed Al Lopez Field for the Reds. Sarasota spent $200,000 to improve their ball park to get the White Sox. And Clearwater built a $400,000 field for the Phillies.[26] In comparison, the City of Vero Beach, except for the swimming pool and some work on Ebbets Field #2, had spent nothing on Dodgertown or Holman Stadium.

In July, with the stalemate continuing, the city council asked Merrill Barber, the mayor when the Dodgers first arrived and now a state senator, if he would intercede with his "good friend Walter O'Malley."[27] But O'Malley was busy in Los Angeles with the construction of Dodger Stadium. Four months passed with no resolution. The city council, again by a vote of three to two and with City Attorney Vocelle's encouragement, passed a resolution "to seek an injunction to prevent the Los Angeles Dodgers from using the airport facilities until the validity of its forty-two-year lease could be determined."[28]

O'Malley responded, calling the injunction "a complete violation of good faith and honest dealings" and arguing that the Dodgers "have a valid lease and are not in default." O'Malley stated that the city council not only "double crossed the Dodgers" but had embarrassed Merrill Barber by their sudden action.[29]

Our Friendly City

Local citizens reacted. At a meeting at Waldo Sexton's Turf Club, now the Szechuan Palace restaurant, a petition with nine hundred signatures was presented, demanding that the city council rescind the action against the Dodgers. The Fact Finders, a civic group, proposed a recall of city council members Offutt, Jones, and Simpson, all of whom voted for the injunction. The Fact Finders ran an ad in the *Press Journal* showing the 1953 dedication plaque for Holman Stadium that honored Bud Holman and referred to the "Friendly City of Vero Beach." The ad asked: "What Happened to our Friendly City?" Local Chevrolet dealer Roland Miller talked of forming a Council of 100 to raise the $12,000 that the FAA demanded the Dodgers pay to the airport fund.[30]

Florida senator Spessard Holland arranged a meeting with the FAA in Washington in November. The city council, Mayor Offutt, Vocelle, Barber, O'Malley, newly appointed Dodgertown director Peter O'Malley, Piper Aircraft owner Howard Piper Jr., and plant manager M. L. Blume attended. Everybody returned to Vero optimistic. Merrill Barber said, "It was gratifying to see all of the interests involved working shoulder to shoulder."[31] Out of this spirit of cooperation came the first sign of a solution. Merrill Barber suggested the possibility of the Dodgers buying the land that they leased.[32] This possibility had been considered initially in 1949, but at the time, in at least O'Malley's mind, the Dodgers were conserving cash to replace Ebbets Field.[33]

Then, the Circuit Court and the District Court of Appeals, in sifting through the three-way law suits of Indian River Flying Service, Bud Holman, and the city, ruled: "On the face of the [Holman] lease it is valid."[34]

In December 1961, three new members joined the city council: Jack Sturgis, Robert Holmes, and Fred Prestin. Offutt, Jennings, and Knight chose not to run. Taylor Simpson and Harry Jones, who consistently voted with Offutt on airport matters, remained on the council.

Jack Sturgis, with 67 percent of the votes cast, gained "the strongest mandate ever received by a council candidate in Vero Beach." The council chose Sturgis to be mayor.[35] "The airport controversy," Sturgis stated, "should be settled according to law and not according to the personalities involved."[36] Jack Sturgis came to Vero from Indiana in 1954 and opened a lumber supply business. His wife Josie worked as a counselor at the high school. Jack and Josie Sturgis had seats up from the Dodgers' dugout in section 17, Holman Stadium, until he died in 2001. Josie Sturgis still sits in those seats.

Shortly after the election, former mayor Harry Offutt announced that he and his family were leaving Vero Beach to work for the Presbyterian Church in Mexico.[37]

Things were looking up, but not for long.

◆ 10 ◆

The Dodgers and Vero Prevail

1962

Colored and White

Twenty-six-year-old Peter O'Malley was now director of Dodgertown, advanced by his father a step up the ladder from his position at the Dodgertown boys' camp. Peter, Vero mayor Jack Sturgis, restaurateur Bud Emlet, and banker Angelo Sanchez, head of the Jaycees ticket sales committee, were among the crowd welcoming the team on its arrival at the Vero airport.[1]

The Dodgers flew in on the new Lockheed Electra. Bump Holman had arranged for its purchase at the instruction of Walter O'Malley. This became the Dodgers' fourth plane in twelve years—the DC-3, the Convair 440, the DC-6, and now the four-engine, prop jet Electra—all piloted by Bump. The Electra, named *Kay-O* for Mrs. O'Malley, contained fifty seats, four beds, six card tables, a poker table, and cost $2 million.[2]

On March 29, in the top game of the spring, the Yankees came to Vero. A crowd of 4,602 packed Holman Stadium. Mickey Mantle provided the excitement with a 420–foot home run, as the Yanks won 5–4.[3]

Blacks still sat down right field at Holman Stadium, separate from the whites. The toilet facilities and water fountains, like Vero Beach's courthouse and train station, still read "Colored" and "White." The sentiment in the country, with John Kennedy as president, may have been changing, but not in Vero Beach. Tommy Davis, "scholarly looking in wire frame glasses," with Johnny Roseboro, Junior Gilliam, and Willie Davis arranged a chat with Peter O'Malley. They said, "Peter, Jackie Robinson integrated this thing in 1947, and we still have a problem at Holman Stadium, right now." Peter immediately took the "Colored" signs down and desegregated the stands. Tommy Davis said: "We went and

Pilot Bump Holman mans the controls as Walter O'Malley and Bud Holman board the Dodger plane at the Vero Beach airport. (Courtesy of Indian River County Historical Society, Vero Beach, Florida.)

took the people out of the right field area and told them to sit in left field, sit behind home plate, sit over there. And they wouldn't believe us. 'Oh no, we can't do that,' they said. So we just took them and told them to sit wherever they wanted from now on."[4] Holman Stadium became integrated and not a peep came from the town.

Gifford resident Ralph Lundy and the pastor of the Community Church of Vero Beach, Arnold Wettstein, as leaders of the community's newly formed Biracial Committee, also approached the Dodger management about ending segregation at Holman Stadium. "When the blacks," Lundy said, "started to sit with the whites, there were some stares. But that's all there were—stares."[5]

Ralph Lundy first visited Dodgertown in the early days, covering the black players as a reporter for the "Negro News" section of the *Jacksonville Journal*. He spent a week in Vero every spring for four years. The players included Robinson, Gilliam, Newcombe, and Campanella. "They were confident," he said, "but had mixed feelings about being a small minority. They were tight with other players on the field, both black and white, but off the field there were differences. The black guys would stick together more." Ralph Lundy did not like Vero Beach. He couldn't stay in the hotels, and for service at a restaurant he had to go to the back door. But fate brought him permanently to the Vero Beach area. In 1959 he moved to Gifford when his wife took a job as a secretary at the black high school. He initially published a black weekly and later worked for the *Press Journal*.[6] In 1960, Mayor Sturgis asked him to join the Biracial Committee, with representatives from Gifford and Vero Beach, to work on issues of housing, recreation, employment, and education.

Integration pushed beyond Holman Stadium, and the major concern became schools. As Mrs. Willie Mae Darrisaw, a black member of the committee, explained: "[School integration] will come sooner than later, and we would like to be accepted rather than force our way." Reaction from the white community was mixed. One school board member stated that integration was "a certainty and only a question of time." A county commissioner said he believed in segregation and the traditions of the county and urged the committee to get off its "integration jag."[7]

On a lighter note, Johnny Roseboro began giving haircuts at Dodgertown. Barbers in Vero would not cut a black man's hair. Maury Wills refused to go to Gifford to get one, so Maury became Roseboro's first, and perhaps last, customer. Wills came out of it with a shaved head.[8]

A Capricious Action of Irresponsible Bureaucrats

FAA difficulties overshadowed the joys of spring training. The Washington meeting of the previous November seemed forgotten. The FAA arrived in Vero and, stating that the city was in default, again threatened to take back the airport. The FAA said it had been "patient," but claimed the city had "procrastinated" in getting a new lease with Holman and in obtaining rent from the Dodgers. The city received a formal notice reiterating the defaults and giving it sixty days to remedy the problems. Councilman Prestin described the FAA notice as the "capricious action of irresponsible bureaucrats."[9]

Florida senator George Smathers, whose influence in Washington was unquestioned, advised the city that there was no way to prevent the FAA from taking back the airport. The city council discussed buying out Holman's lease, as well as obtaining an injunction against the FAA.

The city hired a Washington legal firm that identified the need for a formal airport authority and the resolution of the Holman lease as critical to satisfying the FAA. Mayor Sturgis talked to Holman about lease modifications. They discussed Holman's retaining exclusive rights to flight-line services, but transferring his lease servicing Eastern Airlines to the city.[10]

Two days before the FAA's June 16 termination deadline, Mayor Sturgis wrote the government agency, stating that progress was being made. The FAA responded with a ninety-day extension, based on "good faith" and "the renegotiation of the Holman lease."[11]

In August, the city again met with the FAA. It wanted assurances that the city would pay $12,000 a year for the remaining thirty-five years of the Dodger lease and wanted more rent from Piper. The FAA approved the city's new lease with Eastern Airlines and looked favorably on the city's recent decision to replace the old Navy control building with a new terminal.[12]

Two days before the ninety-day extension ended on September 16, the FAA granted the city a one-year grace period in which to repair runways, runway lights, the ramp, and other items. With rental income of $100,000 per year from all the approved leases, only the Dodger and Piper rent payments remained the outstanding issue.[13]

A Taj Mahal of a Ball Park

Dodger Stadium at Chavez Ravine opened on April 10, 1962. Seating fifty-six thousand, the four-deck ball park rose from a sculptured setting in the Elysian Hills. Beyond the outfield fence, palm trees provided the backdrop. The fans sat closer to the game than in any other ball park of its capacity in the country. Nationally syndicated sports columnist Jim Murray wrote, "O'Malley built a Taj Mahal of a ball park, setting the tone for subsequent edifices."[14]

Emil Praeger, with O'Malley looking over his shoulder, designed Dodger Stadium, drawing on their joint experience building Vero Beach's Holman Stadium. In both instances, they prepared the site by pushing dirt up to form the sides of a bowl. Both stadiums had unobstructed views; fans were close to the action; and the landscaping, dominated in both cases by palms, gave the sites a natural beauty.[15] O'Malley, the amateur horticulturist who cared for his orchids and other plantings at Dodgertown, placed 3,400 trees on the Dodger Stadium site.

In the new setting, the team played gloriously, winning 102 games. Maury Wills stole a phenomenal 104 bases, a major league record, and won the Most Valuable Player award. Drysdale won the Cy Young Award. Sandy Koufax pitched the first of his four no-hitters. Despite all this,

DODGER STADIUM

Dodger Stadium opens in 1962. Dodgertown's Holman Stadium was in several ways the prototype for the construction at Chavez Ravine. (Courtesy of Los Angeles Dodgers, Los Angeles, California.)

the Dodgers ended the season tied with the Giants. In the championship game, reminiscent of 1951 and Bobby Thomson, the Dodgers blew a ninth-inning lead and lost.

Speculation took off: Alston would be fired and replaced by Leo Durocher, Chuck Dressen, or whoever. O'Malley discussed firing Alston with Bavasi, who declared that he would have to be fired too.[16] That next spring in Vero, Bavasi signed Alston to another one-year contract.

Bavasi recounted the story that after a poor season, Walter O'Malley invited Walter Alston to go on a turkey shoot, probably out on the Holman ranch. Rumors spread throughout Dodgertown: "One of the Walters is not coming back." Bavasi thought O'Malley started the story himself.[17] But Alston's one-year contracts continued on and on.

1963

FAA Pussyfooting

Vero mayor Jack Sturgis kept the FAA satisfied in 1963 by notifying the agency that the city was talking with the Dodgers and Piper Aircraft about buying the property they leased. This would solve the long-standing rent problem. The city further committed to build a $150,000 air terminal.

In February, Mayor Sturgis asked the FAA to declare the airport free of all defaults. The city was ready to build the new terminal and issue long-term leases or sell the property for industrial development if it wouldn't be needed for aviation purposes. Both the Dodgers and Piper wanted to buy their property. The city prepared appraisals to send to the FAA. Meanwhile, until the sales could be completed, the city guaranteed the $12,000 "Dodger rent" payment. Most of that money would come from the proceeds of an exhibition game being promoted by the Jaycees and other civic organizations.[18]

The Dodgers increased the number of exhibition games at Holman Stadium from four to six. But Dodgertown director Peter O'Malley expressed disappointment that the attendance averaged only 2,769 per game.[19]

In this the Dodgers' fifth year in Los Angeles, only five players remained from Ebbets Field days: Jim Gilliam, Johnny Podres, Sandy Koufax, Don Drysdale, and Johnny Roseboro. For Roseboro, in spite of the changes, "We were always a family, black and white." Not everyone loved "one another," he added, "but no one loves everyone in the family."[20]

Moose Skowron came to the Dodgers from the Yankees in 1963. To make him feel at home, Don Drysdale, Ron Perranoski, and Frank Howard took him out for a beer before dinner one evening in Vero. Having tossed down a few, the boys forgot dinner. They ended up at the Palomino Club on the way to Fort Pierce. The crowd consisted mostly of couples, all having a marvelous time doing the twist. Drysdale, after another round of beers, convinced Howard and Skowron, with a combined weight of almost five hundred pounds, to join the crowd on the dance floor. With arms swinging and butts bumping, it didn't take long to clear the floor. On the way back to Dodgertown, a hungry Howard threatened to eat the cab driver's Chihuahua.[21]

The team redeemed itself in 1963. The Dodgers won the National League Championship and then swept the Yankees in the World Series.

After the Series, Bump Holman flew Walter O'Malley, Bud Holman, and other O'Malley friends to Africa in the Electra for a big game hunting expedition. Bump described it as one of his dad's "happy times."[22] The trip was most successful. Bump has a picture of the interior of the Electra with what looks like half the animals of Africa sitting in the seats. (Bump had gone to Denver to pick up from the taxidermist the stuffed trophies and had strapped them in the seats to bring back to Vero.)

Meanwhile, the FAA did nothing. Councilman Fred Prestin charged that the city seemed to be a "stepchild" of the FAA and that the agency was "arbitrary" in opposing land deals at the airport. "It's time we stop pussyfooting with the FAA," he said. Mayor Sturgis remained hopeful of settling the longstanding difficulties so the city could retain full control of the airport and encourage its further development.[23]

1964

The Final Resolution

Sandy Koufax received many accolades for his 1963 performance besides the Cy Young and Most Valuable Player awards. One award that didn't receive national publicity was the coveted Barrett Belt, a rhinestone-encrusted jock strap presented by Barrett's Steakhouse on U.S. 1 in Vero. The Barretts and their restaurant were local institutions.[24]

During spring training, Walter Alston used sportswriters to manage the teams in intrasquad games. Sports editor Joe Hendrickson managed the Hendrickson Horribles and won the camp championship. Walter O'Malley invited Joe to sit at his table at dinner. The other sportswriters booed. Later, O'Malley sent Joe a letter of congratulations: "When Alston retires, you are my next manager."[25]

Disappointed with the Dodgertown attendance the previous spring, the team tried to improve their exhibition game income by taking a junket to Mexico City. With an attendance of seventy-five thousand for three games, O'Malley judged the trip a success. Bud Holman, who accompanied the team, did not. A pickpocket stole his wallet.[26]

The City of Vero Beach reached an agreement with both the Dodgers and Piper Aircraft to sell them airport property. The Dodgers would

Bud Holman and the O'Malley family. From left to right: Peter, Walter, Kay, Terry O'Malley Seidler, and Bud Holman. (Courtesy of Indian River County Historical Society, Vero Beach, Florida.)

buy 110 acres, which included all the Dodgertown buildings and fields, for $134,000. Proceeds would go into the airport fund. The FAA needed to approve the deal. Part of the arrangement required that the Dodgers transfer the Ebbets Field #2 property, including the adjacent practice field, to Piper, which needed it for an employee parking lot.[27]

On June 1, Bud Holman died at his Blue Cypress ranch. He had brought the Dodgers to Vero and done the most to keep them there. Reverend Arnold Wettstein conducted the service at the Community Church. Pallbearers included Merrill Barber and Peter O'Malley. Walter O'Malley, James Mulvey, *Press Journal* publisher J. J. Schuman, and Mayor Sturgis were among the honorary pallbearers. A large white baseball with "Dodgers" printed across its top stood out among the floral arrangements.[28]

Terry O'Malley Seidler remembered "Bud Holman [as] everyone's favorite Vero Beach friend. His warm smile was always the first we saw as the plane landed at the airport, and it represented the bond between the Vero Beach community and the Dodgers."[29]

Bud Holman did not live long enough to see the final resolution of the airport problem. Shortly after his death, the FAA approved the airport property sales to the Dodgers and to Piper. The city and the county added

Dodgertown to their tax roles. The FAA stipulated that nothing could be done to the property to endanger flight operations. One wag suggested that slugger Frank Howard would have to shorten his swing to lower the height of his home runs.[30]

With matters settled, Walter O'Malley stated that he never had any intention of leaving Vero "no matter how sticky the relationships became, because the weather is better than California and there is more competition—furthermore, we had an understanding with the weatherman that it only rains at night in Florida."[31]

Jack Sturgis, looking back years later at his time as mayor, said, "Those of us who always realized the value of the Dodgers and Piper to Vero Beach prevailed. I have enjoyed my relationship with the O'Malleys and the Dodgers. I have seen them contribute to Vero Beach in many ways. O'Malley was a master at letting the community know he cared about them. His policies stimulated good will."[32]

While the Dodgers wallowed in the second division that summer, Vero experienced some excitement. A hurricane came up the coast in August. It was small in comparison with a history-making hurricane that had assailed the area 250 years earlier. That storm destroyed a Spanish treasure fleet, blowing the ships onto the reefs along Indian River County's coast. For years, beachcombers had occasionally found isolated gold pieces. But it took famed treasure hunter Mel Fischer to discover the location of the wrecked ships and their valuable cargoes.[33] With gold and artifacts still found to this day, this area is known as the Treasure Coast. The publicity surrounding Fischer's find matched that generated by the Dodgers during their annual spring training.

Peter O'Malley completed his third year as director of Dodgertown and was off to Spokane, Washington, to become the top farm team's general manager—the next step in his father's process to prepare him for the presidency of the Dodgers.

Wins and Losses

1965

A Year of Rage

Spring training proceeded innocuously enough. Members of the pitching staff attempted some fishing on the Indian River. According to Don Drysdale, "Polish captain" Ron Perranoski and "Lithuanian outdoor expert" Johnny Podres led the expedition. They caught no fish, but a thunderstorm caught them, and they arrived back in camp soaked.[1]

One Dodgertown recreational activity was of a more intellectual nature. Manager Walter Alston and players Jim Gilliam, Wes Parker, and even Don Drysdale formed a group that played bridge in the barracks' lobby. World-renowned bridge champion Charles Goren visited Dodgertown. He and Alston played Gilliam and Parker. Alston figured he must have been "pretty much of a liability" as he and Goren lost. But then Parker, a slick fielding first baseman, was a master player. Goren handed out a small card to the winners that said, "I beat Goren."[2]

There was rage that year, not only in the nation but also on the baseball field. Giants' pitcher Juan Marichal attacked catcher Johnny Roseboro with a bat during a game at Dodger Stadium. In Watts, a few miles from Chavez Ravine, riots and fires exploded following a black driver's arrest by a white policeman during a traffic stop. A long-standing atmosphere of racial tension and mistrust, coupled with a mob presence, magnified what would otherwise have been a fairly routine officer-civilian interaction. The smell of smoke drifted through Dodger Stadium. Thirty-four people died as the cry, "Burn, baby, burn," ricocheted through the streets of Watts.

In the black community of Gifford, the *Press Journal* reported that three black youths beat up a white youth. The blacks had been turned away from getting service at a truck stop on the north side of Vero. Earlier in the evening, a white man had thrown a cup of coffee in the face of one of the Gifford youths.[3]

Outfielder Lou Johnson was subjected to an ugly incident at a Vero laundromat. When he placed his clothes in the washer, the woman in charge told him to take them out: blacks weren't supposed to do their laundry when whites did theirs. Johnson responded with some strong remarks. The woman complained to Dodger management. "To their credit they ignored her; to their discredit, they didn't do anything about it," Roseboro explained later.[4]

The blacks couldn't go into the Vero saloons like Podres and Drysdale did. When black players went to a local doctor, they had to wait in a back room away from the whites. Roseboro remembered an unpleasant encounter with a Vero Beach doctor during a visit for a physical exam. When Roseboro—in response to the doctor's request for insurance information—told him about his $200,000 policy, the doctor didn't believe him and treated him "like trash."[5] Local car rental agents wouldn't rent cars to blacks. A bus dropped the white players in Vero and the blacks in Gifford. Eventually, the Dodgers provided rented cars for the players.

Willie Davis, John Roseboro, and Tommy Davis liked to go to the high-school basketball games in Gifford. "It was a good place to pick up teachers. Most of the single women in Gifford were either teachers or servants for the whites," Roseboro said. He noted that the married women were attracted to the ballplayers, who were "throwing dough around." The husbands, who were "having a hard time making it," hated the ballplayers: "We weren't much more welcome in their town than in the white man's town."[6]

Changes came slowly in the sixties. The Florida Theater in downtown Vero still maintained a walled-off balcony section and a back entrance for blacks. John Roseboro said that the black players would go to "a dump in Gifford" to see "some of the first movies ever made," rather than suffer indignities at Florida Theater. Though it was integrated with the help of the Biracial Committee, the insults didn't stop right away. When Roseboro attended a movie one night, he heard someone behind him complain, "There sure are a lot of niggers in here."[7]

The recently formed community Biracial Committee pushed for school integration. The school board began working on a plan. Committee member Ralph Lundy tried to persuade the public: "We are faced with a situation where some people may seek outside help to integrate schools here. . . . Let's try to solve the problem on the local level rather than create bad publicity for the community."[8] The school board issued a half-hearted plan that allowed any student, regardless of race, to apply to the school closest to where he or she lived. Given Indian River County's sharply segregated demographic areas, the plan did little more than maintain the status quo. It would be another four years before the schools would be totally desegregated.

Rebounding

The Dodgers rebounded in 1965 and finished in first place just in front of the Giants. The Dodgers met the Minnesota Twins in the World Series. This was the Series where Sandy Koufax, because of his Jewish faith, refused to pitch the opener on Yom Kippur, but came back to win two games and the Series for the Dodgers.

Dodger coach Danny Ozark, who had asked Koufax to pitch the final, crucial game with only two days' rest, had been a minor leaguer in the first days of Dodgertown. His story was similar to Tommy Lasorda's. He never made the big team as a player, never went further than playing first base for St. Paul, but became a scout and managed Omaha and St. Paul. In 1961, while he enjoyed the spring at Dodgertown, his wife and children were snowed in for three days at the family home in Buffalo. She called him and asked," How's the weather down there? Nice and warm? Well, I'm selling the house."[9] Vero became the Ozarks' home.

Bud Holman's son Bump retired as Dodger chief pilot to run his dad's flight line service business. He had started as copilot on the Dodger DC-3 almost fifteen years earlier. He saw a lot of baseball games, waiting to fly both the Dodger major leaguers and the minor leaguers all over the country. Captain Lew Carlisle, a former Eastern Airlines pilot, took over for Bump.

The city dedicated the municipal airport terminal, which replaced the old Navy control building. With 2,500 local citizens attending, the FAA's Cole Morrow, who dealt with the city in the early stages of the airport fiasco, spoke. He praised the community: "We in Washington join you in your enthusiasm. . . . The people who worked so hard to make this airport what it is today deserve great credit."[10]

The city council dedicated a plaque in front of the terminal to the memory of Bud Holman: "For His Contribution to Aviation."[11] The perceived villain of the four-year airport battle that split the community was exonerated, the year after he died.

1966

Collective Bargaining

When the Dodgers arrived in Vero, Koufax and Drysdale weren't there. They sat in Los Angeles, holding out. They wanted salaries of $100,000, plus three-year contracts. To make it worse from management's standpoint, they even hired a Hollywood agent to advise them. This was collective bargaining; unions did this, not baseball players. Multiyear contracts and agents: this was blasphemy.[12]

Bavasi tried to stay blasé through the whole affair: "Come on down to Vero, throw a little bit, and we'll work it out here."[13] The agent told Koufax and Drysdale, "Don't fall for that old ploy. Don't budge."

Scout director Al Campanis described the atmosphere at Dodgertown: "These guys were 50 percent of our starting pitching. Not only 50 percent but arguably the best two pitchers in baseball. So at first our players were sure it would get handled. Then as spring training went on, panic set in."[14]

As the season opener approached, Bavasi flew to Los Angeles to talk with his errant boys. Chuck Connors, the former Dodger minor leaguer, Dodgertown entertainer, and now an actor, served as intermediary.[15] Bavasi offered $110,000 to Drysdale and $125,000 to Koufax, but no three-year contracts. They accepted. The Dodgers announced the settlement as the team flew from Vero to Los Angeles.[16]

Maury Wills didn't arrive in Vero at the beginning of spring training either. He wanted the same salary as Drysdale and Koufax. After all, he stole ninety-four bases the previous season. Wills, however, made the mistake of going to Vero. Bavasi offered him $85,000, and he accepted it on the spot.[17]

Go Easy with the Rough

Teammates may have missed Koufax and Drysdale at Dodgertown, but they had something else—the Dodgertown Golf Course, a nine-hole, thirty-six-par course that wrapped around the west side of Holman Stadium. Walter O'Malley decided that he and the players needed a diversion. On the new course, outfielder Ron Fairly shot a 71, playing two rounds, to win the player tournament.[18] The Dodgertown course was inclusive, as Maury Wills noted: "Black players, who couldn't play on local

Holman Stadium and the new Dodgertown Golf Course are shown in this promotional card. (Courtesy of Dick Bird, Vero Beach, Florida.)

courses, could play there."[19] Plus it was open to the public and provided another source of income, always an O'Malley consideration.

Dodger Stadium resident engineer Ira Hoyt laid out the course. O'Malley told Hoyt, "Go easy with the rough. I don't want any alligator jungles." O'Malley delayed the installation of the traps until he got the "feel" of the course. He wanted the traps placed to his advantage and to the disadvantage of his fellow Dodger owner and golf partner Jim Mulvey, who tended to hook the ball. O'Malley wasn't above having a bunker moved overnight to surprise a competitor.[20] It amazed golf writer Joe Buttitta that the official rules of neither the United States Golf Association nor the Royal and Ancient Golf Club of St. Andrews applied.

Walter O'Malley made his own rules, and penalties did not pertain to him. If O'Malley's ball lay beneath one of the bridges that crossed a swale, only he could pick up without penalty and toss the ball out on the fairway. But as Buttitta said, "What can you say to the man who owns the course?"[21] "Dodgertown was his little empire," said Buzzie Bavasi of his boss. Kay O'Malley liked Dodgertown as well. She and Walter spent their vacations there. Peter O'Malley said, "Dad loved every tree, every plant. Dad loved Dodgertown."[22]

Walter O'Malley's Baby

Walter O'Malley wanted more property for another golf course, this one with eighteen holes and the potential for country club development. The FAA approved his purchase of 220 acres, adjacent to Dodgertown, from the City of Vero Beach.[23]

With this golf development in mind, O'Malley hired twenty-five-year-old golf pro Dick Bird as director of Dodgertown. Dick became the first director without a baseball background, as well as the first full-time director. The job was typically part time, with groundskeeper Bob Summers and a skeleton crew maintaining Dodgertown during the off-season. Dick replaced John Stanfill, who filled in when Peter O'Malley left to become the general manager at Spokane.

Dick Bird, a local boy, played golf for Vero Beach High School and the University of Florida, and became the pro at the Riomar Country Club.[24]

Bird met Walter O'Malley at Riomar. It is interesting that O'Malley would give the responsibility of managing Dodgertown to such a young fellow. Yet it was not out of character. O'Malley had made Bump Holman, just out of college, the Dodgers' head pilot, even authorizing him to negotiate the sale of the Convair to the Spanish airline Avianca and then purchase million-dollar airplanes like the DC-6 from Western Airlines and the Lockheed Electra from General Motors. O'Malley also gave significant management responsibilities in the Dodger organization to his own son, Peter, when he was still in his twenties.

Sitting in his Vero Beach real estate office and looking back almost forty years, Dick Bird talked about his relationship with the Dodgers and Walter O'Malley. Yes, he was young when he took the Dodgertown position. From his high school days, Dick remembered local male jealousy of the good-looking, young Dodger athletes. The Dodgers would walk downtown to go to the movies or hang out at the drugstore to meet girls. Dick and his friends would drive by in a convertible and plaster the players with oranges. Soon he was in a reverse role, trying to keep those young Dodger players from getting into confrontations.

Peter O'Malley gave Dick a crash course on how to prepare for spring training. Supported only by a small staff of local retirees, Dick found his job challenging. He contracted for food services, hired waitresses, handled preseason ticket sales, sold game tickets, added additional ground crew, and found ushers. At one point, the minor league coaching staff did the ushering. But that became difficult when he had to tell minor league manager Duke Snider, "one of the finest center fielders in the game," that he was supposed to usher. Dick said that one of the most difficult jobs was putting together the program. He sold ads, bugged publicity director Red Patterson to get the content on time, and then rushed the program through printing. Interns didn't exist then to do the dirty work, and there wasn't the staff of two hundred that keeps Dodgertown going today.

As Dick Bird said, "Walter O'Malley had a love affair with Vero Beach. Dodgertown was his getaway from the pressures of being one of the most successful owners in professional sports. If he had to make a trip to the East Coast on business, he would find a way to come to Vero for a few days. He and I would play a round of golf in the morning. He would go back to his Dodgertown apartment for lunch, nap, and then take care of a little business. In the evening he liked to go to a restaurant, either the Ocean Grill, Emlet's, Barrett's Steak House, or the Menu to enjoy good food and fellowship and to get to know the owners. This was one of the things he loved about Vero."

Dodgertown was Walter O'Malley's baby: his to play with. The baseball training was taken very seriously, but the orange trees, his orchids, his attempt to grow papayas for profit, the golf were things to have fun with. When he and Mrs. O'Malley stayed during spring training, he prided himself on being the first one up. He would go talk with the kitchen crew, get a cup of coffee, and sometimes do his own laundry. He used the siren on his golf cart to make sure everyone was up.

Walter O'Malley wanted the additional property for a new course, because the Dodgertown Golf Course had become instantly too popular. At times, even the boss couldn't get on it. He told Dick to write out a check for $148,500 for him to sign to buy the property. The amount's magnitude made Dick nervous, and he had to write the check twice.

O'Malley hired a consultant to lay out the new eighteen-hole course. The consultant was Scottish and stubborn; O'Malley was Irish and stubborn. That didn't work. Walter said to Dick, "You and I are going to design this course." And they did, with assistance from Dodger Stadium engineer Ira Hoyt.

Dick Bird and Walter O'Malley spent a lot of time together. Dick described Mr. O'Malley as "a second father to me, like a grandfather to my

Dodgertown director Dick Bird and Walter O'Malley properly attired for the annual Dodgers' Saint Patrick's Day party. (Courtesy of Dick Bird, Vero Beach, Florida.)

children." Mr. and Mrs. O'Malley became the godparents for Dick's son Bobby.

When Dick worked on the new course, Mr. O'Malley stood close by, looking over his shoulder, watching him as he ran the grader. Dick said, "If there was a rough side to Walter O'Malley, I never saw it."

O'Malley wanted to buy another thirty-six acres in 1968 as an extension to the new course. Walt Disney, after his experience with Disneyland, had told O'Malley to make sure to always have a buffer for future development. (Disney would do that with Disney World in Orlando.) But the FAA issued the caveat that if the property use ever changed from recreation to development, it must revert back to the airport.[25] According to Bird, O'Malley responded in essence "To heck with 'em."

Trying to Forget That One

Missing spring training had little effect on Koufax in 1966. But Drysdale couldn't duplicate his previous season. Rookie Don Sutton picked up the slack. In a game that spring at Holman Stadium, Sutton pitched against the Tigers. He struck out Al Kaline who said to him, "Kid, isn't it a little early to be throwing a curve that hard. You won't last long [in the majors]."[26] Don Sutton pitched the next fifteen years for the Dodgers.

On the last day of the season, Koufax beat the Phillies to win the National League pennant. Vero Beach sent a fifty-foot telegram to the Dodgers saying, "Congratulations to our favorite ball club. With our best wishes you will take the series." It contained 1,100 names collected by the *Press Journal* and radio station WTTB.[27]

The Dodgers faced the Baltimore Orioles and played miserably. Coach Danny Ozark said later, "The 1966 Series? I'm still trying to forget that one. But I do remember Mr. O'Malley's reaction. He was very irate that we lost four straight."[28]

O'Malley planned another excursion to Japan at the end of the World Series. The trip included a five-day stay in Hawaii for wives and other members of the Dodger organization. Mrs. Dick Bird, wife of the Dodgertown director, and Mrs. Danny Ozark of Vero Beach made the trip. During the tour, Emperor Hirohito presented Walter O'Malley with the prestigious "Order of the Sacred Treasures (Third Class)" medal in honor of his efforts to promote friendly relations between the United States and Japan. The Tokyo Giants would return to Dodgertown for another visit in 1967.[29]

Stung by the Orioles' Series win, O'Malley's players showed as little eagerness for this journey as they had for the 1956 Japan trip that followed their loss to the Yankees. Maury Wills left in the middle of the trip and returned home, presumably to have some medical treatment for his legs. Instead, he went back to Hawaii to play his guitar in a nightclub. For O'Malley, such behavior could not be tolerated, and he traded Wills to the Pirates. Maury couldn't believe it. He had been the leader of the Dodgers.[30]

Sandy Koufax shocked the sports world by announcing his retirement on November 17, 1966. He was thirty years old and at the peak of his career, having just won the Cy Young Award for the third time. But he had survived for three years on cortisone shots, Empirin with Codeine, and a dangerous anti-inflammatory drug.[31] After every game, he packed his arm, swollen double its normal size, in ice cubes. He began to drop things. He faced losing the use of his arm for the rest of his life. Sandy Koufax had to quit, had planned it a year earlier, but mentioned it to only a few people.

Maury Wills said of Sandy, whom he considered a close friend, "Too nice to be so great."[32] Their friendship had developed from quiet talks during the long interludes after games while one soaked his leg, the other his arm.

After he retired, Sandy broadcast the NBC *Saturday Game of the Week* for several years. In 1979, he showed up at Dodgertown and became the organization's minor league pitching coach. He traveled around the Dodger system for nine years working with the young pitchers. He lived in Vero (and still does), but was rarely seen except in the early mornings when he used the workout room at Dodgertown. He continued to work with pitchers during spring training: with the Texas Rangers, with the Mets when they moved to Port Saint Lucie, and with the Dodgers.[33]

Glad the Sixties Were Over

1967–1969

Dodger Departures

The 1967 Dodger Press Guide optimistically portrayed a cartoon of a Dodger stacking a '67 National League pennant crown on top of the ones for '66, '65, '63, and '59.

Responding to this optimism, a large number of the media, a crowd not seen since the Brooklyn days, covered Dodgertown. Bob Hunter of the *Los Angeles Herald Examiner*, George Lederer of the *Long Beach Press Telegram*, and Joe Hendrickson of the *Pasadena Star-News* reigned as deans of the press corp. They had visited Dodgertown every spring since the team moved to Los Angeles. In addition, eleven other writers, all representing Los Angeles– area papers, occupied the Holman Stadium press box, and renowned *Los Angeles Times* columnist Jim Murray occasionally dropped in. Shooting the action on the field was Dodgertown's favorite photographer Herb Scharfman. Vin Scully and Jerry Doggett provided the radio play by play to Los Angeles and Vero Beach over local station WTTB.

Despite the media coverage, the Dodger success of the early sixties waned. The team dropped to eighth (now out of ten teams) in '67 and to seventh in '68. The team recovered some with a fourth-place, over .500, finish in 1969 in the new six-team West Division.

Not only had Koufax departed, but Johnny Podres, Tommy Davis, and Johnny Roseboro were traded in the latter part of the sixties. Dodger players found it tough to leave the team. Podres couldn't believe it and got drunk. All the same, that was baseball. Despite being traded, Roseboro always felt that he was a Dodger, as did most of the players who had been with the team. He appreciated the consistency, the same manage-

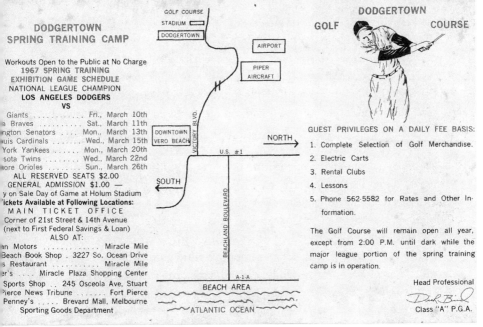

Flyer promoting the 1967 Dodger spring schedule and Dodgertown Golf Course.
(Courtesy of Dick Bird, Vero Beach, Florida.)

ment during his eleven-year stay—a management that didn't give up on players who had a bad year, that displayed patience, not panic, after the team had a rough season, and that treated the players fairly, inspiring loyalty to the team.[1]

Jim Gilliam and Don Drysdale retired. Gilliam became a Dodger coach, Drysdale a baseball broadcaster. Drysdale thought highly of both Walter Alston and Walter O'Malley. He has a story about testing his boss once in Vero. With the team playing over on Florida's west coast, he and Johnny Podres had a day off. They wanted to go to the races in Miami but were short of cash. O'Malley had a so-called open-door policy. Drysdale and Podres got up their nerve and walked into see him, hemming and hawing. O'Malley dropped his head and peered at them over his glasses. "You guys need some money. Is that it? I'll get it back, won't I?" he asked. O'Malley called down to the auditor and arranged for each of them to get $200.[2]

Don Drysdale died of a heart attack in 1993 at age fifty-six in Montreal, where he'd gone to broadcast a Dodger game.

The departures continued. Buzzie Bavasi left the Dodgers in 1968. He knew it was time. Room needed to be made for Peter O'Malley. The new San Diego Padres offered Bavasi an ownership opportunity. Peter O'Malley ascended to the position of executive vice president. In preparation, he spent two years as vice president of Dodger Stadium operations. Fresco Thompson filled the player personnel position but died a few months later. Thus, the old Dodger triumvirate, running major league and minor league operations, of Bavasi, Fresco, and Al Campanis was no more. Bill Schweppe became vice president of minor league operations and Campanis moved from director of scouting to vice president, player personnel and scouting.

The Dodger family suffered yet another loss. Mrs. James (Dearie) Mulvey, the wife of the Dodger vice president and co-owner, died. She loved to come to Dodgertown every spring with her children and grandchildren and hadn't missed an exhibition game in twenty-two years. In Mrs. Mulvey's honor, the Dodgers established the Dearie Mulvey Award to go to the outstanding rookie at Dodgertown each spring. Second baseman Ted Sizemore won the first award in 1969 and become the National League Rookie of the Year that season.[3]

Despite the Local Government

Despite concerns about integration and the Vietnam War, Vero Beach's economy grew. Flight Safety, a nationwide company training professional pilots, joined Dodgertown and Piper at the airport. A Holiday Inn replaced the old Windswept Hotel on the beach. Developers bulldozed the Sunny Surf Cottages, which dated back to the 1930s, and built an apartment and motel complex. Peter O'Malley joined in the real estate boom, buying nearby beach properties. Work began on an ocean-to-river development to be known as The Moorings. Palm Beach developer Lloyd Ecclestone announced the development of Johns Island, a two-and-a-half-mile stretch of oceanfront property straddling A1A.[4]

Young professionals and their families began to move to the area. One of those was Doctor Hugh McCrystal. Hugh had grown up in Brooklyn with ties to the Dodgers. His family had belonged to the same beach club as the Mulveys, and Hugh had lived in the same neighborhood as Gil Hodges, attending an elementary school that later would be named after Hodges. Hugh remembered Gil standing at the back of the neighborhood Catholic Church so he could get outside easily to smoke a cigarette.

Like all of Brooklyn, Hugh had prayed for Gil during his 1952 slump. Hugh attended medical school at the old Long Island College of Medicine, near Ebbets Field. He left Brooklyn about the time the Dodgers did to pursue a medical career. After completing his internships, an opportunity came up in Vero and, by chance, the team he had followed since boyhood trained there.

At Dodgertown, Hugh reestablished his connections with the Dodgers. He went to dinner with Buzzie Bavasi, who he had known from the past. Bavasi asked him how he liked Vero. Hugh said, "It's great, spectacular." Bavasi replied, "Yeah. It survives despite its local government."[5]

Eastern Airlines, which Bud Holman had brought to Vero almost forty years earlier, shocked the community by applying to the FAA to stop service.[6] Eastern, like the Dodgers, was regarded as a local institution. The city fought the loss of Eastern into the '70s and then gave up. The airports at Melbourne, Orlando, and West Palm Beach were too close. If Holman had been alive, something might have been done.

Vero Beach did not escape the turmoil of the '60s. Seven Indian River men died in Vietnam. People were being arrested locally for possession of marijuana. And the courts ruled in December 1966 that all Indian River County schools be desegregated. This "freedom of choice" desegregation plan stated that any child was free to attend any school in the county.[7]

What You Guys Did in Baseball

The murder of Martin Luther King Jr. occurred on April 4, 1968. Riots erupted across black communities in Chicago, Baltimore, Washington, and Cincinnati. Violence in Vero Beach was limited. A fight in Gifford resulted in the arrest of several blacks. Brush fires burned. Arson was attempted at two Gifford nightspots. Bars were closed.[8] Gifford civic leaders and local ministers issued an appeal for calmness and peace among residents. No further violence took place.

Many years later, Don Newcombe would recall a dinner with King a month before he was killed. King said to Newcombe, "Don, you, Jackie, and Roy will never know how easy it made it for me to do my job with what you guys did in baseball."[9]

Ralph Lundy, as president of the Gifford Civic League, wrote a piece in the *Press Journal* stating: "There are citizens who feel proud of the peaceful relationship that has existed here the last few years." He wrote about the progress being made. Job opportunities existed because the

Dodgers, Piper, and local department and grocery stores began hiring qualified persons, regardless of race. Students could select the schools of their choice; facilities, including Holman Stadium, became integrated.[10]

But ultimately, as in many southern towns, freedom of choice did not work. No white students attended the black schools. Another court decision ordered the Gifford schools to integrate or be closed. The Indian River County School Board came up with a new plan. All high school students, black and white, attended Vero Beach High School. All middle school students attended the upgraded Gifford schools. Elementary students were dispersed among the existing, formerly white, elementary schools.[11] Full integration began in September 1969 with students bussed to the designated schools.

With the encouragement of Dick Bird and Peter O'Malley and through appearances by Dodger players like Jim Brewer and Manny Mota, Little League baseball became integrated. Ralph Lundy, the Jaycees, and the Dodgers joined together to build a Little League field in Gifford.[12]

The Dodgers set the example in Indian River County by first bringing Jackie Robinson, Roy Campanella, and Don Newcombe to Dodgertown and then by taking down the "Colored Only" signs at Holman Stadium. Whether that made what followed easier isn't clear. But Indian River County, once integration began, seemed to have fewer problems than other places. Alma Lee Loy, who served as president of the Chamber of Commerce and then on the County Commission during that time, remarked, "The community was not proud of its segregated past, but we were blessed that it worked out as well as it did."[13]

Both Vero and the Dodgers had to be glad that the sixties were over. Vero Beach survived both the FAA and integration battles and stood poised to grow in ways that no one could imagine. The county's population had doubled in the 1960s from 12,000 to 25,000.

The Dodgers hit a peak in 1965, then crumbled with the end of the Koufax-Drysdale-Wills era. The future rested with a group of guys who were being trained at Dodgertown and were playing in the minors, mostly for Tommy Lasorda.

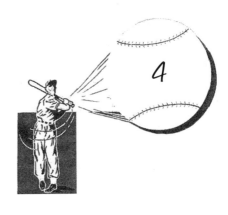

4

The Seventies

13

A Team and a Town in Transition

1970

The Green Phantom

After three down years, the 1970 Dodger Press Guide portrayed the hope for a Dodger turnaround in the seventies. The front page highlighted 1969's individual performers: Willie Davis and his thirty-one game hitting streak, a Dodger record; National League Rookie of the Year, second baseman Ted Sizemore; and twenty-game winners, Claude Osteen and Bill Singer. But the future of the Dodgers was not on the front page of the press guide but in the spring training roster with names like Joe Ferguson, Bill Buckner, Ron Cey, Steve Garvey, Bobby Valentine, Tom Paciorek, and an outfielder, who had come up the year before, Bill Russell. Davey Lopes and Steve Yeager would soon join them. For the near term, Maury Wills again wore a Dodger uniform. He and Manny Mota had arrived from Montreal in a 1969 midseason trade.

The Green Phantom struck Dodgertown. It started when Spokane manager Tommy Lasorda, pitching batting practice, irked some of the regulars by saying how soft they were compared to the players of his time in the fifties. Suddenly things began to happen to Lasorda. The whirlpool where he soaked his sore arm was tagged the "USS Lasorda." A green uniform appeared with a note attached daring him to wear it; the note was signed, "The Green Phantom." He wore the uniform and vowed to catch his tormentors. During the St. Patrick's Day party, a green baseball appeared in his room with a series of clues that led him to look under his bed. There he found the wheels to Walter O'Malley's golf cart. During the Yankee game at Holman Stadium, the phantom filled Lasorda's barracks room with toilet tissue and other debris. Lasorda became furious. The climax came the last day of spring training at a barbecue party at the swimming pool. A figure dressed in green and wearing a mask appeared. Lasorda rushed the figure hollering, "I'll get you." Before Lasorda could make the tackle, a bunch of guys pushed him into the pool. The Green Phantom removed his mask and grinned. It was Jim Lefebvre. The wet Lasorda could only laugh.[1]

Tommy Lasorda gave as well as he received. When Tommy was a scout, he and John Carey, who ran the on-field operations at Dodgertown, came back from dinner in Vero one night extolling the virtues of a first baseman they'd discovered. "Hit two of the most tremendous home runs I've ever seen," said Lasorda. "Potentially the best player I've seen," agreed Carey. The phenom had the perfect name for a Dodger—Pee Wee Mullins. Lasorda and Carey had stashed Mullins away in a Vero motel. Having gotten the news going, Lasorda and Carey went to pick up their man. As word spread around Dodgertown, a big crowd gathered to greet Pee Wee. Lasorda described the arrival: "Dressed in a Dodger uniform that almost fit and carrying a bat, he started getting out of the back seat of the car, then continued getting out of the back seat of the car, and still continued getting out of the back seat of the car. Nobody could stop laughing." Kay O'Malley laughed so hard tears came to her eyes. Pee Wee stood almost eight feet tall! His real name was Harry Hite, and he worked for a local meat company. Lasorda said, "Although we didn't sign Pee Wee Mullins, it was still the finest moment of my scouting career."[2]

There were other pranksters at Dodgertown as well. Walter Alston in a conversation with writer Joe Hendrickson said that the "top prankster" among the players he managed was Jim Brewer, ace relief pitcher in the late '60s and early '70s. A great outdoorsman from Oklahoma, Brewer trapped armadillos and put them in the other players' rooms. Brooklyn native Al Ferrara entered his room to find a strange creature with a shell on its back crawling around. Brewer and Claude Osteen made the most of being in proximity to the Florida wilderness. They fished, hunted bobcats at night, and caught snakes.[3]

At the annual Saint Patrick's Day party at Dodgertown, Walter O'Malley, surrounded by his board of directors, announced the promotion of his son, Peter, as president of the Dodgers. Now thirty-two, Peter had worked his way up through the organization: at Dodgertown, in Spokane, in stadium operations, and as executive vice president. Reporting to Peter were Red Patterson, in charge of promotions and public relations; Al Campanis, handling player personnel; and Bill Schweppe, in charge of the minor league system. Peter's father became chairman of the board, a timely move. The Mayo Clinic performed abdominal surgery on Walter O'Malley that spring.[4]

The Dodgers finished second in 1970, well behind the Reds in the West Division. The rookie crop still had a couple of years to go before they matured.

An Irritating Moratorium

With pressure from developers, the Vero Beach community squabbled over building height limits, and it ended up irritating Walter O'Malley. The city and the county finally agreed on a five-story limit, which still applies today. At some point, a dishonest out-of-town developer slipped a permit through and built the Village Spires—twin, thirteen-story condominiums on the beach, the only high rises in the county.[5]

During the height discussions, a building moratorium was put in place. It delayed O'Malley's plans for new facilities at Dodgertown, which would increase income and offset training expenses. City manager John Little and mayor Art Neuberger warned that Vero could lose the Dodgers.[6] The moratorium was soon lifted.

1971–1972

Running into a Palm Tree

The Dodgers arrived in Vero in the spring of 1971 in a new plane, a jet airliner. The Boeing 720-B, named the *Kay-O II*, was the fastest commercial plane flying and the largest jet under corporate ownership. Captain Lewis Carlisle captained the *Kay-O*, with his wife Millie serving as cabin attendant. The Dodgers purchased the jet from American Airlines and had it modified to include seventy first-class seats and four lounges. It made the flight from Los Angeles to Vero in four hours and fifteen minutes—quite a change from rookie Don Drysdale's thirteen-hour, first trip to Dodgertown from Los Angeles in 1959.[7]

The Dodgers pulled off the "bombshell deal" of the winter. The team acquired Richie Allen, described by Dodger publicists as "one of the greatest sluggers of modern time." Allen almost ended the season before it started. On the first day of spring practice, chasing a fly ball, he ran into one of the Holman Stadium palm trees and was knocked out.[8] But the Allen deal, along with one for American League pitching ace Tommy John, was not enough to win a pennant. The team finished second in the West Division in '71 and third in '72.

Vero Beach had made progress with integration in the 1960s, but still had a ways to go. Jim Lefebvre asked teammate Willie Crawford to go into town for dinner and a drink. The owner of a local establishment sent the waitress over to tell Willie, "We don't serve you here." Willie said, "I didn't like it. . . . but I didn't want to make an issue of it. I didn't go anywhere I wasn't wanted. I just dined in Dodgertown and went to the movies there or just watched TV. I figured I'd soon be in Los Angeles where I could go anywhere I wanted."[9]

Bobby Valentine, hitting .340 at Spokane in 1970, became the organization's top prospect with expectations of replacing Maury Wills. At Dodgertown, Bill Russell, not Bobby Valentine, became the Dodger shortstop. Walter Alston thought Valentine too cocky, so he was traded. He endured several injuries and never lived up to his potential, but he went on to become a manager and led the New York Mets to the World Series in 1999. He married Ralph Branca's daughter, a Mulvey-McKeever descendant, and the Dodger organization considered him almost family despite his short stay with the team. Rumors circulated in later years that he would manage the Dodgers.

An Unusual Guest

In 1972, Marvin Miller, director of the Major League Players Association, arrived at Dodgertown on Saint Patrick's Day. He came to conduct a vote among the players on whether to strike for increased pension benefits. Player representative Wes Parker reported that the Dodgers voted strongly for the strike. At one point early in Miller's reign when he proposed that all player grievances be subject to arbitration, he was not well received by Walter O'Malley.[10]

While Miller reviewed the strike vote count, he received an invitation from a more gracious O'Malley to attend the annual St. Patrick's Day party. Miller described O'Malley as "a power house among the owners" who "with his large jowls had the look of a Cheshire cat, if not a lion." Miller called the party "a big league bash" with everything green: "water, scotch, beer, potatoes, tablecloths, you name it." It disappointed Miller that, while Sandy Koufax and Roy Campanella attended, none of the current players were invited. Miller and O'Malley talked at the party. Miller couldn't understand why "the most rational businessman among the owners didn't understand that their non-negotiation stance was about to force a strike."[11]

The strike began April 1 and ended April 13. The owners, after talking big, caved. They couldn't stand losing the revenue.

Save the Barracks

Across from the entrance to the Dodgertown barracks on Jackie Robinson Avenue a new phenomenon appeared—the villas. They consisted of ninety units modeled after Holiday Inn rooms. The barracks could house at least 480 people when there had been more than twenty farm teams.[12] Now, with only five to six farm teams, the villas provided adequate space. Vero Beach architect John Schlitt worked with Walter O'Malley to design the units. Local contractor Paul Parent built them in four months in 1972 and said that Mr. O'Malley was an inspiration during the construction.[13] The O'Malleys had their own villa, 162 Sandy Koufax Lane, right across from the swimming pool.

The barracks still stood, and the Dodgertown regulars speculated about their future. Bumper stickers appeared on cars: "Save the Barracks." Who

Ninety villas replaced the old barracks, which were originally across the street and to the left. (Courtesy of Los Angeles Dodgers, Los Angeles, California.)

was running this campaign? Walter O'Malley didn't know. He said to Dick Bird, "Let's have a little fun" and asked him to have bumper stickers and yard signs printed. Then, early in the morning, before anyone was up, O'Malley went around Dodgertown placing them. His "What idiot wants to save the barracks?" campaign went on for two weeks.[14]

Despite O'Malley's joke, real sentiment was connected to the barracks. Would Dodgertown still be Dodgertown without them? Third baseman Ron Cey said he was glad to have come up to the Dodgers early enough to get to live in the old barracks. They meant that much to him.[15]

Betty Miller directed the maids at Dodgertown. She "kept the rooms spic and span for her boys" for twenty years. She particularly liked Jim Gilliam and Dusty Baker because they were "so friendly and down to earth." Despite the villas, which must have made her job easier, she liked the barracks better. She told Joe Hendrickson that there was something "homey" about those rooms.[16]

Peter O'Malley echoed these sentiments: "We don't want to lose the intimacy of the early days," he explained. "Living conditions in the days of the old barracks were crude, but there was a certain primitive romance. Those times are remembered fondly. There was a closeness we all felt, and it brought us all together. I think we are coming close to keeping the basic romance of the past while combining the convenience of modern times."[17] But with the villas in place, the barracks disappeared a year later.

Safari Pines

The new eighteen-hole golf course was completed in 1972. Dick Bird suggested it be named Safari Pines. The clubhouse could be decorated with Walter O'Malley's hunting trophies, which he had accumulated on a couple of trips to Africa in the '60s.[18] The par-72, championship course reflected the creativity of its somewhat amateur designers, Walter O'Malley, Ira Hoyt, and Dick Bird. It included forty sand traps, two lakes, a pond, and a canal—all "carved out of the natural woods with many of the tall pines left in place to add to the beauty and the difficulty of the course." The heart-shaped number four green and the number nine green that resembled a four-leaf clover added to the course's ambiance.[19]

Walter O'Malley decided to take Safari Pines one step further. He would build a high quality, seven-hundred-unit modular home development surrounding the course. Units would sell for $13,000 each. After all, his friend Art Linkletter had been successful with that kind of development in Southern California. The initial forty-six units, called Safari Pines Estates, were built at the entrance to the course. Further development ceased. Dick Bird said, "As nice as those units were, they weren't the best for the property." He admitted that their planning hadn't been the most professional. There was some talk of building condominiums instead of the modular homes. "The city fathers stopped our plans to expand," said Dick. "It was strange politics at that time. There were two city councilmen against growth."[20]

On October 24, 1972, Jackie Robinson, at age fifty-three, died of a heart attack at his home in Stanford, Connecticut. His participation on the team had shaped the initial concept, as envisioned by Branch Rickey, of a totally integrated Dodgertown. The concept continued to expand under Walter and Peter O'Malley with the integration of Holman Stadium and the future addition of a golf course open to all. Jackie Robinson and Dodgertown set the example for Vero Beach and Indian River County to follow.

A New Era

1973

Born to Be a Dodger

A new era began at Dodgertown. The longest-standing infield in major
league history began its first season, and Tommy Lasorda joined the
Dodgers as a coach. The last semblance of the original Dodgertown disappeared with the razing of the barracks.

Bill Russell had already replaced Maury Wills at shortstop. Steve Garvey played third but with difficulty fielding the position. Rookies Davey
Lopes and Ron Cey were ready for the majors. Lopes became the second
baseman and Cey took over third. Bill Buckner moved to the outfield so
Garvey could shift to first. Garvey, Lopes, Russell, and Cey would play
together for the next eight years.

Steve Garvey believed that he was "born to be a Dodger." His Brooklyn
grandfather was a Dodger fan. Steve grew up in Tampa and at age seven,
in 1956, began riding in the bus his father drove carrying the Dodgers to
games on Florida's west coast.[1] Steve served as batboy for the team in
those games. The Dodgers picked him in the first round of the June 1968
draft, and he played for Tommy Lasorda at Ogden that summer.

Tommy Lasorda finally made the big team, becoming one of Walter
Alston's coaches after a twenty-five-year career as a Dodger minor league
player, scout, and manager. Tommy replaced Danny Ozark, whom the
Phillies hired as their manager.

In spring training, Lasorda, in his typical fashion, initiated an incen-
tive program for the nonroster players. A group of coaches selected several nominees for the best hustle of the day, and the players would vote
the winner. Rewards included using Lasorda's personal electric heater
for the night, assisting in feeding the ducks in the pond next to Holman

Stadium, enjoying the honor of riding to Melbourne to pick up Don Drysdale, and dining with Walter O'Malley with permission to say, "Walter, please pass the salt."[2]

With the new infield; the catching depth of Joe Ferguson and Steve Yeager; a pitching staff of Don Sutton, Claude Osteen, Tommy John, and Andy Messersmith; and the soon-to-be-acquired outfielders Jim Wynn, Reggie Smith, and Dusty Baker, the Dodgers stood poised to win three National League titles in the next six years. But this year, the Dodgers finished second in their division, again behind the Reds.

Jim Mulvey, the son-in-law of Ed McKeever, a Dodger director since 1940, and Walter O'Malley's favorite golf partner, died in 1973. The Dearie Mulvey Award for the best rookie performance in the spring at Dodgertown was renamed the Jim and Dearie Mulvey Award.

1974

Someone Else Can Have a Chance

Spring brought with it several notable events: Peter O'Malley's in-laws, who lived in Denmark, visited Dodgertown for the first time; lady umpire Christine Wren worked some of the exhibition games; Fred Claire, a former Southern California sportswriter, became the Dodger publicist; and fifteen-year-old Eric Olson retired as the Dodgers' spring-training batboy so that, as he put it, "Someone else can have a chance."[3]

Eric Olson particularly liked Jim Gilliam. Eric's mother invited Jim to come play golf at the Riomar Country Club. Jim declined. Given its racial climate, he knew Vero Beach wasn't yet ready. The Olsons represented the attraction the Dodgers exerted not only for visiting Vero but for moving there. The Olsons came every spring to see the team. In the late sixties, Norris Olson sold his business in Columbus, Ohio, and brought his family to Vero. He started a new career there as one of the area's first stockbrokers.[4]

Former Dodger publicist Red Patterson had resigned to become president of Gene Autry's California Angels. Once vice president of publicity and promotions, Red had some favorite memories of Dodgertown: Maury Wills helping his wife Helen brighten up their room by adding drapes and seat covers; a Long Beach sportswriter driving back to Dodgertown one night, missing the bridge, and plunging unhurt into the canal; walking late at night with an angry Walter Alston after he broke his

World Series ring during the Koufax-Sherry incident; Al Ferrara's setting a davenport to smolder with ashes from his cigar, which triggered a fear of fire in the barracks.[5]

Dodgertown night watchman Glen Joyce could remember only one fire and that occurred in the old lobby from a cigarette dropped on a couch. Joyce had come to work at Dodgertown about 1960 and was in his eighties. During his many years of service, he discovered no burglaries, only an occasional prowler. But he did "put a flashlight on occupants of parked cars where nobody had anything in mind but stealing affection." Before going off duty, Glen blew the whistle in the barracks in the mornings to wake up the players.[6]

The Saints

The National Football League's New Orleans Saints trained at Dodgertown in the summer of 1974. Dick Bird swung the deal in another Dodger effort to expand the revenue-producing potential of Dodgertown. The Saints returned to Louisiana for training in '75. But the weather was so awful there that they came back to Vero the next year and stayed for several years. Coach Dick Nolan liked the family atmosphere at Dodgertown, though the players' wives stayed over on the beach. The team practiced early in the morning and late in the afternoon to avoid the August heat. The Saints held an annual practice game with the Miami Dolphins, the local National Football League favorite. The Vero Beach Exchange Club sold tickets, and two thousand fans stood around a field converted from baseball to football. Archie Manning quarterbacked the Saints, Bob Griese the Dolphins. Saints owner John Mecom liked Vero and kept his yacht at the Riomar Bay Yacht Club during the summer.

With Steve Garvey as the National League's Most Valuable Player and reliever Mike Marshall as the Cy Young Award winner, the Dodgers won their division and beat the Pirates for the National League Championship. In the World Series they lost to the Oakland A's.

By the end of the year, a new Dodger administration building stood across from the villas on the site of the old barracks. It included a clubhouse for the major leaguers and one for the minor leaguers, a dining room and kitchen, press facilities, trainers' rooms, and laundry rooms. The Dodgertown of 1948 was no longer recognizable.

Dick Bird resigned as director of Dodgertown in 1974. As Dick said, despite his years with the Dodgers, his background was golf not baseball. Walter O'Malley's health had declined, and his son Peter was now more

Charlie Blaney became Dodgertown director in 1974. He would
diversify operations by adding the
conference center. (Courtesy of
Los Angeles Dodgers, Los Angeles,
California.)

in charge and "really not that fond of golf." "My future was limited," Dick
explained. There also may have been some question as to whether or not
Dick was to blame for the City of Vero Beach's refusal to approve further
development at Dodger Pines. But Dick had another opportunity, a part-
nership with a local beverage distributor. Later he went into real estate
and served several years as an Indian River County commissioner.[7]

Charlie Blaney replaced Dick as director of Dodgertown. Charlie came
from the Albuquerque farm team, where he had spent eight years as general manager. During that period he won a Minor League Executive of
the Year award. The Blaneys arrived in Vero with a bevy of children and
quickly became active in the community.

1975–1976

The New Dodgertown

The clubhouse for the eighteen-hole golf course was completed and
named Dodger Pines. With Dick Bird gone, the name Safari Pines applied
only to the modular home development. Instead of wild animal heads,
huge pictures of great Dodger moments decorated the clubhouse walls.
The waitresses wore Dodger shirts with the names of Dodger greats—

like Reese, Robinson, Snider, and Koufax—printed across the back. The place became a popular Vero institution, particularly its buffets. Paul Parent Construction, following its work on the Dodgertown villas, built the clubhouse. Parent said, "Mr. O'Malley personally projected his ideas. He drew plans himself. To illustrate his insight, he built the clubhouse on a level above the golf course so people could look out over the action."[8]

To introduce the public to its new layout, the Dodgers ran an ad in the *Press Journal*: "The Los Angeles Dodgers cordially invite you to an OPEN HOUSE AT THE 'NEW' DODGERTOWN, this Sunday, Feb. 22nd. Take a free tour of the 'New' Dodgertown. Learn how the Dodgers live and what they do to prepare for the National League season."[9]

The next year Dodgertown gained another addition—a conference center. Peter O'Malley had instructed Dodgertown director Charlie Blaney to find other uses for the Dodgertown facilities. Blaney toured the country looking at alternatives and came up with the conference center concept. The Dodgers invested $500,000 to make Dodgertown competitive with the major hotels that received this type of business.[10] They modified the villas and the administration building where the barracks once stood, upgrading the dining room and adding conference rooms. Each conference room carried the name of a Dodger legend—the Koufax Room, the Alston Room. Conference guests had available for their use the swimming pool, the tennis courts, the golf courses, and an elegant lounge, the Stadium Club. The facility could handle 180 conferees and had its own 130 employees. During spring training, the conference center reverted back to being the major and minor league clubhouses and the baseball offices.

Blaney selected Harrison Conference Services to operate the facility. Over the next few years, five hundred companies came to Dodgertown, including corporations like DuPont, Kodak, and General Electric.[11] A young man from Brooklyn, Craig Callan, managed the operation for Harrison and would later join the Dodgers as Dodgertown director.

In 1975 and 1976, the Reds manhandled the West Division, leaving the Dodgers far behind in second place both years.

1977

The Emotional Cheerleader

After the 1976 season, sixty-five-year-old Walter Alston retired. He had managed the Dodgers for twenty-three years and in that period led the team to seven National League titles and four World Series championships. Only Connie Mack and John McGraw had managed a team longer. A feeling existed in the Dodger organization that "the game had passed him by." The younger players didn't relate to him. As bullpen catcher Mark Cresse said, "Since most of the guys had played for Tommy Lasorda in the minors, Tommy had more control of them than Walt did."[12]

In the spring of 1977, Tommy Lasorda returned to Dodgertown, this time as the new Dodger manager. The emotional cheerleader replaced the stoic and methodical Alston. No one knew Dodgertown and the players better than Lasorda. First arrived in 1949, he had been a coach with the team since '72 and had managed five of the starters and three of the pitchers in the minors.

On the first day of spring training, Lasorda told his players, "I'm tired of watching someone else in the World Series. What we're striving for is to win the World Series. That is our supreme objective. If you believe as much as I believe, then I have the utmost confidence we'll do it."[13]

Tommy Lasorda instituted a new policy in spring training. Before each game, he had his eight starters—Yeager, Garvey, Lopes, Russell, Cey, Smith, Monday, and Baker—run together in left field, loosening up. It was part of a plan. These eight players practiced together, played in the games as a group, and came out of the game as a group.[14] The new manager with his new approach led the Dodgers to victory in the National League. It was the year Steve Garvey, Reggie Smith, Ron Cey, and Dusty Baker each hit thirty home runs as the Dodgers outdistanced Cincinnati's Big Red Machine by ten games in their division. They then whipped the Philadelphia Phillies, managed by Vero Beach resident and former Dodger coach Danny Ozark, for the league championship. Lasorda was selected the National League Manager of the Year.

Hail to the Chief

1978

Phenomenal Turnouts

Despite losing to the Yankees in the World Series, the Dodgers set an attendance record in spring training. In ten exhibition games at Holman Stadium they drew a record 45,256 fans. The Vero Beach Junior Women's Club sold a thousand season tickets, the most ever. Games in Holman Stadium with the Yankees and the Reds each drew over seven thousand. Charlie Blaney called the turnouts "phenomenal."[1] Average attendance had almost doubled since 1963, the year Dodgertown director Peter O'Malley publicly expressed disappointment with the lack of local support for the exhibition games. The Holman Stadium attendance would be a prelude that year to the Dodgers becoming the first major league team to draw three million fans at home in one season.

Baseball commissioner Bowie Kuhn came to Dodgertown to visit Walter O'Malley who had been ill. The commissioner, described by the *Press Journal* as a "tall, superior gentleman," had encountered controversy with the owners. In a press conference, Kuhn said he felt his job was secure. (O'Malley had always been his strong backer.) He hoped to see the designated hitting rule applied to the National League, and he was concerned that "the runaway spending on free agents could cause a problem in the future [an accurate prophecy]."[2] He attended the Dodgers-Braves game with 5,381 fans, the largest opening day crowd in Dodgertown history.

Two hundred-and-twenty-five players, coaches, and staff resided in camp, along with thirty-five members of the Southern California media. *Good Morning America*'s David Hartman and NBC-TV's Bryant Gumbel visited. The annual Dodger family barbecue was held at the Dodgertown pool. With a Christmas theme, twenty-seven children of players and staff received presents from Santa Claus.[3]

While the team emphasized family at Dodgertown, a problem flared up in the clubhouse that involved Steve Garvey, of all people. In Vero Beach, Steve was a favorite. He was the player most generally accessible to the fans, perhaps too accessible according to his teammates. "Spring is really your closest contact with fans," wrote Garvey. "During the season you perceive 'fans' as tens of thousands of screaming people in the stands. At Vero you get to know people as individuals."[4]

This always-friendly approach and his all-American boy image caused resentment within the team. Teammate Davey Lopes said, "The problem was that he was presented as better than we were. The press did that; the organization did that. . . . It created a tension that never went away."[5] The situation came to a head during the season, when Garvey and Don Sutton got into a brief scuffle in the Dodger clubhouse.

Despite the Garvey situation, the Dodgers won the West, edging the Reds and the Giants by a slim margin. Again they beat the Phillies for the National League Championship. But again they lost to the Yankees in the World Series.

Two days before the World Series started, Jim Gilliam, at age fifty, died of a brain hemorrhage. He joined the Dodgers in 1953, played in seven World Series, and then became a coach. Steve Garvey served as a pallbearer, reflecting a relationship that went back to when Steve was a batboy for the Dodgers.

Also at Jim Gilliam's funeral was longtime Dodgertown bus driver Ben Grier. He drove the minor league teams to games around Florida on an old bus. Ben liked Jim Gilliam: "I was a poor boy when I started my job here. Jim was a fancy dresser. He would give me the clothes he didn't care to keep any longer. He would accompany me on my trips at night to keep me awake. We were like brothers. He also took me to restaurants I had never been in." The Dodgers flew Ben Grier to Los Angeles for the funeral.[6]

Jim Gilliam became the fifth Dodger to have his number retired, joining Jackie Robinson, Roy Campanella, Sandy Koufax and Walter Alston. Pee Wee Reese, Duke Snider, Don Drysdale, Tommy Lasorda, and Don Sutton would later join the group.[7]

Running and Eating with Tommy

With construction booming on Vero's beach, including the new Saint Edwards Upper School and the Riverside Theater, a high-rise, second bridge now spanned the Indian River. After it was built, drivers would often watch as Tommy Lasorda, leading the way, ran his pitchers up and across what he called "the Hill" to get them in shape during spring training.[8]

To all appearances Tommy enjoyed eating more than running, and his favorite Vero restaurant was Bobby's. Restaurateur Bobby McCarthy came to Vero in the '70s and managed the Bamboo Lounge, a favorite Dodger hangout. He had gone to high school in the Williamsburg section of Brooklyn and attended games at Ebbets Field. He was really a Yankees fan but in Vero became friends with the Dodger players. He occasionally joined them on road trips, particularly in Atlanta. After the night games, he would go out with the players, party till four a.m., and then sleep in until they had to go to the ball park. Steve Yeager became a particular friend of his. He said that Steve may have batted .200 something in the majors, but with the ladies he batted .700. Bobby McCarthy opened Bobby's Restaurant on Ocean Drive in 1981, and it became a Dodger favorite. Lasorda, whose autographed picture hangs in the bar, brought his sport celebrity friends there and still does.[9]

After Bobby's, Tommy Lasorda's second choice was Vincent's and its Italian food. He also remembered a place called The Pit on U.S. 1, a bar that "was more the beginning of the sports bars we have today." He added, "There use[d] to be one over here [by Dodgertown], too, that we could walk from to get back to the barracks at night."[10] That would be Lennie's Bar.

1979

A "Big-League" Organization

For a Yankee game billed as a replay of the World Series, a record crowd of 8,598 overflowed Holman Stadium on St. Patrick's Day. Toni Tennille of the Captain and Tennille duo, famous for their hit "Love Will Keep Us Together," sang the national anthem. During the game, an incident occurred at the bottom of the berm in left field. No fence circled the outfield then. Lou Piniella played left field for the Yankees and was visibly irritated that fans were behind him. When a long fly came his way, he raced back, peopled be dammed, to catch the ball. The fans scattered.

126   *The Seventies*

Pitcher Tommy John, his wife Sally, and their daughter Tamara pose before a game at Holman Stadium. (Courtesy of Los Angeles Dodgers, Los Angeles, California.)

When a deep fly came to Dodger left fielder Dusty Baker, he looked back to see that the people were okay and gracefully backed up to take in the ball. Dusty was a gentleman; Piniella was not. The Dodgers won 11–9. Piniella hit a home run, but Davey Lopes, Bill Russell, and Steve Garvey batted in runs in the eighth inning to give the Dodgers the win.[11]

Pitcher Tommy John was no longer at Dodgertown. He had benefited from Dodger doctor Frank Jobe's arm surgery (now called "Tommy John Surgery"), given the Dodgers a couple of great years, and then moved on to the Yankees as a free agent. He later wrote about his feelings for the Dodgers and spring training at Dodgertown: "I had my [contract] differences with the Dodgers. But I never lost my respect for the club." He said the team was "big league in their spring training site, in their personnel, in the manner in which they publicize and sell the game of baseball. . . . And certainly in their concern for their ballplayers and the families of the players." Dodgertown had a "grown-up atmosphere where the players were left to decide what sort of work they needed most and how much they needed." And Tommy John liked the Dodgers' "private jet for their players and wives, the only one in the major leagues." Tommy John's wife Sally also appreciated the Dodgers. She liked Peter O'Malley and Al Campanis and their efforts to make her feel a part of her husband's deal with the team. The Dodgers included wives in all club functions and welcomed them on road trips. "They made it clear," she said, "that I was expected—and would be heartily welcomed—at spring training in Vero Beach."[12]

Major league umpires went on strike that spring, and Charlie Blaney picked up some locals to fill in for an exhibition game with the Texas Rangers. The umpiring crew consisted of insurance agent Jim Thompson, Vero Beach Junior High principal Evan Soash, Sebastian Elementary assistant principal Jack Hanawalt, and county commissioner Bill Wodtke. All four had experience officiating—at the high school level! Protests were minor during the game except for an outburst from Ranger Bert Campaneris over a called third strike.[13]

Sandy Koufax reappeared at Dodgertown in a Dodger uniform. The team had hired him as a pitching instructor. During the spring, he joined coaches Red Adams and Ron Perranoski working with the big team pitchers. In Sandy's characteristically humble fashion he said, "I wait for them to ask for help. I just can't come in here one day and start telling everyone how to pitch." When asked if he felt anything special about putting on the Dodger uniform again, he said no. But he added, "There isn't another team in baseball that I would have come back for. Their attention to detail is what sets them apart from other organizations in the game."[14]

Tommy Lasorda became king in Vero. It must have been about this time that "Hail to the Chief" boomed over the loudspeaker whenever he rolled into Holman Stadium in his golf cart before a game. Everyone believed that he would win his third National League Championship in a row and this time a World Series. But there was no championship in 1979. The Dodgers finished with a losing percentage for the first time in eleven years.

Walter and Kay

Walter O'Malley died on August 9, 1979. His wife Kay preceded him by three weeks. The Los Angles Dodgers and major league baseball lost its patriarch. In Walter and Kay O'Malley, Vero Beach lost two of the best friends the community will ever have.

A special edition of *Line Drives*, a Dodger publication, reviewed their lives in pictures: Walter and Kay sitting in their seats at Holman Stadium; Walter helping President Eisenhower throw out the first pitch in the World Series at Ebbets Field; Walter celebrating the 1956 National League Championship with Walter Alston and Pee Wee Reese; Walter

Kay and Walter O'Malley at Dodgertown. (Courtesy of Los Angeles Dodgers, Los Angeles, California.)

being welcomed to Los Angeles by mayor Norris Poulson in 1958; Kay tossing out the first pitch at the opening of Dodger Stadium in 1962; Walter chatting with Ronald and Nancy Reagan; Walter in his golfing togs swinging his driver; and Walter and Kay walking down the ramp from the *Kay O' II* as they and the team arrived in Vero Beach for spring training in 1971.[15]

In a *Los Angeles Times* interview in the early seventies, Kay O'Malley said, "God has been very good to me. I have lived a full life. That's due to my husband, of course." As she described it, that life included "my church, my family, my friends, and baseball." In the *Line Drives* retrospective, she is remembered as that "cheerful, indomitable woman," "the most enthusiastic rooter of them all." Always with Walter at games and even making the road trips, she wouldn't miss spring training at Vero Beach. She kept score in an official scorebook the writers gave her every spring and taught her eight grandchildren to score. She and Walter shared the hobby of growing orchids. They had greenhouses at their homes in Los Angeles and Amityville, Long Island. They also had homes at Lake Arrowhead and in Vero Beach at Dodgertown.[16]

Alma Lee Loy, a community leader and owner of a downtown children's clothing store for many years, spoke about Kay O'Malley: "The minute she got here she made a beeline for the store. She was so nice and so warm. I felt like she was a personal friend. She would come in the store two or three times a week, buying things for other people's grandchildren. With her tracheotomy (which she had as a young woman), it became progressively harder to understand what she was saying, but she didn't worry about it and went right on [talking]." Alma Lee said of Walter O'Malley that despite his prominence, "he was not considered in that light at all. He had done well, and he brought something to the community and enhanced the everyday life of everyone here. We were proud of the way [he and Kay] conducted themselves and what they did—and we were a tiny community then."[17]

After Kay O'Malley had a series of strokes, she couldn't keep score or walk. "She was dad's copilot," said Terry O'Malley Seidler, "in the golf cart or he was behind her wheelchair taking her to Holman Stadium or the dining room." Terry related one of the Dodgertown memories that will stay with her forever: "Dad pushing Mother's wheelchair from a Saint Patrick's Party while everyone sang, 'I'll Take You Home Again Kathleen.'"[18]

Upon his death, many accolades were bestowed upon Walter O'Malley. In the special addition of *Line Drives*, various members of the press were quoted: Joe Hendrickson, "Friendship and associations were important to him. As a result, a great many individuals have belonged to the O'Malley family. . . . He taught that outthinking and outmaneuvering a foe is everything—providing you make it fun"; Chuck Johnson, "He likely will be voted into the Hall of Fame at Cooperstown as owner of the half century, the game's most knowledgeable, far sighted executive"; Bob Hunter, "[He] will take his place along with Judge Kenesaw Mountain Landis and Babe Ruth as probably one of the three most vital forces in baseball history"; Gordon Verrell, "Without a doubt, he was the most influential man in the game. And the most respected."[19] Former Dodger catcher Roy Campanella called him "a true pioneer, who to me was like a father when I first came to the Dodger organization. He stood by me and after my injury he still stood by me and helped me through all my crises."[20]

Flags hung at half-mast at Dodgertown. They signaled a huge change. As Charlie Blaney observed, "Mr. O'Malley was Dodgertown."[21]

Walter O'Malley left behind not only a rebuilt Dodgertown facility, but also the Safari Pines Estates residential development, the nine-hole Dodgertown Golf Course, the conference center, a training facility for the New Orleans Saints, forty-one acres of citrus groves, and the eighteen-hole Dodger Pines Country Club. The entire 340-acre Dodgertown complex employed a full-time staff of 130 and had an annual payroll and expense budget of $2 million. The local government had invested nothing, yet the Dodgers paid taxes exceeding $100,000 a year and, in their support of the community, were an exemplary corporate citizen. Dodgertown would miss Walter O'Malley's "trail of white cigar holders and his deep bellowing voice."[22]

Rumors and a Storm

Indian River Life Magazine, published in Palm Beach, reported that the Los Angeles Dodgers, including Dodgertown, had been sold to the Union Oil Company of California. Their information came from a source close to Peter O'Malley. The announcement would be made after Walter O'Malley's death. The article went on to state that the rumored sale supposedly had been prompted by Walter O'Malley's wish to sidestep the enormous estate taxes that would be due if he left the ball club to Peter. Union Oil sponsored Dodger radio broadcasts and maintained a close business association with the Dodgers and the O'Malleys.[23] The team denied the report, and no sale occurred at that time. The rumor nonetheless forecast the future. The Dodgers would eventually be sold, but this remained well down the road.

Meanwhile, Dodgertown director Charlie Blaney turned another rumor, that Vero Beach was acquiring a minor league team, into fact by announcing that the Dodgers were transferring their Class A team in Clinton, Iowa, to Vero Beach to play in the Florida State League in 1980.[24]

Since the beginning of Dodgertown thirty-one years earlier, Vero's population had grown from 4,646 in 1950 to 8,849 by 1960. Entering the 1980s, it exceeded 16,000.[25] Walter O'Malley's faith in Vero as a growing community, which would support a full Dodger exhibition schedule and a minor league team, was now substantiated.

In a *Press Journal* column called "A Stormy Decade," journalist Jack Fay echoed O'Malley's sentiments. He argued that "despite a lot of weeping and wailing about how Vero Beach was changing from a nice, quiet, small town to a bustling community with a much quicker pace, the changes were good." He characterized Hurricane David that struck on Labor Day 1979 as probably a fitting climax to the '70s.[26] Though a minor hurricane, David did storm damage to the county that totaled $50 million, including the cost of the radio press box that had been blown off the top of Holman Stadium's concession stand. Dodgertown became a Red Cross evacuation center, and Charlie Blaney rode out the storm with 150 residents huddled in the dining room and one of the conference rooms without power.[27]

As a result of the storm and future expectations, the Dodgers spent $200,000 for a new radio press box, an electronic scoreboard, a new home-team clubhouse, and a renovated visitor clubhouse—all in preparation for the Vero Beach Dodgers beginning play in 1980.[28]

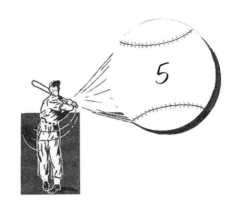

5

The Eighties

We Love Our Vero Beach Dodgers

1980

A Class A First Season

On a muggy, sunny morning in late August 1980, the Vero Beach Dodgers met the Fort Lauderdale Yankees in Holman Stadium for the championship of the Class A Florida State League. A few loyal fans watched. The night before, with a much larger crowd, a thunderstorm struck, drenching fans, players, and field and halting play after the top of the ninth inning with the Yankees leading 4–1. That next morning the Dodgers had a last, but slim, chance to bounce back. It didn't happen. Three outs on four pitches in two minutes and the Vero Dodgers' first season ended.[1]

That season began in April with Vero's opening-day win over the Winter Haven Red Sox before 2,600 fans. Butch Wickensheimer pitched a gutsy 3–0 game. Catcher Bill Sobbe tripled and scored the first run for the new team on a single by third baseman German Rivera.

For the fans, the players on that first Vero team were probably easier to remember than those of any Vero Dodger team since. Stocky left fielder Tony Brewer, who had played at the University of Miami the year before, led the team in hitting with a .285 average. Hustling second baseman Steve Sax stole thirty-three bases. German Rivera batted in eighty runs. Leo Hernandez arrived in Vero in June and brought some badly needed power, hitting ten home runs over the rest of the season. Wickensheimer led the league with fifteen wins.

The fans voted Sobbe the most popular player, and he received a television set from Big Keith's TV. In one game he caught a foul ball, bent double over the waist-high fence on the third-base side of home plate.

Sixty-year-old Stan Wasiak managed the Vero Dodgers. Called both the King of the Minors and the Wizard of Waz, this white-haired, grandfatherly gentleman had managed at every level in the minor leagues. With over two thousand wins, he won the Minor League Manager of the Year award several times. Stan called that first win in Vero one of the most gratifying in his career. "We had a great crowd," he said. "They gave me a hand when I was walking off the field, and fans don't usually do that for managers."[2]

Local banker and Dodger fan Jerre Haffield organized local businesses to provide community support for the team. He said of the team, "They had very good draw appeal. We were thrilled with the quality of the play; the men all seemed to be fine young men. It worked out very well."[3]

In their opening season, the Vero Dodgers drew 85,000 fans, averaging more than 1,200 per game—an amazing attendance for a community of 17,000. Vero became the smallest city in the nation with a full-season minor league team. One game in midsummer drew 3,600 fans. Only St. Petersburg and West Palm Beach drew more fans in the Florida State League. "We Love Our Vero Beach Dodgers" stickers appeared all over town.

Dodgertown director Charlie Blaney selected twenty-seven-year-old Terry Reynolds, a former Dodger intern, to be the Vero general manager. Among his duties, Reynolds was to arrange entertainment at the games beyond just baseball. Boom-Boom Koski, the Human Bomb, blew himself up at home plate. The San Diego Chicken made an appearance. The Clown Prince of Baseball Max Patkin performed. Bob Feller pitched against the media. Reynolds also planned special nights: Tuesday—ladies' night; Wednesday—family night, at two dollars per family; Thursday—men's night, at fifty cents a head; Sunday—bring-your-church-bulletin-and-get-in-free night. Local businesses—the *Press Journal*, Keens Supermarket, Parent Construction, WTTB, Piper Aircraft, and Tripson's Dairy, among others—sponsored games and gave away free tickets all over town. Between innings, fans raced around the bases with shopping carts picking up groceries, scrambled for cash, milked cows, dug for diamonds, and climbed greased poles. Drawings for prizes took place between innings. Children ran races and threw balls through hoops. It was family mayhem and fun.

"We will do just about anything you can do to make it more fun to go to the ball park; maybe you bring out people who normally wouldn't see a ball game," said Terry.[4]

Unfortunately, pig events were less successful. The Dodgers canceled a pig chase when the Humane Society objected. The Daisy Ham and Egg

Revue, featuring a singing pig, was so bad that it made only one appearance.[5]

In the Florida summer heat, Holman Stadium seemed like heaven. Games started at seven p.m. with the sun going down behind the berm bringing a slight coolness to the air. In the glow of the stadium lights, the sky overhead turned from blue to purple to black. Radiant white egrets and ibises flew overhead from the river, going inland to roost for the night. Under the bright lights, nine young men, in crisp white Dodger uniforms and blue caps with the "VB" logo superimposed on a grapefruit emblem, ran to their positions on the field to the applause of the crowd. What a pleasant way to spend a summer evening in Vero Beach, Florida.

And the baseball was always interesting. A visiting team's left fielder disappeared over the berm chasing a fly ball. A minute later, he appeared on top of the berm holding up the ball. The crowd applauded, but the umpire ruled it a home run.

The atmosphere differed from the major league exhibition games where the more elderly fans, sitting in the sunshine, tended to get sleepy and quiet. The minor league games attracted a mixed crowd, both retirees and families with children. Some fans, like Harry and Thea Walker or Bob and Sue Bond and their two boys, came to almost every game, seventy nights a summer. The Walkers were retirees; the Bonds taught at Saint Edward's School. The two couples still have season tickets to this day.

In the major league games the players tried to get in shape, not win ball games; the minor leaguers, age nineteen to twenty-three, tried to win, to impress so they could advance. It mattered whether Vero Beach won.

Adopt-A-Dodger

Unlike during the spring exhibition season, the Dodgertown villas were not available to Vero Dodger players. Instead, the conference center used the villas to house guests. The team ran an "Adopt-A-Dodger" campaign in the *Press Journal* and quickly found private homes where the players could stay. The fans thought of the players as sons. When the Dodgers played at Daytona and beat the Northern Division champs in the playoffs, two busloads of Vero fans accompanied the team.

Joe Sanchez, a New Yorker who moved to Vero to work for a local radio station, became the voice of the Vero Dodgers—the public address

Second baseman Steve Sax relaxes before a game at Holman Stadium. He played on the first Vero Beach Dodger team and quickly made it to the big team. (Photograph by Mark I. Johnson, Edgewater, Florida.)

announcer at home and the radio play-by-play announcer on the road. At Holman Stadium, "Mr. Music," Dave Leitz, assisted Joe by playing the appropriate accompaniment: "The Worms Crawl In, The Worms Crawl Out" when the umpire walked out to break up a conference on the mound. The sound of a splash and a duck quacking from the pond came over the PA system when a foul ball went out of the park down left field. A car window breaking blared forth when the ball went foul down right field. Though Leitz repeated these sound effects over and over, the fans loved them and responded with chuckles.

Steve Sax became the most successful Vero Dodger from that first season. "You just had to like the way he worked," said Stan Wasiak. "I'd go out and hit him a hundred balls a day."[6] Steve Sax made the major league spring roster the next year direct from Vero and went on to Los Angeles after a short stay at San Antonio.

Like Steve Sax, teammate Alejandro Peña joined the Dodgers in '81. He spent twelve years in the majors, ten in Los Angeles. Unfortunately, neither Vero's best pitcher, Butch Wickensheimer, nor most popular player, catcher Bill Sobbe, made the big time.

Publisher John Schuman wrote in the *Press Journal*: "After all these years, the marriage between the Los Angeles Dodgers and Vero Beach has produced its first baby."[7] And that baby, the Vero Beach Dodgers, attracted a lot of local attention.

No Miracle

On the major league front, after being the National League champs in 1977 and 1978 and then having a losing season in 1979, Tommy Lasorda's cry in Dodgertown in the spring of 1980 echoed the words of General Douglas McArthur: "We shall return."[8]

Lasorda based his optimism on several player additions. Rookie Pedro Guerrero hit .333 at Albuquerque and was ready for the majors. Plus the Dodgers had entered the free agent market for the first time and signed pitchers Dave Goltz and Don Stanhouse and outfielder Jay Johnstone. Johnstone carried the reputation of being a prankster, and he showed it quickly. At Dodgertown he tied the doorknob of Tommy Lasorda's room in the villas so that Tommy couldn't leave his room to go to his usual early breakfast.[9]

On March 8, a cold front blew in and the temperature dropped into the mid-twenties, making it one of the coldest nights in Vero Beach history. The freeze made the plantings around Holman Stadium look like a blowtorch had hit them. The next day, the team literally ran through a quick workout. Fifty frigid fans watched. Danny Ozark, returned as a Dodger coach after managing the Phillies, said he felt like he was back in Philadelphia. Pitcher Ken Brett ignored the cold and worked out in shorts.[10]

A day later with the weather warming, teams named for the coaches, the Motas and the Ozarks, played each other before 3,453 fans, a record crowd for an intrasquad game at Dodgertown.[11]

Springtime also saw the ongoing tradition of Dodger involvement in the Vero community. Steve Garvey worked with some little leaguers after practice one day. On another occasion he gave a talk at a father-son banquet at Vero's First Methodist Church.[12] The Vero community–Dodgertown relationship remained tight.

Duke Snider entered the Hall of Fame, and the main access road into Holman Stadium was named in his honor. In his dedication speech, Duke said, "It would have been appropriate if you had given the name Snider Road to the area by the railroad tracks downtown. That's where I cracked up my new car a long, long time ago."[13]

Pitcher Nolan Ryan, with his famed hundred-mile-per-hour fastball, pitched at Holman Stadium after signing a $1 million, annual, free agent contract with the Houston Astros. The Dodgers pounded him. Reggie Smith hit a home run. Garvey, Mike Scioscia, Lopes, and pitcher Burt Hooton hit doubles. Ryan left the game after the Dodgers scored five runs in the third inning.[14]

The Dodgers may have beat up on the Astros in spring training, but during the season, they finished one game behind them in the race for the West Division title. In the final series of the season, the Dodgers beat the Astros three straight to tie for the league lead. However, in a one-game play-off, the Dodgers could not win a fourth straight and accomplish a miracle.

Escaping the snow, the Buffalo Bills trained at Dodgertown for a few days over New Year's in preparation for a National Football League play-off game with the Chargers in San Diego. Some of the practices were open to the public. A tall brunette in skintight slacks and high heels cruised the sidelines, trying to catch the eye of any of the Bills she could. She wasn't having much luck and said to a reporter, "It's not the same as with the New Orleans Saints. These guys are serious; I don't think they're in the mood for playing around." But it wasn't all business. All-Pro guard, balding Reggie McKenzie told reporters he sure didn't want to end the season with a loss to the Chargers but admitted that he "got smashed" in a Vero bar.[15] The community appreciated the Bills' contribution to the local economy

1981

Feeling Like Neighbors

In the opening game of the spring season at Holman Stadium, five thousand fans received lots of sun and an exciting twelve-inning game as the Dodgers played the visiting Tokyo Giants. Jay Johnstone ended the game in the late afternoon with a line drive into the outfield to give the Dodgers a 5–4 win. The Giants had returned to Dodgertown for the fifth time since their initial visit in 1961. Slugger Sadaharu Oh, now the assistant manager, again accompanied the team. During his twenty-two-year career, he hit 868 home runs in the Japanese league.[16]

Commissioner Bowie Kuhn attended the game with Tokyo despite confronting the threat of a player strike. He couldn't stay in Florida for spring training as most commissioners had done in the past. "I have a lot of problems back on the desk in New York," he said. Baseball was "in a turmoil," free agent salaries had become "astronomical," and the teams were losing money and deep in debt, according to Kuhn.[17]

Fernando Valenzuela arrived at Dodgertown as a rookie but already something of a hero. He had joined the big team from San Antonio the previous September and in ten games didn't allow an earned run, won two, and saved another. Dodger scout Mike Brito discovered him pitching in Sonora, Mexico. This nineteen-year-old, with a build like a bull and a ready smile, spoke no English. Steve Garvey described his pitching motion as "an unorthodox windup where he rolls his eyes to the sky, then uncoils with a screwball nobody can hit."[18]

Diehard fan Mollie Thomas of Hamilton, Ontario, visited Dodgertown for the twenty-third consecutive year. She typically flew in the day before the team arrived and stayed at the Beach Motel. She stood in the crowd at the airport when the players stepped off the plane. "It's all so thrilling," she said. "Everyone waves and cheers and has a real good time. They often call out to me and say 'Hi!'" Talking about the early days, she said the team was more like a family. "Now there are a lot of new players, and they just don't have the time to get to know the fans. A smile from Rick Monday, Steve Garvey, Bill Russell, and Steve Yeager can really make your day," she said.[19]

At the Vero Beach High School Math Club Beauty Contest, a good looking young fellow with dark curly hair, carrying a briefcase, walked down the aisle and sat down near the front. It was Steve Sax, and he was the beauty judge. Doing his part in the community, he would make the big team later in the season and replace Davey Lopes at second base.

At the end of spring training, Charlie Blaney announced that the New Orleans Saints had signed a new, five-year agreement to continue to train at Dodgertown. The team had been coming to Vero since 1975. The contingency of 130 players, coaches, executives, staff, and press had full use of the facility. New coach Bum Phillips arrived at Dodgertown to check out the place. John Mecom Jr., president of the Saints, said, "The people of Vero Beach have always made us feel like neighbors, rather than visitors."[20]

A Strange Season

Over ninety thousand fans watched the Vero Dodgers in their second season. But it was strange year. Vero finished last in the first half. Manager Stan Wasiak suffered a heart problem in May and did not return to the team until August. The June player draft strengthened the team with

New Orleans Saints lineman Conrad Dobbler cools off in the summer heat at Dodgertown. (Photograph by Mark I. Johnson, Edgewater, Florida.)

the assignment to Vero of outfielder Lemmie Miller, shortstop Dave Anderson, pitcher John Franco, and first baseman Sid Bream. This group, plus outfielders Ed Amelung and R. J. Reynolds already on the team, provided the punch for a second-half rebound and a second-place finish. Anderson, Bream, Franco, and Reynolds would have major league careers. In fact, Franco was still earning saves for the Mets in 2004 at age forty-three. Al Campanis, in one of his worst trades, gave Franco to the Reds for an infielder named Rafael Landestoy.

The L.A. Dodgers experienced a strange year too. The strike that Bowie Kuhn was so worried about when he visited Holman Stadium shut down play for two months in the middle of the season. The Dodgers were the first-half winners (before the strike), and then beat the second-half winner, the Houston Astros, for the division championship as Fernando Valenzuela's pitching sparked the team and earned him the Rookie of the Year and Cy Young awards. The Dodgers played the Montreal Expos for the National League title and won. In the World Series, the Dodgers met their old nemesis, the Yankees, beat them, and brought another World Series championship to Dodgertown.

Ups and Downs

1982

Dodgertown Doings

Economic growth took a breather in Indian River County. A national recession impacted the area. A freeze caused a reduction in the grapefruit crop. Piper Aircraft encountered a dismal sales year and laid off nine hundred employees. Tourism declined.[1]

However, on the Monday morning when Dodger exhibition game tickets went on sale, three hundred people stood in line. Some arrived at four a.m. Average crowds at Holman Stadium for the World Champions hit a high of 5,416.[2] In the coming season, attendance at Dodger Stadium also would set an all-time high—3.6 million.[3] But the Vero Dodgers, perhaps more accurately reflecting the local economy, suffered a decrease in attendance.

Gold Glove shortstop Mark Belanger, after seventeen years with the Orioles, joined the Dodgers as a utility infielder. Dodgertown's friendliness impressed his wife Dee. She said, "Jo Lasorda has been wonderful. And I got my Lasorda hug." The Belangers rented a house in The Moorings, the upscale development south of Vero on the island. To keep up with their studies, the Belangers' two sons were being tutored during the training season.[4]

Dodgertown was active as always. Coach Danny Ozark good naturedly told veteran Steve Yeager, who was cutting corners running around field #1, to rerun some laps. Yeager did what he was told. Hall of Famer Sandy Koufax, the minor league pitching instructor, caught balls for bullpen coach Mark Cresse, who was hitting infield practice. Steve Garvey "did a little dance" at first base as "Music Man" Dave Leitz played tunes over the public-address system. Al Campanis, in his sixties, gave a demonstration in the sliding pits. When Tommy Lasorda tried a slide, his players jumped him. In an intrasquad game, Tom Niedenfuer, who made the big team one year out of college, was the winning pitcher, while young Sid Fernandez, destined for the Class A Vero team, was the loser. Comedian Danny Kaye visited Dodgertown. The Dodger wives plus some press and staff flew over to Nassau on the Dodger plane for a day of sightseeing and shopping. Reverend John Ryan of St. Helen's Catholic Church conducted the annual memorial mass, remembering departed members and friends of the Dodger organization. The Dodgers named a Dodgertown street Vin Scully Way to honor the popular broadcaster and new member of the Hall of Fame.[5]

The Dodgers traded Davey Lopes to Oakland, and former Vero Dodger Steve Sax took over second. Thus ended the eight years of Garvey, Lopes, Russell, and Cey playing together. Meanwhile, the one member of this infield who would last the longest with the Dodgers, Bill Russell, had a memorable afternoon at Holman Stadium. He made five errors in an exhibition game against the Tigers.[6]

Trouble at Lennie's Bar

Pitcher Bob Welch had a problem. Like Don Newcombe before him, he was an alcoholic. Incidents occurred: lonely drinking in hotel rooms; teetering on a hotel ledge, not knowing how he got there; and a late night golf cart mishap at Dodgertown. Night watchman Glen Joyce roused Guy Wellman, a veteran coach in the Dodger minor league system, and took him over to the deep drainage ditch by the batting cages where an abandoned golf cart hung over the edge. The players occasionally used the golf carts to run over to Lennie's Bar. Wellman swore that the boy (who took the cart) would be on his way home in a hurry. Wellman later discovered that the culprit was Bob Welch. In time the Dodgers asked questions. Don Newcombe helped. Bob Welch entered a rehabilitation center, joined Alcoholics Anonymous, and went public with his problem.[7]

Bob Welch wasn't the only one who got in trouble at Lennie's Bar. The bridge over Main Canal on the way to Lennie's was familiarly known as the Bobby Castillo Bridge. A relief pitcher in the late '70s and early '80s, Castillo frequently had difficulty walking a straight line as he crossed the bridge coming back to camp.[8]

No-Hit Sid

Vero Dodger manager Stan Wasiak missed the entire 1982 season because of complications from his heart condition. Vero pitching coach Dave Wallace (the interim L.A. Dodger general manager in 2001) substituted for Wasiak, followed by Terry Collins, who played for Wasiak at Albuquerque. Collins became a major league manager with the Houston Astros, 1994 to 1996, and with the Anaheim Angels, 1997 to 1999. He returned to the Dodger organization to become director of player development.

A nineteen-year-old pitcher from Honolulu, named Sid Fernandez, sparked a good Vero team. With an 8–1 record and a 1.91 earned run average, he dominated the Florida State League. He struck out twenty-one batters in a game with Lakeland. He threw two no-hitters, including a perfect game against Winter Haven at Holman Stadium. The Dodgers quickly moved Sid Fernandez up to Albuquerque.[9]

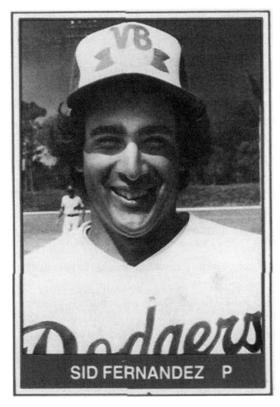

SID FERNANDEZ P

Sid Fernandez pitched two no-hit games for the Vero Beach Dodgers and went on to a successful major league career with the Mets. (Courtesy of Vero Beach Dodgers, Vero Beach, Florida.)

Sid Fernandez appeared in two games in Los Angeles in 1983. The Dodgers then traded him to the Mets for utility infielder Bob Bailor. Fernandez, or "El Sid" as he was known, pitched as a starter for the Mets for nine years. He enjoyed his best season in 1986 with a 16–6 record.

Three Vero players, Sid Bream, Cecil Espy, and Stu Pederson, hit over .300. Espy also stole seventy-four bases. (He would steal forty-five bases for the Texas Rangers in 1989.) Pitcher Kenny Howell, with only five wins, made it to the majors with Bream, Espy, and of course, Fernandez. One of the players on this "star-studded" team of 1982 had his career end abruptly. He was convicted of distributing cocaine and sent to federal prison.[10]

The Vero Beach Dodgers made the play-offs but lost to the Fort Lauderdale Yankees. The Los Angeles Dodgers came close as well, finishing one game behind the Atlanta Braves.

1983

Errors and Drugs

While Walter Alston was visiting Dodgertown, the announcement came that he had been voted into the Baseball Hall of Fame. Alston joined such managerial greats as Connie Mack, John McGraw, Joe McCarthy, Casey Stengel, and old-time Dodger managers Ned Hanlon (1899–1905) and Wilbert, "Uncle Robby," Robinson (1914–1931) at Cooperstown.[11] In the future, Tommy Lasorda would also join the group.

A salary arbitration decision delayed Fernando Valenzuela's arrival at Dodgertown. He won, receiving a record judgment of $1 million for the 1983 season. As a rookie two years earlier, the Dodgers paid him $42,000—not a bad increase for a "naïve" twenty-two-year-old Mexican kid.[12]

Ron Cey and Steve Garvey were gone. Following the old Branch Rickey theory of it's better to trade them a year early than a year late, Al Campanis sent the thirty-five-year-old Cey to the Cubs, where he enjoyed three more good years.

Steve Garvey and the Dodgers could not agree on a contract. Garvey wanted to remain with the team. He reminisced at the time about being a Dodger, about Dodgertown: "You have to have stayed in the old Navy barracks in March when the air smells of orange blossoms and you sneeze your head off. And all that as a Dodger—my whole life as a Dodger." But Steve Garvey felt that Peter O'Malley and Al Campanis didn't try hard enough to keep him. He signed as a free agent with the San Diego Padres.[13]

Vero resident Hugh McCrystal knew Garvey well. Steve frequently visited the McCrystals' home. Prior to Steve leaving the Dodgers, he and his wife Cyndy had separated and were on the way to a divorce. Steve, missing his own two daughters, would come to Hugh's house and play games with the McCrystal children on the living room floor.

Garvey told Hugh that if Walter O'Malley had still been around the negotiations would have worked out so he could have remained a Dodger.[14]

The team felt comfortable letting Cey and Garvey go because they had two sluggers in camp ready for the big leagues—outfielder Mike Marshall and first baseman Greg Brock. However, Guerrero, replacing Ron Cey at third, had problems fielding the position; Steve Sax with a mental quirk couldn't make the throw from second to first base; and reliever Steve Howe had a drug problem. Yet the team won the West Division, though losing to the Phillies for the league title. Tommy Lasorda was named National League Manager of the Year, a well-deserved honor for the adversity he faced.

Florida State League Champs

With Manager Wasiak returning to the team, the Vero Dodgers won the Florida State League championship in 1983. The team beat Fort Myers and Daytona in the play-offs. Reggie Williams and Ralph Bryant paced the offense, and Mariano Duncan stole fifty-six bases. Two fellows with Vero connections led the pitching staff. Rob Slezak had a 9–4 record. He would pitch for Vero again in 1984 and then marry a local girl. He is now the director of recreation for the City of Vero Beach. Chris Thomas, who grew up in Vero, won five games and had a 1.94 earned run average. After his baseball career ended, he became an Indian River County firefighter.

Despite winning the championship, only one member of the team, Mariano Duncan, made the majors. He played thirteen seasons, five with the Dodgers at shortstop and second base. General manager Terry Reynolds said, "That was a team of overachievers that jelled at the right time. They really had no business winning the championship, but the last month of the season, nobody could beat them."[15] However, after the 1983 league championship, the team would not reach the play-offs again during the remainder of the 1980s.

1984

Holman Stadium Grows

When the Dodgers arrived for spring training, Holman Stadium had a new look. Seats added down right field and left field increased capacity from 5,100 to 6,400. New concession stands stood at the bottom of the berm behind first base and third base. The first base concession stand included a beautifully landscaped entrance to the stadium. As single game tickets went on sale in mid-February, over 3,100 season tickets already had been purchased.[16] This enthusiasm reflected the Dodgers' good year in 1983, as well as the presence of twelve Vero Dodger alumni on the major league spring roster. When the Yankees came to town, the enlarged Holman Stadium handled a crowd of 8,051, second only to the 8,200 for a Yankee game in 1979.[17]

The Dodgers had initiated their Adult Baseball Camp at Dodgertown in the fall of 1983. In 1984 they had ninety-six campers. After the camp and utilizing Dodgertown to the fullest, Peter O'Malley brought their entire front-office staff from Los Angeles to Vero Beach for meetings.[18]

The 1984 Dodgers finished fourth with a losing record. Rookies Dave Anderson and German Rivera, both ex-Vero Dodgers, shared third, allowing Pedro Guerrero to return to the outfield. Another ex-Vero Dodger, Alejandro Peña, won twelve games, including four shutouts, and had the lowest earned run average in the league.

This was the last summer the New Orleans Saints trained at Dodgertown. A new coach wanted to move the training camp closer to New Orleans. However, National Football League teams, including the Green Bay Packers, the Cleveland Browns, and the Buffalo Bills came to Dodgertown for short periods to escape the cold as they prepared for play-off games.

1985

Questionable Decisions

The 1955 World Champion Dodgers held a thirty-year reunion at Dodgertown. The players dressed in Dodger uniforms with the Brooklyn "B" on their caps. The players reminisced. Pitcher Clem Labine, who had moved to Vero, said that when you speak about 1955, you have to speak of the "demise" of the borough of Brooklyn and the Brooklyn fans who attached themselves to the team. "There are still world champion Dodger clubs," said Labine, "but unfortunately or fortunately, depending on how you look at it, they were all in L.A." During the three-day festivities, the team named a Dodgertown street for another Hall of Famer—Pee Wee Reese. Deceased members of the team were remembered, including Jim Gilliam, Don Hoak, Gil Hodges, Coach Jake Pitler, Vero resident Karl Spooner, Jackie Robinson, and Walter Alston.[19] Longtime manager Alston had died in 1984, the year after entering the Hall of Fame.

Peter Uberroth, the new baseball commissioner and former head of the successful 1984 Los Angeles Olympics, visited Vero. He tossed out the first ball; then the Dodgers played the Samsung Lions, a Korean professional team training at Dodgertown. The game represented the first-ever encounter between professional teams from America and Korea. Sam Rolfing of the *Press Journal* said, "If Peter Uberroth can conduct the business of baseball as well as he manages an unruffled, calm demeanor and a low-key delivery, he's got it made." He politely refused to talk about individual players, such as Steve Howe who had drug problems, saying, "We're to fight drugs not baseball players."[20]

The Dodgers bounced back in 1985, led by Orel Hershiser's phenomenal 19–3 record. The Dodgers won their division and faced the Cardinals for the National League pennant. In the deciding game, Tommy Lasorda chose to pitch to slugger Jack Clark rather than walk him. He promptly hit a home run, and the Cardinals went to the World Series.

In local news, Vero's no-growth sector won a victory. The city council voted down rezoning oceanfront property, which killed a proposal to build a $40 million, 276-room Marriott Hotel just north of the beach business area. Building trades groups, the chamber of commerce, the board of realtors, and retailers supported the hotel. The civic association, which successfully placed its members on the city council, opposed it.[21]

All in all, 1985 went down as a good year, except for a couple of questionable decisions—to pitch to Jack Clark and, among locals, to reject a Marriott Hotel for Vero's beach.

1986–1987

The Farm or Free Agency

Inconsistency and injuries prevailed. The Dodgers fell into a pit and experienced two losing seasons in a row, finishing fifth in '86 and fourth in '87.

After the '86 season, Tommy Lasorda promised a Johns Island gathering in Vero that the Dodgers would appear in the 1987 World Series.[22] Instead, Lasorda and Al Campanis at Dodgertown were still trying to find a winning infield combination, using former Vero Dodgers: Steve Sax, German Rivera, Dave Anderson, Mariano Duncan, Franklin Stubbs, Tracy Woodson, and Jeff Hamilton. Sax remained a fixture at second. Anderson, followed by Duncan, shared shortstop with Bill Russell until he retired and became a Dodger coach. Stubbs moved from the outfield to first base to take over for Greg Brock, who never met expectations. Third base was a merry-go-round, despite an appearance there by veteran Bill Madlock. The Dodgers had traded top prospects Sid Bream, R. J. Reynolds, and Cecil Espy—all former Vero Dodgers—for Madlock, a four-time, league batting champ. But Madlock stayed with the team only one full season.

With the player round robin going on, Al Campanis expressed the Dodger philosophy: "You have to look at it in a five or ten-year plan. Teams that go for the quick one-year deals are bound to fail. We develop players in the farm system and make projections where they will fit in our system. So far we have been successful."[23]

But other teams were signing free agents and winning. In Vero in the spring of 1987, Peter O'Malley also talked about the Dodger philosophy. Team payroll had climbed from $11 million to $15 million in two years. O'Malley explained that ticket prices had been flat from 1958 to 1976 "until free agency came along, that's when Dodger Stadium ticket prices went up": "Our policy on free agents has been pretty much the same for the last ten years. We prefer to give the opportunity to a young player that we have signed, coached, and developed. If we don't have the talent

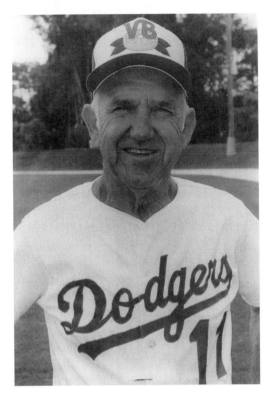

Vero Beach Dodger manager Stan Wasiak holds the minor league record for career wins with 2,561. (Courtesy of Vero Beach Dodgers, Vero Beach, Florida.)

in the organization, then, yes, we have to go out for a trade or the acquisition of a free agent."[24]

Richer in Many Ways

Before he retired after the 1986 Vero Dodger season, Stan Wasiak won game 2,561—amassing the most wins for a manager in minor league history. Wasiak achieved 429 of those wins with the Vero Beach Dodgers.[25] With complications from heart bypass surgery, he had missed the '82 season, though he took the field for one game that enabled him to manage a record forty-four consecutive years. Stan Wasiak died at age seventy-three in 1992.

During a twenty-year reunion for Wasiak's 1983 Florida State League championship team, the Vero Dodger administrative office was named for him. He and his wife Barbara had spent the seasons living near that office in what they called their "honeymoon cottage," a doublewide trailer located just beyond the Holman Stadium right field berm.[26]

Wasiak protégé, John Shoemaker, replaced his mentor in 1987 and led the Vero team for the next two seasons. Shoemaker played for Stan at Class D Lodi, New Mexico, and coached under him at Vero from the team's beginning. John Shoemaker lived in Vero and in the off-season did substitute teaching, while coaching junior-varsity basketball. John remains with the Dodger organization to this day, handling a variety of minor league assignments, including a turn at managing Albuquerque.

To promote the flow of more talent, the Dodgers opened a baseball school, Campo Las Palmas, in the Dominican Republic. The facility—in essence a junior Dodgertown with two fields (one named for Manny Mota), a dormitory, and a dining room—provided training to Dominican players signed by the Dodgers. Alumni of the academy would include Pedro Astacio, Adrian Beltre, Juan Guzman, brothers Ramon and Pedro Martinez, Raul Mondesi, Jose Offerman, and Henry Rodriguez. Even Mike Piazza received catcher training there the winter of 1989–1990, before he joined the Vero Beach Dodgers. Alumnus Ramon Martinez would say at the tenth anniversary of the academy, "The Dodgers don't just make baseball players, they make people who are apt to live in society."[27]

In Vero Beach, the Dodgers initiated a relationship with another school just a few blocks from the baseball complex. It became Dodgertown Elementary. Trimmed in Dodger blue and white, the classrooms bore the names of Dodger greats, and the students called themselves the Little Dodgers. The team invested $30,000 for an outdoor classroom, added landscaping to improve the school's appearance, and provided signs with a baseball motif. Dodger players and management visited the school and talked with the children. The school chorus sang the national anthem at L.A. and Vero Beach Dodger games at Holman Stadium. The school's Valentine's Day carnival featured a "hug-a-Dodger" booth. The team adopted a school in Los Angeles as well, and the Vero Little Dodgers became pen pals with the L.A. Little Dodgers.[28]

Dodgertown director Charlie Blaney and his wife Dawn cochaired the annual Indian River County United Way drive and raised the most money ever. The *Press Journal* editorialized, "It's been another Dodger spring in Vero Beach, and we're richer in many ways for it."[29]

An Unfortunate Remark

On a TV program commemorating the fortieth anniversary of Jackie Robinson's debut in the major leagues, Al Campanis responded to a ques-

Dodger general manager Al Campanis talks with Peter O'Malley beside a practice field. Campanis had been at Dodgertown every spring since its inception. (Courtesy of Los Angeles Dodgers, Los Angeles, California.)

tion as to why there were no black managers and general managers in baseball. He said, "It's just that they lack some of the necessities."[30]

Al Campanis had been with the Dodgers since the days of Branch Rickey. He played shortstop side by side with Jackie Robinson at Montreal in 1946. He recommended that the Dodgers make Jim Gilliam a coach. No one had ever accused him of prejudice in his eighteen years in charge of player personnel, black and white.

"The comments Al made Monday night," said Peter O'Malley, "were so far removed and so distant from what this organization believes that it was impossible for Al to continue his responsibilities with us."[31]

Tommy Lasorda sobbed at the news.[32] Like Buzzie Bavasi and Fresco Thompson, Al Campanis had been an institution at Dodgertown. But his departure brought changes in the Dodger organization and a new team attitude at Dodgertown.

Refuse to Lose

1988

My Name Is Kirk Gibson

Pulitzer Prize–winning sports columnist Jim Murray, visiting Dodg-ertown, wrote about Peter O'Malley. He described Peter as unlike the other owners: "He inherited a smooth-running organization with im-peccable community. He was groomed for the job since birth. He has no entourage. . . . You see him around the Dodger camp here; he's reading a report—alone. . . . Peter O'Malley does not hobnob with his players; he goes in the locker only when they win a World Series. He's a three-piece-suit sort of guy." But a rumor kept surfacing, according to Murray, that Peter O'Malley "had had his fill of baseball" and might be looking for something else.[1]

Meanwhile, Peter O'Malley made changes in the "Dodger Way." With Campanis gone, he put Fred Claire in charge of baseball operations, gave the go-ahead to sign a high-profile free agent, and replaced a part of the management group.

Fred Claire was not a baseball man like Bavasi or Campanis. Though Claire had been with the Dodgers since 1969, his background lay in sports writing, public relations. "His specialty was Chamber of Com-merce lunches," as Jim Murray put it. Rumors circulated that Lasorda wanted the general manager's job. But Peter seemed more comfortable with Claire. Lasorda was too "blue collar" for Peter, one writer said.[2]

New general manager Fred Claire took immediate charge, as the Dodgers made their first significant venture into the free agent market in eight years. Claire spent $4.5 million to sign free agent outfielder Kirk Gibson to a three-year contract.[3]

Kirk Gibson expressed his excitement about joining the team by calling the Dodgers "a sophisticated organization with a fabulous sense for making people feel good about themselves and by extension, the ball club." On reporting to Vero Beach for spring training, he said, "It was incredible to see Los Angeles' fabulous complex, Dodgertown. It's a dream baseball facility, built on the concept that comfort and hospitality are central to a baseball club's success. Everything is perfect."[4]

Quickly, he found that things were not perfect—that maybe the Dodgers lacked a winning attitude. After all, they had just come off two losing seasons.

In the first team meeting at the start of spring training, Tommy Lasorda asked each of the rookies and new players to introduce themselves. Gibson, tall, heavily mustachioed, dark stubble on his face, stood and said, "My name is Kirk Gibson. I played football at Michigan State. I was a first round draft choice by the Detroit Tigers, and I've been there my entire career. We won one World Championship when I was in Detroit. I came to Los Angeles for one reason only and that's to win a World Series trophy and ring. That's what's fun to me about baseball. I hate to lose. I refuse to lose."[5]

In a practice session, fielding bunts, Pedro Guerrero at third nonchalantly threw a ball into right field. Everyone laughed. Kirk Gibson didn't. He "burned inside." This happened in a serious workout. What kind of attitude did this team have?[6]

In the pregame warm-ups for the opening exhibition game at Holman Stadium, Gibson prepared himself for his first game as a Dodger. He removed his cap to wipe the sweat away. His new teammates began laughing. He asked bullpen coach Mark Cresse what was so funny. Cresse said, "I think somebody played a joke on you." Gibson realized that he had eye black on the inside of his cap. He had wiped it all over his face. He exploded; he stormed off the field. He passed Lasorda, who asked him what was going on. "Find that son of a bitch who did this," Gibson said. "I can't take this atmosphere any longer."[7]

Lasorda tried to excuse the incident by saying they were just trying to make him part of the team. Gibson kept on going, right out of Holman Stadium and across the practice fields to the clubhouse.

The next morning, Gibson demanded to talk to the team. Relief pitcher Jesse Orosco, who had just joined the Dodgers from the Mets, was the jokester. He tried to apologize. Gibson brushed him off.

In the clubhouse in an atmosphere of "cold stone silence," Gibson spoke, "On a bunt play you guys throw balls into right field. . . . You laugh. . . . We're here to be world champions. You don't become world champions by stumbling into it. . . . If we haven't got heart, we haven't got a prayer. . . . If I'm wrong, then I'm on the wrong team. . . . I'm here to sacrifice in order to become world champions.[8]

The laid back, fun-loving atmosphere at Dodgertown changed. The Dodgers, with a 21–11 record, won the most spring games in their Los Angeles history.

A crowd of 7,900 turned out for a game with the Mets at Holman Stadium. The New York team became almost a neighbor to the Dodgers. They now trained at Port Saint Lucie, a rapidly growing community twenty miles south down I-95. A developer built an $11.5 million facility for them and then turned it over to the community, who paid for it over time with a resort tax.[9]

The Holman Stadium outfield had a different look. A waist-high, chain link fence circled the bottom of the berm. New Dodgertown director Terry Reynolds said that people could still sit on the bank and see right through it. He said it would bring more excitement with more home runs, yet keep fans safe from fielders chasing long fly balls.[10]

In a game of musical chairs, Terry Reynolds, previously the Vero Dodger general manager, replaced Charlie Blaney as Dodgertown director. Blaney moved to Los Angeles to become director of minor league operations, stepping in for Bill Schweppe, who retired. Reynolds soon followed Blaney to the West Coast to take a position as assistant director of scouting. Craig Callan replaced Reynolds as Dodgertown director.

Craig Callan first arrived at Dodgertown in 1978 to manage the Harrison Conference Center. Prior to coming to Vero, he worked at a Harrison facility in the Pocono Mountains. One day while pushing cars out of the snow, his boss asked if he would like to go to Florida and take over the center at Dodgertown. Being from Brooklyn, he accepted immediately.[11]

Improbable and Impossible

In 1988, the Dodgers surprised the National League and won the West by seven games. Orel Hershiser won twenty-three games and pitched fifty-nine scoreless innings in a row to beat Don Drysdale's 1968 record. Kirk Gibson provided the spark and earned the National League Most Valuable Player award.

In the league championship, the Dodgers played the heavily favored Mets and won. Kirk Gibson batted in the winning run in the second game, but experienced muscle strains in both legs and appeared to be sidelined for the World Series.

The Dodgers, again the underdogs, faced the Oakland A's in the World Series. In game one, in the bottom of the ninth, the injured Kirk Gibson came out of the clubhouse and hit the game-winning home run. The Dodger Stadium fans leaped to their feet as Gibson, in a historic image of arms pumping, limped around the bases. Gibson's home run set the tone, and the Dodgers won the Series. It was a magic moment and a magic season. And unfortunately, no Dodger team since has appeared in the World Series.

1989

The Revolving Door

On Saturday, February 25, 1989, three thousand fans turned out at Holman Stadium to greet the World Champions. Tommy Lasorda arrived by helicopter and said, "We've grown as an organization and we have seen Vero Beach grow." Mayor Ken Macht and Indian River County Commission chairman Gary Wheeler presented proclamations honoring the team and declaring the occasion "Dodger Day." Lasorda and executive vice president Fred Claire presented bats signed by the team to Macht, Wheeler, and Chamber of Commerce director J. B. Norton. The team was introduced, and twenty-four little leaguers came on the field and threw back and forth with the major leaguers.[12]

This was not the only hoopla in Vero Beach that winter. Four thousand spectators, the Saturday before "Dodger Day," watched Britain's Prince Charles play polo at the new and elegant Windsor development. The prince scored a goal, and after the game he enjoyed a reception with the local citizenry. Was the community changing? Was polo rivaling baseball, and did Vero now think of itself as another Palm Beach?[13] Time would tell.

Orel Hershiser, whom Lasorda called "Bulldog" despite his meek appearance, won the 1988 Cy Young Award. He arrived at Dodgertown as baseball's newest salary champ. He signed a three-year contract exceeding $3 million a year. Orel talked about his negotiation with the Dodgers:

"The only thing I can relate it to is when I was a kid and I wanted a raise in my allowance or a new bicycle. I'd talk to my dad about it, but after it was over I'd still love him." (His mom and dad had just moved to Vero.) Orel said that with the way salaries were going up, his wouldn't last long as the highest.[14] After his interview, Hershiser joined twelve little leaguers at Indian River County's Hobart Park to film a Pizza Hut commercial.

Members of the 1959 World Series came to Dodgertown for a thirtieth anniversary get-together. Buzzie Bavasi made a comparison between the 1959 champs and the 1988 team. Both teams had come off a losing year, both had acquired hard-hitting outfielders (Wally Moon in '59 and Gibson in '88), both had endured changing lineups, and no one had given either a chance to win.[15]

In a trade with Baltimore, the Dodgers received future Hall of Famer Eddie Murray. During batting practice at Dodgertown, Coach Manny Mota told Murray to take two bunts. Murray leaned on his bat and said, "I want you to know that in twelve years I haven't bunted yet." Mota waved him to hit away.[16] With Gibson still hobbled by injuries, Eddie Murray at first base would add power.

The heroes of the '88 season became mere mortals in '89. The Dodgers slipped back to fourth place with another losing season.

Making the Majors

Of the twenty-four major league roster players, only ten came out of the Dodgers' farm system.[17] Furthermore, the number of players developed by the Dodgers' playing on other major league teams dropped to the lowest level in thirty years. And despite the infusion of Vero Dodgers, who reached the major league roster in the early '80s, the situation indicated a decline in player development.

By 1988, two hundred players had worn the Vero uniform, forty-six had made a forty-man major league roster, and fifteen had played at least one season in the majors.[18] Instructor Norm Sherry, a former Dodger pitcher from the '50s and '60s, put the chances of making the majors in perspective. He said, "About 3,000 players get drafted each June. Of those, maybe a hundred get a shot at the major leagues and of those maybe thirty get major league careers."[19]

Some players did well at Vero and never made the majors. Michael White hit .340, the highest of any Vero Dodger to date and was considered the best hitter in the Florida State League in 1988. Tony Lachowetz's fifteen homers in 1982 led all other Vero Dodgers in the '80s.

Dodgertown director Charlie Blaney, who later became head of Dodger minor league operations, said that making the majors takes "heart." Attitude was more important than the physical tools. There is no way of knowing who is going to make it. "It has to be the right confluence of circumstance, timing, talent, hard work and luck. You can never figure this game out," said Blaney.[20]

Pitcher Jay Ray on the '88 Vero team said that the odds were "stacked against everybody" to make the big leagues. "If it happens, it happens. All I can hope for is a chance to show that I can play," he said.[21] Jay Ray never made it.

While the Vero Dodgers failed to reach the play-offs, they continued to produce future major leaguers: Chris Gwynn from the '85 team, Dave Hansen '88, Jose Offerman '88, and Henry Rodriguez '89. In 1989 alone, five pitchers who played for Vero had significant major league careers: Darren Holmes, John Wetteland, Juan Guzman, James Poole, and Ramon Martinez. Holmes and Poole each pitched for eight major league teams. Wetteland had 330 career saves. Guzman had ninety-one career wins. But Martinez, mostly pitching for Los Angeles, led all Vero alumni with 135 major league victories. Martinez and Poole had exceptional years at Vero. It was fun to watch Ramon Martinez lead the Florida State League with sixteen wins. Jim Poole as a relief pitcher won eleven games and saved nineteen.

But the Vero Dodgers did more than just produce talent for the parent Dodgers. After ten seasons they continued to provide fun, excitement, and drama to the community. Former *Press Journal* sports editor Randy Phillips, still official scorekeeper for the Vero team, enjoys many memories of the early days: a Vero player robbing an opponent of a home run by catching the ball on the top of the berm; an inside-the-park home run ricocheting off a palm tree and flying back on the field to be chased by the fielders as the batter sprinted around the bases. On another occasion, Vero trainer "Doc" Rob Glescke rushed onto the field and helped save the life of an opposing catcher who had swallowed his "chew" in a collision at home plate.[22]

Things Start to Stir

By the fortieth anniversary of Dodgertown in 1988, Chamber of Commerce executive J. B. Norton had estimated that the Dodgers provided a $20 million boost to the Indian River area economy. With an average per-game attendance exceeding six thousand, half of that from out of state, visitors spent over a $150 per day in the community. The Dodgers paid $180,000 a year in local taxes. Dodgertown employed two hundred people full time and added another fifty during spring training, which amounted to an annual payroll of $1 million. Add in the rent the major leaguers paid for beachfront condominiums for their families and the $20 million annual expenditures looked reasonable. "The Dodgers have paid their own way," said Norton. (In the 1980s, a developer and Saint Lucie County had built the Mets a stadium, as did the taxpayers of Osceola County to get the Astros.) "I'd hate to think what the city would be like without the Dodgers coming here each year. We'd still have some tourism, but life would be quieter. One can tell when the Dodgers are in town—people's spirits perk up and things start to stir."[23]

Bump Holman, whose father Bud had originally promoted the Dodgers to Vero, said, "With the Dodgers making Vero Beach their spring training home, the time table for the development of the area has been advanced by at least 20 years."[24]

One of the reasons Branch Rickey brought the Dodgers to Vero in the first place was to escape the big-city atmosphere of places like Havana and Miami. But in the 1980s, Vero experienced its own Miami-type crime wave. Crack cocaine use became epidemic, causing the sheriff's department to expand to get drug sales under control. An ex-auxiliary sheriff's deputy murdered six women in the county. Two escaped felons shot four people to death in a Domino's Pizza in Vero Beach. And two female clerks at two different convenience stores were murdered.[25]

On the other hand, the Center for the Arts (now the Vero Beach Museum) opened in 1986 near the Riverside Theater, expanding Vero's cultural scene as more and more people moved into the county. During the decade, the population almost doubled, increasing to 88,000.[26]

And while all this activity reflected change, the 1990s would bring even more change, plus turmoil, to the Dodgers and their relationship with Vero Beach.

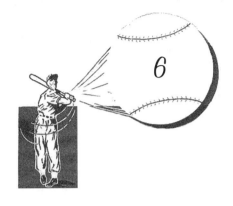

6

The Nineties

Not for Sale

1990

Peter Goes Fishing

Spring training in 1990 started three weeks late for the major league team. The owners locked the players out of the spring training facilities until the two sides reached a new, four-year collective bargaining agreement.

Despite the delay, activity proceeded at Dodgertown. Manager Tommy Lasorda showed that at age sixty-two he still had a "rubber arm" and a curve ball. In a simulated game on field #2, he pitched the equivalent of nine innings against a group of minor leaguers. They spotted him a 5–0 lead and, with batting coach Reggie Smith calling balls and strikes, Lasorda beat the young players 5–1. Future Dodger first baseman Eric Karros, up from Class A Bakersfield, scored the only run against Lasorda with a homer.[1]

Vero resident Sandy Koufax gave up his role as the Dodger minor league pitching instructor, a position he had held since 1978. The official announcement said that he "wanted to take some time off." According to one story, he became fed up with the performance of the Dodgers' player development system.[2] Minor league director Charlie Blaney received press criticism that the forty-man spring roster contained only twelve players with major league experience who had been developed by the Dodger farm system. But Blaney pointed out that the minor league teams were winning and predicted that things would improve.[3]

One day, Peter O'Malley chartered a boat and took a dozen guests on a deep sea fishing trip out the nearby Sebastian Inlet. The group included a few minor league coaches, some sportswriters, and Peter's two teenage sons. With the sea bumpy, part of the group spent time at the rail. During the trip, Peter chatted with writer Kevin Modesti of the *Los Angeles Daily News*. Modesti wrote that, unlike George Steinbrenner, Peter was "comfortable out of the spotlight" and that "stability and continuity" were important to him. The three losing seasons wrapped around the World Championship of 1988 concerned O'Malley. Lean player drafts put Fred Claire in the position of building the team from free agents. But emphasis would continue to be placed on the farm system to develop players.

With the player lockout under way, Peter told Modesti, "The biggest issue facing baseball is our [the owners'] inability to work in a civil, businesslike atmosphere with the players' association. Whatever we're doing isn't working." O'Malley felt sorry about the owners' collusion effort to avoid signing free agents in 1986. "We're paying for it by the mistrust of the players," he said. Though he knew it was a disaster at the time, he went along with the majority of the owners. He concluded his chat with Modesti: "Yes we've been down. . . . But we won more championships than anybody else in the '80s. It isn't just happening. Somebody must be doing something right."[4]

A year later, Peter O'Malley would say: "If I didn't care [about baseball], I wouldn't have stayed as long as I have. . . . I've had the opportunity to leave every year. . . . someone calls interested in buying the team, and we tell them it's not for sale."[5]

Dodgertown fans hardly knew the 1990 team. They weren't the Dodgers. The only Dodger-developed starter was catcher Mike Scioscia. The rest of the starters had been acquired from other teams. What was Fred Claire doing? Had the farm system really deteriorated that badly? Ex-Vero Dodger Ramon Martinez did win twenty games. No Dodger pitcher has won twenty since. With his conglomeration of players, Lasorda finished second in the division, five games behind Cincinnati.

A Sixty-first Round Draft Pick

The Vero Beach Dodgers under manager Joe Alvarez won their second Florida State League championship. They beat the Saint Lucie Mets, the Port Charlotte Rangers, and the West Palm Beach Expos in the play-offs for the championship. The team stole 304 bases led by Eric Young, who set a team record with seventy-five. Young would enjoy a successful major league career, stealing over four hundred bases. Pedro Astacio went 1–5, returned to Vero in '91 for a 5–3 record, and made the Dodger staff

STAR

MIKE PIAZZA

VERO BEACH

Catcher

Mike Piazza, a back-up catcher for the Vero Beach Dodgers, starred with the Dodgers before the Fox ownership traded him in 1998. (Courtesy of Vero Beach Dodgers, Vero Beach, Florida.)

in '92. Through 2004, he won 118 major league games. But the most successful major leaguer from the '90 Vero team would be Mike Piazza.

As a favor to Tommy Lasorda, the Dodgers chose Piazza in the sixty-first round in the 1988 draft. Lasorda grew up with Mike's father, Vince, in Norristown, Pennsylvania. Mike received so little respect at Dodgertown that a coach ran him out of a batting cage so that two better-known prospects could use it. He went to another cage and hit balls for two and half hours until his hands were raw.[6] At home, Piazza had his own batting cage in his family's house. Vince Piazza, a self-made millionaire with a series of car dealerships, led a group who tried to buy the San Francisco Giants and move them to St. Petersburg. Major League Baseball rejected the bid.

With Mike assigned to the Vero Dodgers, his father questioned the coaching staff as to why they didn't play his son more often. During one of the play-off games, Mike replaced the regular catcher. Vince Piazza and Dodger catching instructor John Roseboro sat together in the stands. Roseboro hugged Vince: "What a game your son caught!" Vince replied, "I hope they realize he's a catcher, not a part-time first baseman or outfielder or wherever they're playing him."[7] Though he had been almost a nonentity all season, Mike Piazza's hitting helped Vero win the championship series.

1991

All the Hype and All the Problems

The big team's record didn't change much in 1991. But one move caused some excitement. The team signed Mets superstar outfielder Darryl Strawberry to a five-year, $20 million contract. With a return to his Los Angeles roots and with Lasorda's cajoling, Dodger management hoped Strawberry would achieve his full potential. One *Los Angeles Times* columnist characterized him as "almost like the Dodgers' first modern ballplayer, with all the problems and all the hype that went with it." One observer who saw him hit six balls over the Holman Stadium flagpoles said, "The fans were crazy for him in Vero Beach."[8]

During the season, Strawberry hit .265 with twenty-eight home runs and ninety-nine runs batted in, but this would be his best performance in his abbreviated stay with the Dodgers. Even with Strawberry in 1991, the Dodgers finished one game behind the Braves, who had begun their streak of winning consecutive division titles.

Dodgertown expanded with the addition of fields #5 and #6, east of the villas. These fields were for the use of the minor leaguers and included a coach's observation tower. Craig Callan had secured the property from the city in a trade. He had wisely purchased the old Ebbets Field #2 property from Piper at a time when they were in need of cash. He then exchanged it with the city for the property where the new fields were placed.[9] Ebbets Field #2 and the adjacent practice field had been acquired by Piper for employee parking when Walter O'Malley bought Dodgertown from the city in 1964.

1992

Holman Stadium's Section 17

The Dodger section at Holman Stadium, directly behind the team's open dugout, was where the Dodger brass, visiting dignitaries, and the owner's friends sat. A guard made sure only authorized people entered this section, and a young Vero Dodger intern served the group with programs and drinks.

Across the aisle from the Dodger section and closer to home plate was section 17.[10] Most of the people there were old-time Vero residents, largely retirees who had been season ticket holders for years. They knew each other well.

An advantage of these section 17 seats was that they allowed observation of interaction in the Dodger section, which was sometimes more interesting than the action on the field. Tommy Lasorda, usually fan friendly, once chewed out a woman who stretched over the fence hounding him for an autograph. The seats were so close to the bat rack that one could see the sweat on Darryl Strawberry's brow as he selected a bat. When the first team left the field after playing their five to six innings, the players opened a gate and ran up the aisle between the two sections. When Darryl Strawberry came out of the game once, he stopped, bent over, and exchanged pleasantries with his boss Peter O'Malley, not more than ten feet away from row 5.

Peter O'Malley, often with his wife Annette by his side, sat in the first row. Tommy Lasorda and his coaching staff sat in folding chairs at the end of the dugout in front of him. Tommy occasionally leaned over the fence and talked with Peter.

By 1992, the crowd in section 17 began to change as people got too old to come to the games anymore, were living in nursing homes, or had died. Some seats switched to the next generation or, heaven forbid, to people no one knew.

As the O'Malleys had done for years, Peter invited his Los Angeles friends to Dodgertown every spring. Along with a few close Vero Beach friends, they sat in the Dodger section. Local friends of the O'Malleys, who went back to the early days of Dodgertown, included the Holmans, Fairburns, Emlets, Corrigans, Semons, Clements, Schumans, Tripsons, Birds, Wodtkes, and Chandlers. Peter's sister, Terry O'Malley Seidler, commented on these friendships: "The hospitality of Vero Beach families like these and so many others had always made Vero Beach a second home for Dodger people."[11]

The Dodger farm system started producing, and the team took a first step back to internally developed players. Former UCLA star Eric Karros took over first base and with twenty home runs became the first Dodger Rookie of the Year since Steve Sax. Jose Offerman played shortstop, and ex-Vero Dodger Dave Hansen became the third baseman. Bringing in another free agent slugger, outfielder Eric Davis, to join Darryl Strawberry helped increase the payroll to $44 million, more than double what it had been in 1990. But the team still lost ninety-nine games. As Tommy Lasorda said: "Let me put it this way. I was the first Dodger manager to finish in last place since 1905."[12]

1993

Looking to the Future

At the beginning of spring training in 1993, the big team took batting practice in Holman Stadium as usual. The regulars stood around the batting cage, waiting to hit. Among them, stood a broad shouldered fellow with Piazza lettered across his back. After a nondescript year at Vero three years earlier, Mike Piazza suddenly blossomed during a second year in Class A. He hit twenty-nine home runs at Bakersfield. In 1992, he jumped from San Antonio to Albuquerque and on to Los Angeles in September. Now on the Dodger spring training roster, Piazza batted .500 in nineteen games and received the 1993 Mulvey Award for best rookie in camp.[13]

This was Roy Campanella's last spring at Dodgertown. He had been coming there for thirty-five years. The Hall of Fame catcher died later that year. Mike Piazza would follow Campanella's footsteps with the potential to become a Hall of Fame catcher. In this his first year, Piazza hit .318, walloped thirty-five home runs, and batted in 119 runs to become the National League Rookie of the Year.

The farm system had produced talent for the '90s in addition to Piazza: infielders Eric Karros, Jose Offerman, Dave Hansen, and Eric Young; outfielder Raul Mondesi; and pitchers Ramon and Pedro Martinez and Pedro Astacio. Karros, Piazza, and Mondesi won consecutive Rookie of the Year awards beginning in 1992.

But Eric Young, who became an accomplished major league second baseman, was lost in the 1992 expansion draft to the Colorado Rockies. Needing to fill that position, the Dodgers acquired Delino DeShields from Montreal for Pedro Martinez in a most disadvantageous trade. Martinez would prove to be, with Koufax and Drysdale, one of the best pitchers ever developed by the Dodgers. DeShields didn't work out, and Eric Young returned to the Dodgers from the Rockies in 1997 in exchange for his old Vero Dodger teammate Pedro Astacio. Such are the vagaries of developing and trading baseball talent.

With the 1993 team playing .500 ball and again finishing far behind the Braves, Lasorda and Claire took criticism for the Dodgers' performance. Strawberry and Davis never met expectations. Despite the addition of the young players, concern existed over an "interruption in the flow of talent." Peter O'Malley stated that despite a very tough time for baseball and his team, he saw "light at the end of the tunnel," and again he said that he would not consider selling his franchise.[14]

The Vero Dodger production had peaked in 1990 with Piazza, Astacio, and Young, but output declined after that. The '91 team, with ex-Dodger Jerry Royster managing, won a first half, lost in the play-offs, but set a local season attendance record of 95,900. The next year, the Vero team under manager Glenn Hoffman finished last in both halves of the season. (Seven years later Hoffman would briefly manage the major league Dodgers.)

Disney Comes to Town

While the Dodgers floundered in the early '90s, Vero Beach moved on. The Grand Harbor development on the mainland side of the river expanded to a point where it matched the success of Johns Island and The Moorings. Construction began on the new Barber Bridge. A new library and a new courthouse opened with hopes of sparking the downtown economy. Developers initiated plans for two major malls.[15]

Hurricane Andrew, at one point aiming for the Indian River area, veered south with its 170-mile-per-hour winds and drastically damaged the area south of Miami. Andrew tore up the University of Miami Hurricanes' practice facility, and the team moved to Dodgertown to prepare for the 1992 football season.[16]

The Indian River County United Way raised over $900,000 for the first time, and a note on a newspaper clipping to Peter O'Malley, presumably written by Craig Callan, stated that the Dodgers were a driving force in the success of the fund. Callan, as president of the United Way, followed in the footsteps of previous Dodgertown directors, Terry Reynolds and Charlie Blaney, both of whom served the community in that position. The Chamber of Commerce selected the Dodgers and Piper Aircraft (on the rebound once again) as the County Businesses of the Year. Area economic development director Alan Campbell said, "Whenever I ask Craig Callan for anything, his response is, 'If it's good for the community, we're for it.'"[17]

When a rendering of a proposed Disney resort on the beach appeared on the front page of the *Press Journal*, the community erupted as if Disney World itself were moving from Orlando. As one letter to the editor noted, some people thought it an "obscenity" to place Mickey Mouse between the exclusive developments of Johns Island and Windsor. Another letter wondered what would have happened if the Dodgers had come to Vero in 1993 instead of in 1948. Would there have been opposition?[18]

The two hundred-unit resort survived the controversy and gained the approval of the County Commission, unlike a proposed Marriott Hotel ten years earlier. Commission chairman Dick Bird, the former Dodgertown director, said, "Let's hope today is the beginning of the blending of the quality of the Disney organization and the quality of Indian River County."[19] As an advertising sponsor for the spring training games, Disney's Florida Beach Resort worked with the Dodgers at Holman Stadium with promotions for their new operation.

1994

Afghanistan

On a bright Sunday afternoon at Holman Stadium with an overflow crowd sitting on the berm, Darryl Strawberry took up his position in left field. A fence at the bottom of the berm now separated the fans from the field. A couple of the attendees with New Jersey accents heckled Darryl from the berm about his tax troubles. He responded by making a leaping, reaching catch over the fence to prevent a home run. The fans on the berm gave him an appreciative round of cheers, and he flashed a thumbs up. The New Jersey couple shut up.

The Dodgers released Strawberry two months later; he had a drug problem.

In a fundraiser benefiting Vero's Samaritan Center for Homeless Families, current and former Dodger players and coaches roasted Tommy Lasorda. Patrons donated $100 a person to attend. Tommy always had given to the community, and he enjoyed the spotlight. Dr. Hugh McCrystal tells a story about one of Lasorda's talks. The Indian River Memorial Hospital, of which Hugh had been chief of staff and a board member, held an affair for their major benefactors at The Moorings' club. A Washington snowstorm prevented TV anchor David Brinkley from attending as the guest speaker. Hugh asked Tommy on the spur of the moment to speak in Brinkley's place. Tommy said, "Sure. What was he going to speak about?" "Afghanistan," said McCrystal. "I can handle that," said Tommy. As usual, he wowed the audience.

Hugh occasionally traveled with the Dodgers as the team doctor. He attended the 1988 World Series in that role. He watched Tommy smoothly handle the TV interviews, but when he got with the team's beat writers, who didn't use tape recorders, every other word was f—ing this and f—ing that. Tommy was a dichotomy.[20]

The Dodgers stood in first place in August when a players' strike over the owners' demand for revenue sharing between teams and a proposed salary cap canceled the season and the World Series.[21]

The owners' committee dealing with the players' strike did not include Peter O'Malley. "I have no knowledge of what's going on," he said.[22] In major league baseball ownership circles, Peter O'Malley now stood on the outside looking in. He had been part of the owner power elite at one time, though not to the extent of his father who all but ruled the game. Acting commissioner Bud Selig surrounded himself with owners with whom he felt comfortable. As one Dodger observer noted, the story was that Selig's ownership clique did not return O'Malley's phone calls.

Like Leaving Your Spouse after Fifty Years

1995

A Scab Spring

The spring was like no other for the Dodgers and for Vero Beach. The major league players stayed on strike, as did a lot of fed-up fans. Local merchants, hotels, and restaurants suffered. One hotel operator said he lost $40,000. Seasonal home rentals and even real estate sales took a dip. While this drop in business revenues couldn't be attributed wholly to the Dodgers, one real estate executive noted, "The Dodgers have a lot more impact than we realize." The Chamber of Commerce estimated a $2 million economic loss to the community. With a large number of the fans at spring games coming from out of state, the average attendance for teams training in Florida dropped 63 percent.[1]

Spring training became a split season. A replacement team represented the Dodgers during March. When the strike ended, the major league team began an abbreviated twelve-day session. Attendance for exhibition games played by both the replacements and the major leaguers at Holman Stadium averaged 2,200, down from 5,800 the previous season.[2]

Fred Claire signed Japanese pitcher Hideo Nomo and introduced him at a Dodgertown press conference with much fanfare. The Japanese media requested forty press credentials. With the strike still going on, Nomo was scheduled to be the opening-day pitcher for the Vero Dodgers.[3]

Tommy Lasorda fielded the replacement team with vigor. Some, however, would call the substitute players scabs. Half of those on the roster had no more than Class A minor league experience. Each player was promised a $5,000 bonus and guaranteed a job in the organization. Five of the starting lineup played or would play for the Vero Dodgers. First baseman Jay Kirkpatrick, a Vero Dodger, hit two home runs in the opening game against the Yankees. The most experienced player on the team was third baseman Mike Busch, who made the Dodgers spring roster the year before. (When Busch was called up to the big team later in 1995, his major league teammates ostracized him for being a scab.)[4]

In a game where the young Dodger team beat the Houston replacements 11–1, Tommy Lasorda turned to the crowd and yelled, "Isn't this good baseball?" Two thousand people agreed with an enthusiasm that you didn't see in traditional spring games. This young team produced a 20–7 record, traveled to Los Angeles to play the Angels in the Freeway Series, and stood ready to open the season at Dodger Stadium.[5]

The strike ended, and some local fans were disappointed. They wanted to see the replacements play in the big leagues. A federal judge issued an injunction that stopped the owners from applying new work rules and a payroll cap. On April 10, when the big team should have been in Los Angeles playing the regular schedule, they were playing an intrasquad game in Holman Stadium, trying to get in shape. Piazza hit two home runs and Hideo Nomo threw two great innings. For the second go-around of the exhibition season, the major leaguers played six games at Holman Stadium. Reserved seats sold for a bargain $3.50. In the first game on April 13 against the new Florida Marlins, only 1,700 showed up. The crowd improved to three thousand for a game with the Yankees.[6]

Four Home Runs

This strange spring ended with a bang. Former Vero Dodger outfielder Henry Rodriguez provided some great excitement on a warm Sunday afternoon at Holman Stadium. Henry hit a home run in the first inning, again in the third, and again in the sixth. Henry's brother was sitting in section 17 next to the Dodger section, and he and the crowd got excited over the third one. Manager Tommy Lasorda left Rodriguez in, which was unusual in an exhibition game. In the ninth, Henry came to bat. What was left of the crowd buzzed. His brother hollered for another homer. Sure. What are the odds of that? Henry Rodriguez then drove the ball over the berm. The crowd stood, hollered, and applauded loudly as Henry circled the bases. His brother jumped up and down with excitement, then shook hands with everyone around him.[7] (Shortly afterwards, Henry Rodriguez was traded to Montreal where, in 1996, he hit a career-high thirty-six home runs.)

Outfielder Henry Rodri-
guez hit four home runs
in a game at Holman
Stadium. (Courtesy of
Los Angeles Dodgers,
Los Angeles, California.)

By the latter part of April, with the exhibition games still going on, it was too hot for afternoon baseball in Holman Stadium. The regular season opened on April 26 in Miami in the first-ever major league game for the new Marlin team. The Dodgers won 8–7 and went on to win their division as Hideo Nomo became the Dodgers' fourth consecutive Rookie of the Year. But the glory didn't last. In the play-offs, the Reds whipped the Dodgers three straight.

1996

Tommy's Heart Attack

During an intrasquad game, outfielder Karim Garcia chased a long foul ball and disappeared beyond the end of the right field stands into the vicinity of the men's room. He ran back on the field, holding the ball high as if he had caught it. Garcia had hit twenty-one home runs for the Vero

Dodgers two years earlier and was now on the big team spring roster as a top prospect. But it was outfielder Todd Hollandsworth who won the Jim and Dearie Mulvey Award for best rookie in camp. And he would go on to become the Dodgers' fifth consecutive Rookie of the Year.

At the end of June with the team leading the division by two games, Tommy Lasorda suffered a heart attack. His heir apparent, Bill Russell, stepped in to manage the team. Russell, after playing eighteen years with the Dodgers, became a coach in 1987, managed Albuquerque in '92 and '93, then returned to the team as bench coach and Lasorda's number-one assistant. When Lasorda recovered, he moved into the front office as a vice president and goodwill ambassador.

Bill Russell led the Dodgers to a second-place finish behind the Padres. But in the new, crazy, three-division system, the Dodgers won sufficient games to be the wild-card team. However, as in 1995, the Braves beat them three straight in the play-offs to end the season.

The Vero Dodgers won their first half but lost in the play-offs. Future L.A. favorites Paul Lo Duca and Alex Cora caught and played the infield respectively. John Debus, a Vero Dodger alumnus, managed the team for the third year in a row. His '94 Vero team had produced slugger Karim Garcia and pitcher Matt Herges. Garcia never fulfilled his promise as be bounced around the majors. Herges won eleven and lost three for L.A. in 2000, then went to the Expos for reliever Guillermo Mota.

1997

The Time to Sell

On January 6, 1997, Peter O'Malley announced that the Los Angeles Dodgers were for sale. In a press conference at Dodger Stadium he said, "It finally occurred to me that this is the time. The thought has been in my mind for a while, but with a lot more frequency." He credited estate planning as the primary reason. "It's a pretty good idea not to have all your eggs in one basket," he said.[8] The Dodgers remained the only major league team owned by a single family—Peter and his sister Terry Seidler.

But there were other reasons for the sale. Peter O'Malley, now fifty-nine, had spent the past year working on a plan to build a football stadium at Chavez Ravine and bring back to Los Angeles a National Football League team. But the city leaders decided that, if a team could be found,

Tommy Lasorda was inducted into the Hall of Fame in 1997 and in Dodgertown tradition had a street named after him. (Courtesy of Los Angeles Dodgers, Los Angeles, California.)

it should play in the Coliseum. The decision deeply disappointed Peter. Four months later, he put the Dodgers up for sale. "You can't fight city hall," he would say.[9] Of course, his father had fought city hall in New York, Los Angeles, and Vero Beach. Dodger general manager Fred Claire felt that if the football deal had worked out, Peter O'Malley would have never sold the team.[10]

"It's like a death in the family," said former L.A. city councilwoman Roz Wyman responding to the sale announcement.[11] She had worked with Walter O'Malley to bring the Dodgers to Los Angeles and had come to Vero Beach in 1957 for the meeting at the Holman ranch.

The Dodger "old guard" took the announcement hard. Billy DeLury, who went to work for the Brooklyn Dodgers at sixteen in 1950, when Walter O'Malley took charge, said, "It was like somebody threw a cold bucket of water on me."[12] Ben Wade, a former director of scouting who had joined the Dodgers in 1951, said, "I knew Peter was upset with the way things were going with the players and the owners and with the commissioner thing [Bud Selig]. I think somewhere along the line he got fed up with it."[13] Tommy Lasorda, who had just been voted into the Baseball Hall of Fame, said, "When people like him want to sell their ball club it's a very bad sign. I think that Peter has just been unhappy lately with the situation, the direction the game of baseball is going."[14]

Director Craig Callan was concerned about Vero: "The relationship between the Dodgers and Vero Beach is directly tied to the O'Malley family. There have been things done in the past fifty years that have not been done for business but for the relationship with the community."[15] Vero Beach mayor Jack Grossett was "shocked." A *Press Journal* editorial summed up the situation: "The whole idea just doesn't sound right. After all baseball is steeped in tradition. . . . Much of what Vero has become over the past fifty years can be traced to the Dodgers. . . . How could the Dodgers ever hope to sell their entire complex and pull out of Vero Beach? It would be a mind-boggling divestiture, one that would hurt our area." The editorial continued, comparing the Dodger–Vero Beach relationship to a "love affair" and its breakup, like "leaving your spouse after fifty years."[16]

Peter O'Malley had concluded his announcement by saying, "I will do everything possible to identify the most quality ownership to follow our family."[17]

Boys of Summer author, Roger Kahn, talked with the *Los Angeles Times* about the sale and the O'Malleys. He said that Peter did not "possess his father's style or combative cunning." He "lacked a passion for baseball" that his father and Branch Rickey had. Kahn concluded: "Peter is a decent man, probably one hell of a lot better than what will follow."[18] What a prophecy that became!

During spring training in Vero, Peter O'Malley met with mayor Bill Jordan, city manager Rex Taylor and county commissioner Ken Macht to discuss the sale. He said that new ownership, whoever it might be, would likely reexamine existing arrangements, but he hoped that the Dodgers would stay in Vero Beach. He gave an "advance signal" to the city and the county that they "should examine available options to keep the Dodgers here."[19]

In May, Rupert Murdoch, CEO of the News Corporation, confirmed that he had talked with Peter O'Malley about buying the Dodgers for an approximate price of $350 million. The Dodgers would be a part of the News Corporation's Fox Television organization. O'Malley immediately offered three-year personal service contracts to his front-office staff so they could not be arbitrarily fired.[20]

Manager Bill Russell took over the team for his first, full season in 1997. At Holman Stadium he sat in the manager's seat, a folding chair between the end of the open dugout and the bat box. He was quiet, certainly no Lasorda. The razzle-dazzle was gone. But the team won eight out of their first nine spring games. A thrill that spring was seeing the tall, almost stately Cal Ripken playing for Baltimore with his consecutive game record surpassing two thousand.

At Dodgertown, rookie Wilton Guerrero and veteran Eric Young replaced Delino DeShields at second. Rookie Korean pitcher Chan Ho Park made the pitching staff, having worked his way up through San Antonio and Albuquerque. The Dodgers finished the season in second place again, but did not repeat as the wild-card winner.

In a Vero Beach Dodger game in April, local fans saw nineteen-year-old Adrian Beltre hit perhaps the highest, longest home run ever seen at Holman Stadium.[21] Beltre batted .317, hit twenty-six home runs and batted in 104 runs to become the Florida State League's Most Valuable Player and *Baseball America's* Class A Player of the Year. John Shoemaker returned as manager, and with Beltre's performance the Vero team won the first half but lost the championship series. Adrian Beltre had the potential to be the career third baseman the Dodgers had lacked since the departure of Ron Cey.

Where is Vero Beach?

The big news in Vero, besides the pending sale of the Dodgers, involved a rumor that the troubled former sports star O. J. Simpson had bought a $2 million house on the beach. Florida law states that the courts can't take away a person's home no matter what his or her legal situation might be. And the rumor included a Dodger connection. From the medical community came the story that Dodger surgeon Frank Jobe, supposedly a neighbor of O. J.'s, had recommended Vero Beach. The O. J. rumors stirred up emotions like an approaching hurricane—exciting, but you didn't really want it to come. When the press asked O. J. about Vero, he responded, "Where is Vero Beach?" He moved to Fort Lauderdale.[22]

Beating Peter O'Malley to the punch, John Schuman Jr. had sold the *Vero Beach Press Journal*, in his family for three generations, to Scripps Howard, a national newspaper chain. This company bought other papers along the coast with a plan to produce a regional newspaper. It was the beginning of the end of Vero's own paper.

Facing the loss of two old-time institutions, the Dodgers and the local newspaper, to the corporate world, the Indian River County populace could find some solace in what had been gained: the Disney resort, the new Barber Bridge, a second high school west of Sebastian, and the Indian River Mall west of downtown. A Super Wal-Mart and other big national box stores sprung up in the vicinity of the mall, making Route 60 a mile-long shopping corridor.

Vero Beach could no longer be called a small town.

The Mystique Is Gone

1998

Dodger Deal is Done

During spring training, the *Press Journal* issued a special edition commemorating the fiftieth anniversary of Dodgertown. The paper ran a series of articles about Dodgertown over the years. One piece told about three Dodger wives, all close friends, whose husbands Ralph Branca, Duke Snider, and Carl Erskine were at Dodgertown for the winter fantasy camp. Ann Branca, Beverly Snider, and Betty Erskine had all come to Vero with their husbands in the early years. They remembered the shopping in downtown Vero that was limited to Alma Lee's Child's Wear, a gift shop, and a lady's clothing store. The Sniders and the Erskines shared a two-bedroom house in Vero for several years even when they each had two babies. They alternated cooking dinner. "Basically we were in the background as wives," said Betty Erskine. "But it was a wonderful adventure. You accepted what circumstances you were in. It was the era."[1]

Today the players' wives have more options in Vero. Alma Lee's was no longer in existence, but the Indian River Mall out Route 60 housed ninety stores and a twenty-four–screen movie theater. Players and their families rented furnished condominiums for the spring, which were easier to find than houses. Compared with the other Dodger wives, manager Bill Russell's wife Susan was something of an exception. The Russells had no children, and Susan was a consultant for the Centers for Disease Control and Prevention. She and Bill had an apartment in the Dodgertown villas and didn't have to cook. "Down here, it's much more relaxed," Susan Russell said. "If you stay on base there's no travel, everything is available here at Dodgertown. Every convenience is here. You get spoiled."[2]

While stories in the *Press Journal's* special issue portrayed the long-standing relationship between the Dodgers and Vero Beach, this association would soon be in jeopardy. Talk circulated that should the sale to Murdoch go through, his organization would move the Dodgers to Arizona for spring training.

Another Albuquerque rookie phenom, in the tradition of Mike Marshall and Greg Brock, arrived at Dodgertown. First baseman Paul Konerko hit thirty-seven home runs and was selected by the *Sporting News* as the 1997 Minor League Player of the Year. He hit five home runs in the spring and won the Mulvey rookie award. But the Dodgers had Eric Karros and by July traded Konerko to Cincinnati for closer Jeff Shaw.

Tommy Lasorda, fully recovered from his heart attack, worked with the minor leaguers. Tommy didn't believe Vero Beach had anything to worry about, despite the pending sale to Murdoch and talk of the Dodgers going to Arizona. "Dodgertown was just voted [by *Baseball America*] as the best spring site in America," Lasorda said. "I think Fox and everybody knows what a mistake it would be to leave Vero Beach." Tommy talked about the O'Malleys: "Mr. O'Malley played a vital role in making baseball what it is today. And Peter O'Malley continued the high level of success." Lasorda praised Peter for promoting major league baseball globally. He built baseball fields in China, an academy in the Dominican Republic, and a stadium in Nicaragua. He helped to put baseball in the Olympics. And he signed South Korea's Chan Ho Park and Japan's Hideo Nomo.[3]

A crowd of only 3,400 showed up at one of the exhibition games, the first sign that something had happened to Dodger baseball in Vero Beach. Except for the "replacement" games in 1995, Holman Stadium hadn't seen a crowd that small since the '70s. Could it have been concern about the new ownership and the possibility of losing the Dodgers? Vero Dodger season attendance plummeted to 50,094 from its record high of 94,000 in 1990.[4]

Fox Television chief executive officer Chase Carey, a key figure in putting major league baseball on the Fox network said that he expected that the major league owners would approve the Dodger sale: "Fox has had a good, positive, instructive relationship with baseball." His organization owned local cable contracts with twenty-two of the thirty major league teams. In buying the Dodgers, Fox positioned itself to beat out Disney in creating a sports network in the Los Angeles area.[5] Some of the teams worried that as an owner, Fox would have a conflict of interest with Major League Baseball itself, especially as Fox's $11 billion parent News Corporation had the resources to further escalate player salaries.

On March 19, it rained in Vero Beach, canceling the game with the Cardinals at Holman Stadium. That morning, across the state in St. Petersburg, the major league owners voted to approve the Fox buy of the Dodgers. From the Renaissance Vinoy Resort where the owners met, Fox Group CEO Peter Chernin told the press "how extremely happy" Fox was and that they considered the Dodgers the "crown jewel of American sports." Chernin said, "Fox will attempt to continue the traditions of the Dodger organization and has no plans to move its spring training site out of Vero Beach." Fox was "absolutely satisfied" with general manager Fred Claire and wanted to re-sign Mike Piazza, who was eligible for free agency at the end of the current season. Chernin announced that Bob Graziano, the Dodger vice president of business operations, would become Dodger president, reporting to him.[6]

"The overriding objective is to have a seamless transition," said Graziano. Peter O'Malley would stay on as a consultant. Of Dodgertown, Graziano said, "We have a terrific relationship with Vero Beach and have no immediate plans to do anything there." But he hedged his statement, adding, "And with everything, the economics of the game will dictate where spring training is in the future." Chernin concluded, "We haven't even considered moving them: Dodgertown is a great facility and a great place."[7]

In Vero, Fred Claire watched the St. Petersburg activities on the large-screen TV in the Dodger lounge. With the exhibition game canceled, a few of the players watched on the clubhouse TV. Most didn't seem to care. "I didn't pay any attention to it," said pitcher Ramon Martinez. Shortstop Jose Vizcaino, outfielder Raul Mondesi, and utility player Wilton Guerrero wandered off to the batting cage.[8] Mike Piazza said, "No one knows what's going to happen." His two-year, $15 million contract expired at the end of the season, and he wanted a seven-year, $105 million deal.[9]

That afternoon, after the approval of the sale, Chernin, Carey, Graziano, and O'Malley flew on the Fox corporate jet to Vero to address the Dodger front-office staff. Claire, Lasorda, and Russell listened as O'Malley thanked everyone for their service. Graziano assured the group that O'Malley's "family-oriented ways would not be abandoned," and Peter "would always be there if we need his guidance."

The next day, the headline in the *Press Journal* blurted, "DODGER DEAL IS DONE." An accompanying photo showed forty-six-year-old Peter Chernin wearing a golf shirt and gesturing with a cigar as he addressed the Dodger group. Peter O'Malley stood looking on pensively, his hands touching each other at the finger tips.[10]

Shortly afterwards, the Fox crowd announced that they were considering moving the team from Vero to save the operating cost of "the most expensive spring-training facility in baseball."[11]

Piazza is Gone

In May, Mike Piazza—the Dodgers' most popular player, who batted .362 the previous season and who after five spectacular years already was slated for the Hall of Fame—was gone. Fox executive Chase Carey traded Piazza in a multiplayer deal for outfielder Gary Sheffield, a good hitter but a malcontent. Speculation circulated that Carey's deal had more to do with trying to expand the Fox Sports Network to Miami rather than to improve the Dodgers.[12]

Carey made and announced the trade without general manager Fred Claire's knowledge. Claire reacted by telling Bob Graziano, "There needs to be two announcements, because this organization obviously doesn't need me."[13] But Claire stuck around to clean up after Carey. Carey didn't seem to know that Sheffield had a no-trade clause in his contract. This caused some consternation and the Dodgers more money before Sheffield agreed to join the team. Fred Claire wrote, "I didn't want to turn my back on the team. . . . I agreed to stay and see if I could repair the damage."[14]

The Father's Day Massacre

In mid-June, with a .500 record, the Dodgers stood twelve games out of first place. On June 21, Dodger president Bob Graziano called general manager Fred Claire and manager Bill Russell into his office and told them they were being "transitioned," a corporate word for fired. Columnist Ross Newhan called it the "Father's Day Massacre." The *Los Angeles Times* questioned whether Graziano was "running the Dodgers or ruining them."[15] Graziano had been with the team thirteen years as a "finance guy." He had little experience with baseball operations. Graziano fired Claire and Russell with Peter O'Malley's support and no apparent intervention by Fox. O'Malley said, "I've been disappointed in the team's performance, felt we were flat and have been for some time. I think it's time for a change." One writer noted that the Dodgers under O'Malley management had not fired a manager in forty-five years.[16]

Tommy Lasorda, being in good favor with the Fox management, became the "interim" general manager. He had long coveted the position.[17] Management blamed Fred Claire for the team's poor performance in the '90s, though he operated with a limited player-salary budget set by O'Malley. Of course, this was the same Fred Claire who won the 1988 Executive of the Year award for acquiring Kirk Gibson and bringing the Dodgers a World Series championship.

Albuquerque manager Glenn Hoffman became the Dodger manager. Graziano spoke of Hoffman as "interim" while Fox declared him "the" manager. Hoffman had played for the Red Sox in the '80s and then became a Dodger minor league manager, which included the assignment with the Vero Dodgers in 1992. Management expressed the hope that Hoffman would bring the intensity that Russell lacked. Longtime bullpen coach Mark Cresse said, "Tommy spent three seconds a day not talking. Billy spent three seconds a day talking. . . . It wasn't like Billy was a bad manager, but there wasn't a lot of fire there."[18]

Tommy Lasorda said, "I nurtured Bill Russell. . . . he was like a son to me . . . I wanted him to be the manager of the Dodgers." But when Russell became manager, Lasorda felt ignored by his protégé. On the other hand, Russell said, "Tommy has been second guessing me ever since I took over for him." They hadn't spoken for months.[19]

Over the rest of the season, Hoffman improved slightly on Russell's record, and the Dodgers finished third. During this awful year, a positive occurred. Former Vero Dodger star Adrian Beltre jumped from San Antonio to the big team and took over third base.

New Sheriff in Town

In September, Fox and Bob Graziano chose Kevin Malone as the Dodger general manager. Tommy Lasorda received a "promotion" to senior vice president. Malone, forty-one, came from Baltimore where he served as assistant general manager. In 1994, as the Montreal Expo general manager, his team achieved the top record in baseball until the strike canceled the season. *Baseball Weekly* named Malone the best general manager in the game.

Malone didn't get off to a great start. Shortly after being hired, he declared on a Los Angeles radio show, "There's a new sheriff in town and the Dodgers will be back." The "new sheriff's" words would came back to haunt him.[20]

It now became Malone's job to find a manager. Forget Hoffman. He really was "interim." Malone said, "I need my own guy, a proven winner with experience."[21] Both Jim Leyland, longtime Pittsburg manager, and Felipe Alou, who had managed for Malone at Montreal, said they were not interested. Davey Lopes' name came up as a possible candidate. He had little managerial experience, but was aggressive and part of the Dodger tradition. Lopes, who said he hardly knew Malone, remarked of his former team: "The mystique is gone. It's a new franchise, a new generation, a new corporate world. It's all about change—out with the old and in with the new."[22]

Davey Johnson took the job. He gave up golfing in Florida and settled for being the third-choice pick. Johnson was an experienced manager and had led the Mets to a World Series championship in 1986.

With Malone's antics to find a Dodger manager, columnist Ross Newhan commented, "Dodger blue? The allure is gone, the aura dust, the tradition a distant memory."[23]

Love and the Bottom Line

On September 30, Dodger publicity director Derrick Hall made an announcement about spring training: "We are entertaining all the options, but that doesn't mean we would not be in Vero Beach next year. We love Vero Beach, we love Dodgertown, we've got tradition and we want to stay there." Hall said that a move to Arizona would put all the West Coast teams together; the Dodgers would be near their rivals, the Giants and the Padres. "We're going to give Vero Beach the best crack at anything," he said. But it would be the bottom line that counted in the end.[24] (Hall had begun his baseball career as an intern with the Vero Dodgers in 1992 and had risen rapidly in the Dodger ranks.)

With Las Vegas and several Arizona cities starting to court the Dodgers, Dodgertown director Craig Callan began meeting with Indian River County administrator Jim Chandler and Vero Beach city manager Rex Taylor to see what could be worked out.

What did the Dodgers mean to Vero Beach? A *Press Journal* feature assessed the value of the Dodgers to Vero Beach: a $1.5 million payroll covering 275 regular employees and adding two hundred more during spring training; an annual property tax payment of $317,000; purchases from

170 local business ranging from $1,000 to $300,000 per year; donations to fifty local charities, totaling $50,000 a year, plus $20,000 of in-kind donations annually; and the support to Dodgertown Elementary School. (After the sale to Fox, the O'Malley family sent a $25,000 personal check to the school.) Overall, the Dodgers provided an estimated $20 million boost to the Vero Beach–Indian River County community.[25]

In a late-night meeting at Dodgertown in the latter part of October, Peter O'Malley told the Dodger management staff that he would leave the club on December 31. Fox tried to persuade him to stay as a consultant. He refused.[26]

A week later, the Indian River County Commission and the Vero Beach City Council unanimously agreed to attempt to keep the Dodgers by buying part of Dodgertown and leasing it back to the team. The elected officials authorized county administrator Jim Chandler and city manager Rex Taylor to begin negotiating with Dodger representative Craig Callan. The purchase would include Holman Stadium, all the practice fields, and the clubhouse, together representing an assessed value of $4.8 million. It excluded the villas and the two golf courses. The city would pay for its share with $1 million from an existing surplus fund and lease their part of the property back to the county. The county would issue a bond for the balance to be paid for by two cents designated from the tourist tax. In the meantime, the legislature would have to pass a law allowing the tourist tax to be used to acquire facilities.[27]

The whole concept was contingent upon retaining the Dodgers only, not upon possibly attracting another team. Under no circumstances would the county and the city get in a bidding war to keep the Dodgers. The Dodgers had expressed no terms or conditions but were looking for a "level playing field" in evaluating options.[28]

While the crowd in the County Commission chambers applauded the decision, negative comments from local residents surfaced in the *Press Journal*. One said, "The economy might sag a little if the Dodgers leave. But it will recover." Another said, "It's a tax payer rip off." A fan said that he enjoyed going to the games, but didn't want public money spent to keep the Dodgers.[29]

Spending public money—an old issue. It had come up in Brooklyn over a new Dodger stadium, in Los Angeles over Chavez Ravine, and in Vero Beach in the 1960s over the Dodgers' use of the airport property. And here it was again.

Keep Our Dodgers

Craig Callan announced that the Dodgers and Fox were going to visit the Fort McDowell Indian Reservation outside Phoenix. Arizona had ten Cactus League teams in the Phoenix area—all less than an hour by plane and five-and-a-half hours by car from Los Angeles. The Fort McDowell Yavapai-Apache Indians, already operating a casino, offered to build the Dodgers a training facility with a twelve-thousand-seat stadium, several practice fields, and living facilities. The cost: $20 million. The Dodgers also received interest from the cities of Glendale, Arizona, and Chandler in Las Vegas, Nevada. But by mid-December, the Dodgers stated they were looking at only two possibilities—Vero Beach and Fort McDowell.[30]

A group of concerned Vero Beach citizens formed a Keep Our Dodgers Committee. The thirty members met in banker Bill Curtis' office. Dodgertown director Craig Callan attended the meetings as an observer. The group included architect Tony Donadio; community leader Alma Lee Loy; citrusman Dan Richey; lawyer Robin Lloyd; board of realtors president, Wayne Kleinstiver; police chief (and future city manager) Jim Gabbard; county commissioner Ken Macht; future state representative Stan Mayfield; realtor Ed Schlitt; future mayor Mary Beth McDonald; chamber of commerce director Penny Chandler; and chamber economic development director Milt Thomas.[31]

Milt Thomas had come to Vero with his family as a teenager in the late '50s. He remembered the Dodgers from those times: "They didn't have big salaries then; they were just regular folks." His parents bowled with outfielder Wally Moon, a neighborhood girl dated Wes Parker, and a high school friend went out with Sandy Koufax.

Milt Thomas prepared an evaluation showing that the Dodgers provided a $30 million boost to the local community.[32] Milt's number proved consistent with the $25 million annual boost provided by the Mets to Port Saint Lucie and, as one study found, with economic boons provided to communities in Arizona that hosted major league teams. Milt described the impact: "The job situation here in Indian River County is not good (double digit unemployment in the off-season). The Dodgers are a $30 million engine in a weak economy." He believed that in fifteen years the Dodgertown land "would be worth a hell of a lot more than we [the county and the city] pay for it."

Milt Thomas worked the factual justification for keeping the Dodgers, but it was hard to ignore the emotional side: "The Dodgers are part of our culture. It would be like taking the Metropolitan Museum out of New York. That might not affect the economy of NYC, but it would be a major loss. The Dodgers are as much a part of Vero Beach as the ocean."[33]

Oceanside Business Association representative Laurie Connelly, whose family owned shops on the island, said, "People would do anything to keep the Dodgers here. It's a sentimental thing." Like Milt, she had Dodger ties. She had baby-sat for the Steve Garveys and the Don Suttons when she was a teenager. But Milt and Laurie knew that sentimentality was not a factor with Fox. As Milt said, "Loyalty doesn't seem to have any value anymore."[34]

In this year of O'Malley's sale to Fox, Piazza's departure, the firing of Claire and Russell, the hiring of Malone, the debacle over finding a manager, and the threat to leave Dodgertown, one obscenity remained. The Fox Group Dodgers signed premier pitcher Kevin Brown to a seven-year, $105 million deal—the first baseball contract to crack the $100 million barrier. The commitment to Brown represented almost one third the amount that Fox paid for the Dodgers. Questions arose as to why the Dodgers hadn't spent that money to keep Mike Piazza. Unlike a pitcher, he played every day.[35]

With the millions given to Brown, some people in Vero wondered why Fox seemed so concerned about the relatively piddling cost of Dodgertown.

Big, Bad Media Company

1999

Leaving History and Tradition on the Curb

The cover of the 1999 *Dodger Media Guide* showed Kevin Malone and Davey Johnson smiling. Dodger fans were not smiling.

On the inside cover under "Executives," Peter O'Malley had been replaced by Rupert Murdoch, chairman and CEO, News Corporation; Peter Chernin, president and chief operating officer, News Corporation, CEO, Fox Group; and Chase Carey, chairman and CEO, Fox Television. Mr. Carey's picture showed him with a great, curled, handlebar mustache. However, he received no credit for single-handedly arranging the Mike Piazza trade. On page nine, the first Dodger management names appeared: Bob Graziano, president and CEO, followed by executive vice president and general manager Kevin Malone and senior vice president Tommy Lasorda.[1]

Gone, of course, was Fred Claire. Also missing, after thirty-two years in the Dodger organization, was former Dodgertown director and Vero Beach favorite, vice president of minor league operations Charlie Blaney. Malone had replaced most of the baseball operations people with his former associates. Terry Reynolds, the Vero Beach Dodgers first general manager and then Dodgertown director after Blaney, survived as coordinator of minor league scouting. And Craig Callan, managing director of Dodgertown, remained but was put in the difficult position of negotiating the possible departure from a community that he had been such a part of and given so much to over the last fifteen years. In the coaching staff section of the media guide, last year's manager, Glenn Hoffman, was listed as the bullpen coach.

As Glenn Stout wrote in *The Dodgers*: "Fox bought a business, a product, and a franchise, but when it did, it cut the team off from its history and tradition. Fox left all that on the curb, when it cleaned out the offices. And did it ever clean out the offices."[2]

With the addition of the likes of pitcher Kevin Brown and outfielder Gary Sheffield, Fox increased the payroll from $48 million to $84 million.[3] Peter Chernin praised the planning of president Bob Graziano and general manager Kevin Malone: "I certainly don't think anyone could say we were surprised. We bought the team and then we started the process of trying to figure out how to manage it. . . . People don't like change . . . it's a pretty easy target to sort of say, 'Big, bad media company.'" Fox, he continued, had an obligation to the fans to "build a winning team. . . . we're in this for the long term."[4]

General manager Kevin Malone, a short fellow with a receding hairline and a mustache, arrived in Vero for spring training and immediately predicted that the Dodgers would be in the 1999 World Series. With the Yankees' acquisition of pitching ace Roger Clemens, Malone said, "They will need Roger when they play us in the Fall Classic in October." After Malone gave Kevin Brown the most extravagant baseball contract ever, the other owners criticized him. Malone responded, "I didn't realize they would be so jealous and envious, and they'd be so public about it." Malone predicted that Kevin Brown would help lead the Dodgers to the World Series, as he had the Padres in 1998 and the Marlins in 1997.[5] Meanwhile, the media declared that Brown's contract illustrated what was wrong with baseball.

In his remarks on arriving at Dodgertown, manager Davey Johnson spoke in a more restrained manner than his general manager: "For me this is an opportunity to be a part of getting [the Dodgers] back to being a perennial play-off contender." "It's an honor and a thrill," he said.[6]

At Dodgertown on a typical, bright sunny day before the exhibition games started, onlookers watched the team practice. Kevin Brown was not sighted. Perhaps he was somewhere counting his millions. It seemed Indian River County and Vero Beach were willing to spend millions to keep the Dodgers. The Indians in Arizona were willing to spend even more millions to steal them away. Everything in baseball was about millions, with Fox raising the ante millions more. Fifty years of tradition meant nothing. But the fans were able to see some pure baseball that day—outfielder Todd Hollandsworth taking ground balls and experimenting with playing first base.

Watching newcomer Davey Johnson manage in the spring, he seemed pleasant but no more inspiring than Billy Russell. Next to Davey in the folding chairs at the end of the dugout sat the unknown Jim Tracy, the new bench coach. He had managed in the minor leagues and been a coach with the Montreal Expos. No one could foresee that within two years he would be the Dodger manager.[7]

The Fox millions did not buy success. The Dodgers experienced a losing season and finished twenty-three games behind the Arizona Diamondbacks, an expansion team in its second year in baseball.

Turmoil reigned. Raul Mondesi insulted his manager and his general manager publicly, referring to them as "f—g Davey" and "f—g Malone." Management did not suspend, fine, or publicly rebuke him. He played the next night. The frail Fred Claire had once stood up to the huge Kirk Gibson. Malone did nothing.[8]

The Vero Dodgers also had a losing season—the second in a row—as well as a decline in attendance. A Canadian hockey player named Eric Gagne won nine games for the '98 team. He would join Mike Piazza, Eric Young, Pedro Astacio, Paul Lo Duca, Alex Cora, and Adrian Beltre from Vero teams of the '90s, all of whom produced for the big team.

Hoping for the Home-field Advantage

Meanwhile, the Dodgers' demands for staying in Vero Beach grew. The original $4.8 million deal, based on the tax value of Dodgertown property, had escalated to $19 million. The appraised value of the property, now sixty-four acres with the villas added, rose to $10 million. But the Dodgers wanted more: $7 million for capital improvements and a $2 million reserve for future improvements.[9] The city reserve of $1.4 million remained available, but the county would have to issue bonds for the balance. Help from the state became a necessity.

Florida state representative Charlie Sembler and state senator Patsy Kurth, both representing Indian River County, spent the legislative session in Tallahassee fighting for the money to keep the Dodgers. In April, the Florida Senate approved spending $7.5 million in state money to help the city and the county put together a financial package to satisfy Fox and the Dodgers. Republican governor Jeb Bush vetoed the funds. The governor argued that the expenditure was for a "narrowly focused, local project that has little state benefit."[10]

Fortunately, Bush did not veto the provision that allowed Indian River County to use local tourist tax money to acquire the training facility. Indian River County administrator Jim Chandler and Vero Beach city manager Rex Taylor were grateful for the tourist tax dollars, but restructuring would be necessary. Taylor said, "I'm not going to say the deal is dead. . . . We're working on another concept." Chandler felt that Vero had the "home-field advantage."[11]

Craig Callan seemed discouraged. He said that the $7.5 million for improvements was an "integral part" of the deal." He hoped that "somehow we can salvage keeping the Dodgers in Vero."[12]

In May, Tommy Lasorda met with Governor Bush and "glad handed" his way around Tallahassee, thanking legislators for their support. Led by Lasorda, a feeling existed among many in the Dodger organization that they didn't want to leave Vero.[13] A column in the *Los Angeles Daily News* said: "Don't Mess with the Tradition of Vero Beach."[14]

With the Bush veto, the *Arizona Republic* gleefully ran the headline, "Florida Refuses to Help Dodgers." This rebuff, the paper stated, "clears the way for Arizona to lure the team to the Fort McDowell Yavapai-Apache Reservation east of Scottsdale. While the Dodgers said they would continue talking with Vero Beach, team officials are expected to be in Arizona next week to meet with the tribe."[15]

A month later, the Fort McDowell Indian community came up short in their quest for state funding to help build what had grown to be a lavish spring training facility. A $2.50 county car rental tax, which paid for existing spring training facilities in the Phoenix area, was obligated until 2017 and not available.[16]

In response to a series of "negative and misinformed" letters to the *Press Journal*, Milt Thomas and the Keep Our Dodgers Committee issued an updated "Dodger Facts" to organizations in the community, encouraging that positive letters be written to the paper. On the fax that Craig Callan received, he replied, "Milt, Great job—Thanks. Craig."[17]

The roller coaster ride continued. In July, the Fort McDowell Indian community decreased its offer to the Dodgers. The cost of the facility, originally estimated at $20 million, had grown to $50 million.[18] To hold the cost at $40 million, the housing part of the facility would have to be dropped. The 850-member Indian community considered taking the risk of raising the money themselves, using their casino operations as collateral with the hope of being reimbursed by the state later. The Indians' attorney was encouraging: "The Dodgers are a rare opportunity." As for Vero Beach, he added, "Basically would you rather fly across the country to a fifty-year-old facility or take a one-hour flight to a new one?"[19] Obviously, he had never seen that "fifty-year-old facility."

Dodger officials met with county administrator Jim Chandler and city manager Rex Taylor, but nothing new developed. It became apparent that the Dodgers were looking for other alternatives. Their two top choices, over which they had spent months negotiating, weren't looking too good.

In early August, the *Los Angeles Times* reported that the Dodgers, after receiving a final but "shaky" offer, were no longer considering the Fort McDowell community as a spring training site.[20] As the Dodgers' negotiation leverage with Vero Beach began to weaken, the team's officials continued to imply that the Yavapai-Apache offer could reemerge. However, one thing became certain; the Dodgers had no choice but to train in Vero another year.

Suddenly, Las Vegas jumped into the fray. The Dodgers' lease with Albuquerque, their top farm team, expired at the end of 1999. Las Vegas wanted not only the farm team but also the major league team for spring training.[21]

The Wicked Fox is Dead

On September 28, Fox fired Dodger president Bob Graziano. The *Los Angeles Times* reported: "Peter Chernin, Rupert Murdoch's top lieutenant, is displeased with the team's poor performance and seeming front-office malaise. . . . The perception has been that Graziano has made questionable decisions, foremost among them being the franchise's search for a new spring training home."[22] According to Dodgertown's Craig Callan, Peter Chernin and Bob Graziano never agreed on anything. But it surprised Callan to hear that the spring training issue was a factor in firing Graziano.[23]

In a flattering article, *Business Week*'s Ronald Glover called Peter Chernin "Rupert Murdoch's alter ego" and described him as affable and a great salesman. An investment firm said, "Peter gives us a lot of confidence that the place [Fox News] is run well."[24] Interestingly, Chernin's salary, plus stock options, barely exceeded that of one of his employees, pitcher Kevin Brown.

One month after the Graziano firing, Peter Chernin, finally recognizing the chaos Fox had created in running the Dodgers, gave up. Fox turned the day-to-day operating control of the team over to Bob Daly, one of their executives, who cochaired Warner Brothers. A Dodger fan, Bob Daly grew up in Brooklyn, attended games at Ebbets Field, and in the spring visited Vero to watch the team. He bought a 5 percent interest in the Dodgers from Fox. "Not only is my heart in this, so is my wallet," said Daly. "I will do everything to bring the Dodgers back to the position that they should be at."[25]

Bill Plaschke of the *Los Angeles Times* wrote, "the suits who saw the systematic destruction of their team" are gone. "The wicked Fox is dead."[26]

In an immediate move, chairman Bob Daly hired back Bob Graziano as president. Derrick Hall, the former Vero Dodger intern, also returned as vice president of communications. He had left the team in January to work in TV and radio.[27]

Meanwhile, Kevin Malone ridded the team of Raul Mondesi's temperament problems. He sent Mondesi to Toronto in exchange for Shawn Green. Both were hard-hitting, strong-armed right fielders. But Green had certain advantages. He was a local boy from Southern California with a genteel demeanor. Malone, however, continued his spending binge, bringing the payroll to $98 million—the third highest in the league. A good chunk of that went to Green's $84 million, six-year contract.[28]

The Vero-Dodgertown debacle did not rate as the top local story of 1999. Putting into perspective a true loss, a child's death in a school bus accident took the Dodgers off the front pages of the *Press Journal*. The bus ran a stop sign and crashed into a citrus truck. The accident killed a third grader and the truck driver and injured fifteen children.[29]

In a decade in which the Dodgers were unable to win a championship for the first time since the 1930s, were saddled with ineffective corporate management, and were unable to resolve the Dodgertown situation, could baseball in Vero Beach be any worse than this?

Two Thousand and Beyond

We Don't Like 'Em Much Anymore

2000

Where Have Those Kind of Guys Gone?

To be a Dodger fan had to have been difficult in 1999—the team falling into last place for a while and then finishing twenty-three games back in the division race. One didn't know whether to be glad when the Dodgers won or when they lost. They deserved to lose. After all, Fox ran the team with a fire-them-all mentality. Fox removed Charlie Blaney, Fred Claire, and Billy Russell in '98 and then Bob Graziano in '99. With a disastrous season and their corporate mentality, Fox executives had to act. They couldn't fire general manager Kevin Malone or manager Davey Johnson. It would look as if they didn't know what they were doing.

And then Bob Daly came aboard as chief executive officer. He thumbed his nose at Fox and hired Graziano back as president. This move represented the most decent, encouraging thing to happen to the Dodgers during the Fox reign.

At Holman Stadium, during the spring, Bob Daly sat behind the Dodger bench in Peter O'Malley's seat. He hardly knew the team, but he was in charge, so there was hope. Sometimes, general manager Kevin Malone sat in the Dodger section with his family and kept score. The previous spring he announced that the Dodgers would be playing in the World Series. This spring, Malone remained quiet.

On the Dodger bench there wasn't much family. The players didn't talk to each other. They acted like multi-million-dollar robots, as if their jobs burdened them. Manager Davey Johnson seemed amiable, but he perched quietly in his folding chair much as Billy Russell did before being fired. Bob Daly brought back Orel Hershiser, who was certainly no robot. He smiled and chatted with his teammates. His personality contributed more than even his excellent spring pitching. Hershiser said, "I'm paying back a debt. Everything I know came from this organization. The knowledge this place gave me, I want to give it back."[1]

Tommy Lasorda would never manage a team of robots. He would make those guys talk, act like a team, and have fun. But where was Tommy? He sat in the Dodger section too, signing autographs between innings. He still wore his uniform, but no more did the public address system play "Hail to the Chief" when he arrived in his golf cart.

Baseball is hard to kill. That spring Holman Stadium still generated some wonderful memories. On a Sunday visit by the Cardinals and home-run king Mark McGwire, Orel Hershiser speared a wicked line drive off McGwire's bat. Rookie Matt Herges struck out McGwire on three pitches. And McGwire, despite his rock-star-type fame, took time to sign autographs along the right field stands as he left the game.

But the big question remained: Would the Dodgers leave Vero? A lot of people hoped not. The tradition was too grand. And with Bob Daly, the decision resided in better hands than with Fox. But where were the Reeses, Robinsons, Sniders, Campanellas or even the Bakers, Garveys, or Hershisers? Would those kind of guys ever return to Holman Stadium?[2]

On one of the rare occasions when a Dodger player misbehaved locally, the *Press Journal* announced in a Sunday morning headline that the Vero Beach police, the night before, had found pitcher Carlos Perez snoozing in his maroon BMW at a stop light on Beachland Boulevard. Carlos had pitched poorly against the Cardinals that day.[3] When asked by the police if he had been drinking, he said, "Not many, a couple at the Riverside Cafe." Carlos spent eight hours in jail, paid a $500 fine, and received the opportunity to chat with Chairman Daly and General Manager Malone the next day. On that same Saturday night, police charged a minor leaguer with disorderly intoxication at Bombay Louie's in downtown Vero.[4]

Can't Wait to Get the Hell Out of Florida

Meanwhile, with the Fort McDowell threat disappearing, the City of Las Vegas began to court the Dodgers seriously. With the pressure on, the Florida legislature passed a different bill from the one Governor Bush vetoed the year before. This $75 million, thirty-year funding would help local governments retain major league teams by upgrading or expanding publicly owned facilities. This time, because it did not apply to just Vero Beach, Governor Bush signed the bill. The local county and city could now request $500,000 a year to service a bond issue.[5]

Las Vegas struck back. A rumor circulated that the Nevada city would offer the Dodgers a $5 million bonus to come there. Las Vegas mayor Oscar Goodman denied the rumor but said the Dodgers had received a rough outline of a deal. He planned to bring six major league teams to this gambling mecca with the Dodgers being the prime draw.[6] Don Logan, president of the Las Vegas Triple A minor league team, promoted the plan. He said that the teams he talked with "can't wait to get the hell out of Florida." With regard to the Dodgers, Logan said, "Vegas is a suburb of L.A., basically."[7]

Bob Graziano, the reinstated Dodger president, visited Las Vegas and inspected potential sites. He said, "Our reaction is that it's real. . . . But we are not intent on leaving Vero Beach. We just have to compare the alternatives."[8]

Indian River County administrator Jim Chandler stated that the Las Vegas bonus offer would have no impact on the county's position. He reiterated that the county had "no intention of getting into a bidding war."[9]

On July 27, the Indian River County Commission and the Vero Beach City Council approved a memo of understanding, prepared by Jim Chandler, establishing a $19 million offer. It included $10 million for the property, $7 million for facility improvements, and a $2 million capital reserve. The money came from three sources: a $10.5 million bond issue, serviced by an additional one-cent tourist tax and an available half-cent sales tax from a paid-off bond; a $7.1 million bond issue serviced by the $500,000-a-year state grant legislation; and the $1.4 million City of Vero Beach reserve fund.[10]

The Dodgers would lease the facility for one dollar per year but would continue to operate and maintain it. The lease covered twenty years plus a twenty-year extension. If the Dodgers terminated the agreement, they would have to pay off the bonds. The thirty-year cost of the package totaled $38 million, including insurance and interest.[11]

Despite the Keep Our Dodgers Committee's trying to put the facts out, a misconception persisted in the community that property taxes would be increased to finance the Dodgertown purchase. People began to demand a referendum. But with the use of the sales tax, the tourist tax, the state grant, and the city's reserve, no legal requirement for a referendum existed. This was not like a school bond issue that increased property taxes and thus required taxpayer approval.

In a collateral arrangement, West Palm Beach developer George de Guardiola proposed buying the nine-hole Dodgertown Golf Course from the Dodgers for $3.7 million. He would build a $22 million mini-town on the sixty-two acre site to include a 120-room hotel, a conference center, 250 rental apartments, and retail facilities. With this deal, property taxes paid by de Guardiola would more than offset the taxes the Dodgers had paid.[12]

With the Indian River County–Vero Beach offer established, Craig Callan was asked if this meant that the Dodgers had lost interest in moving to Las Vegas. He replied, "I believe it does, yes."[13]

Las Vegas gave up on getting the Dodgers for spring training, but they did succeed in getting Albuquerque, the Dodgers' number-one farm team, to move there. The team had played in Albuquerque since 1972, and their lease expired at the end of the 2000 season.[14]

Representing the County Well

Several years later in an interview, Craig Callan talked about the buyout. He sat in his office in the new administration building with a view overlooking the manicured outfield and the Holman Stadium stands. The Dodgers had used a portion of the $7 million facility fund from the buyout to construct the building.

Craig said that he had served as a member of the Dodger-Fox team investigating spring training opportunities. Craig knew how spring training worked and what the needs were. He served as the prime Dodger contact with Indian River County and the City of Vero Beach.

Referring to his activities on behalf of Vero, he said, "I was in a situation where personally I would like to keep the Dodgers in Vero Beach. I have been here twenty something years, but I am a loyal employee. I did what a good employee should do. I pursued the opportunity, hoping the county, the city, and the state would find someway to fund us." Governor Bush's veto of the first bill to help Vero concerned him. "It gave the indication that they were not interested in keeping us," Craig said.

Craig talked about the Dodger requirement for new facilities and when that issue came up in the buyout discussions. Nothing appeared in the *Press Journal* until the city and the county approved the "Memo of Understanding" in July 2000, a year and a half after local negotiations began. Craig said, "It was right there from the beginning. Dodgertown was an older facility. It needed to be on a par with its counterparts in Jupiter (the Cardinals' camp) and Viera (the Marlins' camp)." Craig negotiated directly with county administrator Jim Chandler and assistant administrator Joe Baird. They then put together the "Memo of Understanding" and took it to the county commission for approval. "Jim Chandler did a great job," Craig said. "He was tough. He represented the county very well, he and Joe Baird both."[15]

County commissioner Art Neuberger, supporting the buyout, said, "You may disagree with the decision now but look at the deal twenty years from now." Commissioner Ruth Stanbridge concurred, saying later, "I didn't care whether the Dodgers left or not, but it was important to have that property."[16] Caroline Ginn, the lone dissenter on the commission, expressed concern about "helping a very wealthy organization" while not helping "the small businessmen in our community."[17]

City councilman Craig Fletcher cast the only opposing vote, worrying that the city would have zoning problems with de Guardiola's mini-town proposal. His specific concern did not materialize, but his concern about de Guardiola would prove correct.

While tourism leaders applauded the deal, plenty of opposition surfaced. Local attorney B. J. McClure dismissed the idea that the economy would suffer negative impact if the Dodgers left. "After all Piper Aircraft went bankrupt in the early '90s. And did the economy fold? No," he said. That statement brought a response from a member of the overflow crowd in the commission chambers who asked, "Where were you?"[18]

Businessman and longtime activist Frank Zorc said, "The very idea of a community [providing] financial support for a private sports business is an abomination. We could set a national precedent by just saying, No."[19]

There was dissent of another kind—from the residents of Safari Pines Estates, the manufactured home development created by Walter O'Malley and Dodgertown director Dick Bird in the 1970s as part of the Dodger Pines Country Club. These 340 acres were not part of the deal between the Dodgers and the county and city. The Dodgers were seeking a buyer independent of the other arrangements. The residents owned their units but leased their property from the Dodgers. When the property sold, they might have to leave. Resident Jenny Book, who had lived there for twenty-one years and didn't want to live anywhere else, said, "A lot of people worry about this."[20]

In September, the county and the city approved the legal documents defining the Memo of Understanding prepared in July. They now faced an October 1 application deadline for the $500,000-per-year state funds.

Frank Zorc, who had complained earlier about the Memo of Understanding, became a candidate for the county commission. He objected to the way local officials handled the document review, leaving no time for discussion and no time to put the issue to a referendum in the November election. He threatened to organize a court injunction to stop further action. He initiated a petition to force a vote for a city charter amendment "to prevent the city from offering financial assistance to a professional sports organization without voter approval."[21]

With a county commission election, Indian River County took another step toward acceptance of buying out Dodgertown. Incumbent commissioner Ken Macht, who supported the purchase of Dodgertown, edged Frank Zorc, who opposed the purchase, by ninety votes out of sixteen thousand cast.[22] Was this election the referendum that hadn't taken place? Despite the narrow margin, Macht declared he would not change his position on the Dodgers. Zorc said he planned to continue working on a petition to secure a real referendum. "I think I have credibility with getting close to a split vote," he said.[23]

With the county and the city now waiting for the state funds, the deal with the Dodgers seemed set. The *Press Journal*'s special edition "Discover Paradise," exclaimed, despite "some uncertainties," the virtues of Dodgertown. It mentioned the fans from Brooklyn and California who had retired in Vero because of the team. The St. Helen's Catholic Church held it annual harvest festival at Holman Stadium. Dodgertown was a large source of employment for the community. And besides just the Dodgers, there was also the local Class A farm team; Dodgers Adult Baseball Camps; the sports and conference center; the Dodgertown Golf Course; Dodger Pines Country Club; seventy acres of citrus groves; and Safari Pines Estates, a residential community.[24] In the future, though, there would be changes in this list.

Fire the Manager

On September 29, the Dodgers fired manager Davey Johnson. CEO Bob Daly expected more from a team with a $98 million payroll that barely played .500 ball and finished eleven games out of contention.[25] The *Los Angeles Times* seemed amazed that the Dodgers hadn't fired Kevin Malone. He survived despite what the paper called his "record of roster malfunctions and poor judgment." Now Malone and Graziano, after fumbling their way through the selection of Johnson in 1998, had to do it again.

After a three-week evaluation, the Dodgers chose within the organization, selecting bench coach Jim Tracy. He became the fifth Dodger manager in five years, a dramatic departure from the Alston and Lasorda tenures. Bob Daly liked Tracy's low-key approach. Tracy could get along with Kevin Malone, which seemed to be a consideration.[26] Before coming to the Dodgers, Jim Tracy, age forty-four, had served as a coach for the Expos. Tracy played two years for the Cubs and a year in Japan before becoming a minor league manager. He was certainly not a Tommy Lasorda, but with quiet strength he more readily fit the Walter Alston mold—a small-town Ohioan and "unflappable."[27] In his introduction news conference, Jim Tracy talked about "reestablishing pride" and that "there are times when it's all about 'us' and not about 'me.'"[28]

2001

Dodgertown and the Louisiana Purchase

The year began with the State of Florida formally announcing a grant of $15 million over thirty years to Indian River County to keep the Dodgers. Four other Florida communities having long-term arrangements with major league teams also received grants.[29] Indian River County would issue bonds in the spring so that the Dodgers could commence their facility improvement program. Defeated commissioner candidate Frank Zorc continued to grouse that the state had ignored thousands of petitions demanding a referendum: "The only reason a referendum has been denied is they [the county and city administrations] knew it would fail."[30]

The *Press Journal* editorialized that the county commissioners had made "unnecessary concessions" to keep the Dodgers (the $7 million for facility improvements), had approved the deal "before the public understood its financial implications," and had refused "to ask the voters permission to use local tax money for the Dodgers' benefit." Furthermore, the provisions were "decided in secret and sprung on the public." On the other hand, the editorial compared the Dodgertown deal with the Louisiana Purchase where Thomas Jefferson made a decision without much input—"a decision that over time, [proved] to be golden."[31]

In May, the de Guardiola development organization that was to purchase the Dodgertown Golf Course as a collateral part of the buyout asked for an extension in finalizing the arrangement. One of the partners was having legal problems. The *Press Journal* headline read: "Delay May Threaten Dodgertown Deal."[32]

Battling the Turmoil

Meanwhile, immune from what was going on between the Dodgers and Vero Beach, Southern Californians Leonard and Jeri Polmerantz come every spring to watch the Dodgers. Jeri is the fan, a member of the Dodger Booster Club in Los Angeles. The Polmerantzs had an arrangement. Leonard didn't have to go to Dodger Stadium games during the regular season if he would come with Jeri to Vero for a month. "Spring training is so special. You get so close to the players," she said.[33]

At area hotels and motels like Disney's Vero Beach Resort, the Best Western, and the smaller Sea Turtle Inn on the island, 20 to 40 percent of the guests in March were there because of the Dodgers.[34] But Dodgertown vice president Craig Callan expressed concern that the spring attendance, averaging 4,300, had not increased over the 2000 season despite popular games with the Mets and the Cardinals.[35]

Ten years earlier in 1991, Holman Stadium attendance peaked, averaging 6,500 a game. Overflow crowds of eight to nine thousand had attended games with the Mets and the Reds. Season ticket sales topped 3,500.[36] Since then, the population of Indian River County had increased 25 per cent to 113,000.[37] Yet season ticket holders, mostly representing the local fan base, had decreased to 1,900. This drop had occurred after the strike in 1994, the fouled-up "replacement" spring of 1995, O'Malley's sale of the team, Fox's management antics, the threat to move the Dodgers from Vero, and the county's controversial buyout of Dodgertown. As one local merchant said of the Dodgers, "We don't like 'em much anymore."[38]

During the spring and the season, problems and injuries plagued the team. Adrian Beltre developed complications from an appendectomy. Gary Sheffield continued to cause trouble, demanding to be traded because the Dodgers wouldn't give him a long-term contract. Two weeks into the regular season, general manager Kevin Malone departed. He got into a shouting match with a Padre fan at a game in San Diego, which almost led to a fight. In his two-plus years as general manager, Malone made too many missteps. Bob Daly's tolerance came to an end, and he demanded that Malone resign.

Dave Wallace, a special assistant to Daly, stepped in as Dodger interim general manager. Wallace first came to the organization in 1981 as a pitching coach for the Vero Dodgers. In May, Dan Evans, a former assistant general manager for the White Sox, joined the Dodgers as an advisor to Wallace. At the end of the season, Daly made Dan Evans the general manager with Wallace overseeing minor league operations.[39]

Jim Tracy, the little-known, reserved former bench coach, battled the turmoil and gained the respect of the players and the press. The 2001 team won eighty-six games, the same as the previous season, and stayed in the race into September, before finishing third. The Dodgers hit two hundred home runs with Shawn Green pounding an all-time Dodger record of forty-nine.

It's Done

By August, de Guardiola apparently settled his problems, and all parties were ready to sign off on the collateral purchase of the Dodgertown Golf Course. The Vero Beach City Council and the Indian River County Commission could now formally approve the final financial arrangements to buy Dodgertown. Frank Zorc fought the deal to the end. He reported that out of a 1,200-person straw vote 90 per cent opposed the buyout. He talked of a lawsuit, but nothing came of it.[40]

Assistant county administrator Joe Baird, who had worked closely with county administrator Jim Chandler for almost three years to define and negotiate the arrangement said, "To put it simply, it's a real estate deal." The community bought a $19 million piece of property with a total debt service over thirty years of $29 million, a reduction from the original estimate of $38 million because of a more favorable bond rating.[41]

With this reduction, commissioner Caroline Ginn changed her previous no vote to a yes, making the approval unanimous.[42]

On August 29, assistant county administrator Joe Baird announced, "The closing has occurred. It's done." The county wired the $10 million for the property to the Los Angeles Dodgers and took over ownership of Dodgertown.[43] But was it done?

◆ 24

Fear for the Future

2002

The Original Deal Stands

Like the rest of the country, Vero Beach was trying to recover from the 9/11 attacks. The FBI and the media swarmed the community when it was suspected that some of the terrorists had received pilot training at Flight Safety, Dodgertown's neighbor. This proved untrue. But the events impacted the local tourist industry, which included companies canceling conferences at Dodgertown. On top of this, the New Year started with a shock. Craig Callan walked into a county meeting and announced that George de Guardiola had pulled out of the deal to buy the Dodgertown Golf Course and develop a mini-town on the site. With the economy deteriorating, de Guardiola had lost a partner to bankruptcy. Craig Callan was quick to say, "This doesn't affect county funds at all. [The golf course] is a Dodger property."[1]

To help de Guardiola participate in the Dodgertown closing the previous August, Craig Callan said the Dodgers had loaned the developer money temporarily to complete the golf course part of the transaction. But de Guardiola was now unable to meet the loan obligation, and the golf course had reverted back to the Dodgers. In addition, the county and the city would lose indefinitely the estimated $444,0000 in property taxes that the mini-town would have generated, which would have more than compensated for the loss in taxes previously paid by the Dodgers.

The lead on a *Press Journal* editorial read, "Dodger Disaster?" The piece went on: "there is an element of the community that doesn't trust the Dodgers. Some have suggested that the Dodgers floated the mini-town idea to lure the county into buying Dodgertown. Then, when the mini-town fell through, the Dodgers would try to get the county to buy the nine-hole course."[2] Three years later, it was the city not the county that indeed bought the golf course.

City councilman Craig Fletcher, who had been concerned about de Guardiola from the beginning and who had voted against the Dodger buyout, said, in essence, "I told you so." He wanted the buyout canceled and the city's $1.4 million returned. Other council members took a wait-and-see attitude. County administrator Jim Chandler stated that the golf course's development was not restricted to de Guardiola's mini-town and that the original deal stood.[3]

A *Business Week* article indicated that, in spending $6 million to upgrade the Dodger facilities (the $10 million to buy the property wasn't mentioned), Vero Beach's expenditure was low compared to that of other cities. Kissimmee for the Houston Astros and Clearwater for the Philadelphia Phillies were each spending $18 million. Surprise, Arizona, near Phoenix, was spending $48 million for a facility for the Kansas City Royals and the Texas Rangers, who both left Florida. Compared to the State of Florida's $75 million commitment, Arizona's Maricopa County, which includes Phoenix, had committed $200 million over thirty years to upgrade spring training facilities. Florida now had eighteen major league teams training in the state, while Arizona had twelve.[4]

Ninety-two Wins

Prior to spring training 2002, new general manager Dan Evans stayed busy. He got rid of irritable Gary Sheffield, trading him to the Braves. He brought back pitcher Hideo Nomo and recruited Japanese All-Star pitcher Kazuhisa Ishii. But the prize acquisitions were two fellows with very little major league experience: shortstop Cesar Izturis and outfielder Dave Roberts.

At Dodgertown, Roberts sparkled as a speedy leadoff man and a major league center fielder. Izturis won the shortstop position and the Mulvey Award for the best rookie in camp. Manager Tracy converted ex–Vero Dodger Eric Gagne to a closer, and the former hockey player gave up one earned run in nineteen innings during the spring. With Sheffield gone, Roberts' speed, Izturis' play at short, Gagne's pitching, and a stable management, the Dodgers enjoyed the best spring in Vero since Peter O'Malley announced he was going to sell. The only grousing came from the fans over a weekend series with the Yankees at Holman Stadium. Crowds exceeded six thousand for both games, but they saw not the major leaguers but minor leaguers disguised in Yankee uniforms.

During the 2002 season, Manager Tracy upped the win total to ninety-two, the highest for the Dodgers in ten years but only good enough for third place. Converted closer Eric Gagne saved fifty-two games, a Dodger record.

On the local level, pitcher Joel Hanrahan threw two no-hitters for the Vero Dodgers. The Florida State League chose outfielder Jason Repko and Hanrahan for the All-Star Game. Repko would make the big team in 2005.[5]

Golf is Gone

Meanwhile, developers discussed with Craig Callan the possible purchase of the 339-acre Dodger Pines Country Club. They wanted to redevelop the property into an eight hundred–home golf community.[6]

On August 4, Dodger Pines, which at one time had 270 members, closed.[7] Sixty employees lost their jobs. And the people in Safari Pines, the forty-four-home mobile park on the property, waited to be evicted, though they knew they would have two year's notice. Three Vero developers, Don Proctor, Jerry Swanson, and Earl Padgett, paid the Dodgers $8 million for the property.[8] Two years later the Vero group would resell the course to a South Florida developer for $17 million.[9]

At the same time, the Dodgertown nine-hole course sat idle. Craig Callan said three different developers were interested. Eventually, Proctor and Swanson, the Dodger Pines investors, did buy an interest and became joint owners with the Dodgers. They proposed putting the new county administration building on the property, but the county wasn't interested. The course closed on May 31, 2003.[10] While the golf aspects of Dodgertown disappeared with the closure of the two courses, baseball expanded to almost year-round activity. Extended spring training prepared new players for the later-starting rookie league. Dodgertown became the home base for the Gulf Coast League Dodger rookie team. Baseball draftees came to Vero for the June rookie camp, before assignment to the minor leagues. Top Dodger prospects now played at Dodgertown during the three-week Fall Instructional League. Dodgertown provided rehabilitation for injured players with its new facilities.[11]

2003

Dodgertown's New Look

At the Vero Community Center, vice president for spring training and minor league facilities, Craig Callan, spoke to the Indian River Historical Society about the history of Dodgertown. In the beginning there were twenty-six farm teams, and now there were only six. The players in camp once totaled six hundred. Now there were 150 minor leaguers, the forty-man major league roster, plus the twenty nonroster invitees. He mentioned the space heaters that blew the circuit breaker in the old barracks. He talked about the football teams like the New Orleans Saints that trained at Dodgertown and the foreign teams like the Tokyo Giants that came in the spring.

Craig described the joy of the Vero Dodgers as "raw talent, not lavished with large salaries." He reviewed briefly the recent changes in the Dodgers' and Dodgertown ownership, adding "We were fortunate enough to stay in Vero Beach." He described the new administrative building and how he had worked to make it as unobtrusive as possible, giving it a green roof and moving the location to save an oak tree. Craig reminisced about first coming to Vero to run the conference center and thinking he would be here for just a couple of years. "You can't drag me out," he said. "This is paradise."

During the question and answer session, a member of the audience stated that Dodgertown was no longer as fan-friendly as it used to be. Craig responded that Dodgertown is known as the most fan-friendly facility in spring training. "We are proud of that," he said. "Players are going out of their way to sign autographs. We talk about it at staff meetings." He mentioned Dodger aces Shawn Green and Paul Lo Duca readily signing autographs.[12]

Dodgertown got a new look when Callan quickly invested $5.5 million of the county's $7 million for new facilities. Beyond Holman Stadium's right field berm, where pine trees once grew and fans parked and picnicked in the shade, there now stood a thirty-thousand-square-foot, two-story clubhouse and administration building. It became the centerpiece of a campus-like complex that included covered batting cages, practice pitching mounds, and a bunting area, all enclosed by a wrought iron fence. On its ground floor, the new building housed the clubhouse, pressroom, weight-lifting room, and a therapeutic spa, all of which were

Indian River County commissioner Ken Macht, Dodgertown director Craig Callan, Dodger manager Jim Tracy, and commissioner Art Neuberger cut the ribbon at the dedication of the new administration/clubhouse building. (Courtesy of Los Angeles Dodgers, Los Angeles, California.)

described as bigger and better than the facilities at Dodger Stadium. Offices on the second floor accessed a balcony that looked out over Holman Stadium.[13]

"It's a spectacular facility," said general manager Dan Evans, "and Craig deserves all the credit because this is his baby." Callan created the concept and worked with HOK Sport, Inc., a company that designs and builds stadiums. He wanted to give the players what they needed and "didn't want to skimp on anything."[14] Tommy Lasorda arrived for his fifty-fourth spring at Dodgertown. "It's so great to see all the changes," he said. "I've always said this is the best spring-training camp site in all of baseball." He reminisced about his first arrival at Dodgertown and being so cold in the old barracks that he slept in his baseball uniform.[15]

The new building allowed all the major league operations to be consolidated in one place. Minor league operations remained in the conference center building. The major leaguers could now enter and exit Holman Stadium directly from the clubhouse. No longer would they be walking out of Holman Stadium between the practice fields to the old clubhouse in the conference center. Fans lost the opportunity to approach the players and obtain autographs, but one fan said it was still a lot better than the stadium in Port Saint Lucie where a fence totally separated the Mets from the fans.

Disturbing News

In a spring that would bring disturbing news, eighteen-year-old James Loney brought some joy to the exhibition season by playing first base for the Dodgers in the late innings. This 2002 first-round draft choice was robbed of a grand-slam home run by a great catch in a game with the Tigers. In another game he went two for two. A year earlier, this tall, young fellow had played for his high school baseball team in Missouri City, Texas. "Now," said Jim Tracy, "he's playing first base in a major league game and playing it maybe like he belongs out there." The Holman Stadium fans looked forward to watching James Loney advance in the organization and become the Dodger first baseman of the future. But Dodger first-round draft choices, like Loney, had not done well. Only five in the last twenty years, including Chris Gwynn, Darren Dreifort, and Paul Konerko, had played more than two years in the majors.[16]

A feud erupted that had its beginning at Holman Stadium in 2002. Reliever Guillermo Mota hit former Dodger star Mike Piazza in the hip with a pitch in a game with the Mets. As Mota left the field after his pitching stint, Piazza jumped him and had to be pulled away. In a spring 2003 game at Port St. Lucie, Guillermo again hit the Met catcher with a pitch. Piazza charged the mound, but was restrained by the other players. After the game, Piazza roared into the Dodger clubhouse screaming for Mota. He had been whisked backed to Dodgertown. For a joint trip to Mexico City where the Mets and the Dodgers were to play a couple of exhibition games, Mota was left behind.[17]

Another disturbing situation developed. Sandy Koufax terminated his relationship with the Dodgers. One of Rupert Murdoch's newspapers, the *New York Post*, made a fallacious statement in a gossip column that "a Hall of Fame baseball hero cooperated with a best-selling biography only because the author promised to keep it secret that he is gay."[18] The biography was *Sandy Koufax* by Jane Leavy. The *Post* apologized, but Koufax stopped appearing at Dodgertown.

In other news, the Baseball Hall of Fame's Veterans Committee chose no one to enshrine at Cooperstown. The ballot included Dodgers Maury Wills, Gil Hodges, Buzzie Bavasi, and Walter O'Malley. In particular, why hadn't Walter O'Malley ever made it? After all, other Dodger nonplayers such as Branch Rickey, Larry McPhail, Walter Alston, Leo Durocher, and Tommy Lasorda were in the Hall.[19] Columnist Bill Plaschke noted that there were five owners in the Hall of Fame but "none with O'Malley's on-field success and off-field credentials." But none had "the stigma" of having moved the Dodgers from Brooklyn. And while it "may have saved baseball," it was still hurting O'Malley's legacy fifty years later."[20]

Holman Stadium's average attendance fell to 3,400, dropping below four thousand for the first time since 1977 (the '95 replacement team season excluded). A disappointed Craig Callan put the blame on a slumping economy and the lack of any home games with the glamour teams, the Yankees and the Red Sox.[21]

But *Press Journal* editor Larry Reisman, in his weekly column, explained the declining attendance best. He talked about when he first came to Vero to join the paper in 1984 and the excitement of going to Dodger games. He shared season tickets with a coworker, which cost him about four to five dollars a game. It was tough to get good season seats. If he couldn't make the game, he dropped by the parking lot and sold his tickets at face value instantly. Then came "baseball strikes, replacement players, starters not showing up, and extreme costs ($14 tickets, $100 to take the family)," and after nineteen years he "kicked the habit." Reisman said, "As much as I love baseball, I fear for its future."[22]

Fox Gives Up

After five years of chaotic ownership, Mr. Rupert Murdoch and his Fox Group gave up and placed the Dodgers on the market with a $400 million price tag. The sale included Dodger Stadium and the unsold golf-course property in Vero Beach, but not the Los Angeles television rights. Bill Plaschke had previously written: "At least we know one person thinks the Dodgers have been a smashing success. That would be Rupert Murdoch, who finally admitted recently on national television that he bought the team only because he wanted to fuel a new sports TV network that would keep Disney from entering the market."[23]

Just at a point when the team felt some stability and pride after its ninety-two-win season, the announced sale caused concern about another round of changes, especially with regard to the futures of general manager Dan Evans and manager Jim Tracy. "No disrespect for the new owners, but we have a really great organization now," said catcher Paul Lo Duca. "You'd hope that new owners would recognize that, but I guess if someone buys the team, they have the right to do what they want."[24]

The season went on. Eric Gagne saved fifty-five games and won the Cy Young award. The Dodgers finished second but fifteen-and-a-half games behind the Giants, who went to the World Series.

The Vero Dodgers again missed the play-offs. Vero outfielder Frank Gutierrez became the Dodger organization's Minor League Player of the Year. He hit twenty homers at Vero before being promoted to Double A Jacksonville. Spring training favorite James Loney played for Vero and hit .272.

The Only Bidder

The first interest in buying the Dodgers from Fox came from Tampa Bay Buccaneers owner Malcolm Glazier. He even talked about building a football stadium at Chavez Ravine and bringing a National Football League team to Los Angeles. Of course, Peter O'Malley had entertained the same idea, but it failed. Mr. Glazier's bid for the Dodgers would fail too. The NFL had a strict cross-ownership policy, plus the rules prohibited him from using his equity in the Buccaneers to finance the Dodger buy.

Fox found other suitors unacceptable. Former owner of the Seattle Mariners Jeff Smulyan wanted television stations included in the deal. Los Angeles real estate developer Alan Casden had "legal issues."

Murdoch and Chernin wanted a fast deal. During the six years Fox operated the Dodgers, they invested $200 million on top of their $311 million purchase price as the club lost $40 million a year. These losses were driven by the high payroll that increased from $50 million under O'Malley to $117 million under Fox, a high second only to the Yankees.

In October, Boston real estate developer Frank McCourt made a bid. A Red Sox fan, he had never seen a game in Dodger Stadium. Previously, he attempted to purchase the Red Sox and then the Angels, but other bidders with more resources made better offers. McCourt's wealth came from a family construction business and his ownership of parking garages and undeveloped real estate.

In the end, McCourt became the only bidder. He offered $430 million, but despite loans from banks against his own property interests, he needed another $200 million. Fox in its eagerness for a quick sale, agreed to help McCourt by loaning him the balance. The major league owners remained skeptical of the deal. But Fox maintained leverage on Major League Baseball through its control of their TV broadcasts. Dodger fans shared the owners' skepticism, worried that McCourt didn't have the money to compete and would cut payroll. This questionable arrangement went forward, with a vote on the deal by major league owners scheduled for mid-January.

As a fallback position, billionaire Los Angeles developer and philanthropist Eli Broad offered to buy the Dodgers if the McCourt deal collapsed. And Peter O'Malley might just join him and run the Dodgers again.[25]

With approval of the buy pending and the team's funds frozen, general manager Dan Evans could do little to improve his weak-hitting team in the free agent market. He did cut the payroll by trading pitcher Kevin Brown to the Yankees.

Potential owners Frank McCourt and his wife Jamie quietly visited Dodgertown in December for a few hours. Craig Callan gave them a tour. They strolled around the place, stopping to introduce themselves to each employee they met.[26] Their next visit in the spring of 2004 would not be so quiet.

25

What's Up Next, Skip?

2004

Like a Kid's Dream

Major League Baseball, after a two-week delay, approved the Dodger sale on January 31. To alleviate some of the financial concerns about McCourt's finances, Murdoch agreed to convert $40 million of News Corp's $205 million loan to McCourt to equity, thus retaining a minority ownership in the team. McCourt would have to buy out that equity within one to two years.[1]

With the deal done and spring training three weeks away, Frank McCourt spoke at a press conference at Dodger Stadium. He felt "indescribable. . . . It was like a kid's dream. . . . We're going to sign a player that can hit. . . . I'm not afraid to spend whatever it takes to bring a world championship back to Los Angeles." He would not be an absentee owner. He and his wife Jamie, who would become Dodger vice-chairman, planned to move to Los Angeles. Despite the speculation, he would not build apartments at Chavez Ravine. He wanted to bring back "the luster on the Dodger brand."[2]

The *Press Journal* conducted a telephone interview with Frank McCourt based on his Vero visit in December. He thought Vero Beach was a beautiful community. About Dodgertown he said, "I loved the feel of the place. . . . It's a beautiful setting. I loved the history of the place. . . . I can't wait to get back down there when it's full of players and fans." To a question about keeping the team in Vero, he said, "We know we're taking on a civic treasure here, not only in Los Angeles but in Vero Beach, so we are very, very respectful of tradition, and we're going to come in and respect that tradition and build on it." In response to whether he and his wife Jamie would consider maintaining a residence in Vero Beach, he said, "We plan on being part of the community. It's a big part of Dodgers history. . . . We can't wait for spring training to start."[3]

On a Saturday in late January, the local chapter of the Society of American Baseball Research (SABR) held a meeting at Dodgertown. Attendees included Holman Stadium public address announcer Dick Crago; former American League umpire John Shulock; ninety-three-year-old Elden Auker, the last man living to strike out Babe Ruth; and former Dodger coach and Phillie manager Danny Ozark—all of Vero Beach.

After a morning session, in which various baseball topics such as steroids, Pete Rose, and umpiring were discussed, the group lunched in the conference center dining room in front of a mural of Dodger Stadium and then took a tour of the new administration building. The group walked through the large clubhouse, the coaches' dressing room, the manager's office, the kitchen facility, the workout room, and the rehab area with its tubs and a pool featuring a below-water viewing window. Upstairs the group saw the offices of Bob Graziano and Dan Evans. With new ownership, there was a question as to whether these nameplates would still be there when spring training opened. A huge photograph of a 1949 Dodgertown daily-roster blackboard covered part of the upstairs wall. It listed 620 names, including 269 pitchers, and sixty catchers. It showed Tommy Lasorda on the sick list and Danny Ozark injured.

Dodger vice president Craig Callan came out of his office to greet the group. He talked about staffing. Dodgertown had 190 employees, three hundred during spring training, which now included forty to fifty security guards for games. Soon, 220 players and coaches would be in residence, living three to six in a room in the villas. Of course, the major leaguers, with assistance from the Dodger office, rented homes and condominiums, mostly on the island.[4]

A New Breed of Baseball Exec

Frank McCourt began seeking a general manager to replace the much-maligned Dan Evans. McCourt wanted Billy Beane, but Oakland wouldn't release him.[5] Beane's disciple and assistant general manager, Paul DePodesta, became a possibility. McCourt also considered Pat Gillick, an available, experienced general manager who led the Toronto Blue Jays to World Series championships in 1992 and 1993. Even Steve Garvey made the list.[6]

The new owner chose Paul DePodesta, giving him an $800,000, five-year contract.[7] The thirty-one-year-old DePodesta was portrayed in Mi-

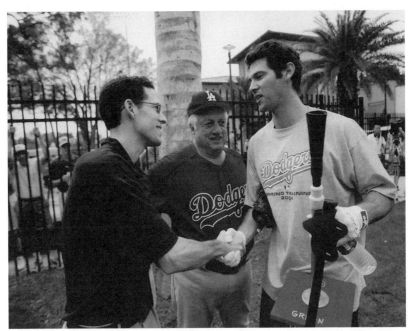

New general manager Paul DePodesta meets outfielder Shawn Green as Tommy Lasorda looks on. (Courtesy of Los Angeles Dodgers, Los Angeles, California.)

chael Lewis' best-selling *Moneyball* as the Oakland A's computer whiz kid. Following Billy Beane's philosophy, the Harvard graduate believed that on-base percentage provided the key to baseball success and that a computer analysis might be a better evaluator of a player's ability than a baseball scout's gut feeling.[8] *Business Week* described DePodesta as "personifying a new breed of baseball exec: Ivy League sharpies often younger than players for whom they're wheeling and dealing. . . . The economics grad developed statistical models to rate players—helping to find bargains, just like a value-stock investor." After graduating from Harvard, DePodesta turned down a lucrative consulting job to work as an intern in the Canadian Football League. He then joined the Cleveland Indians before going to the A's.[9]

On one of the early days of spring training, as pitchers threw off the practice mounds by the administration building, Paul DePodesta stood talking to Tommy Lasorda as they watched. DePodesta, slim in a sport shirt and khaki pants, looked more like a college student who'd dropped by to see Dodgertown during spring vacation than a general manager. Fans looked on from behind a wrought iron fence. Shawn Green, handsome, smiling, wearing shorts, carrying a bat, stopped and shook hands with DePodesta, then headed for the batting cage.[10]

A couple of days later, with the whole team in residence, Frank Mc-Court spoke to the players and staff on field #2. The press was not invited. The Dodger press release quoted McCourt: "This is a good team. . . . We're not rebuilding. My goal is to win this year." McCourt said that players on his team must "really have drive, really have courage," and have "respect and pride" for the Dodger uniform.[11]

The talk impressed team leaders Paul Lo Duca and Shawn Green. "He's passionate and he wants to win," said Lo Duca.

"I think they have a great mindset, wanting to bring back the family feel and tradition," said Green.

Later, Shawn Green practiced at first base. For the good of the team he had agreed to move there from right field on the condition that an impact hitter was added. DePodesta and Manager Tracy stood nearby. A whistle blew. DePodesta asked Tracy, "What's up next, Skip?" He followed Tracy over to field #1, where the pitchers and infielders worked together on covering first and third.[12]

Vero resident Sandy Koufax dropped by Dodgertown for the first time since one of Murdoch's papers maligned him two years earlier. He didn't work with any of the pitchers as he had in the past; he came to see Dr. Frank Jobe about a leg injury.[13]

In the second week of spring training, on Read Across America Day in honor of Dr. Seuss' birthday, a hundred Dodgertown Elementary students in red-striped Dr. Seuss hats gathered on the Holman Stadium berm where various Dodgers read to them. Players' wives and children milled about. Reliever Paul Shuey's little girl beaned a writer with a nerf baseball. Shuey had caught a twenty-pound snook in the Indian River, and a picture of him holding it appeared in the paper. He and his family were staying in a condominium at Grand Harbor.[14]

We Wish People Knew Us Better

On March 3, the Dodgers played the Mets in the spring's first exhibition game. Frank McCourt threw out the first ball. He then joined his wife Jamie, sitting directly behind the Dodger bench where Peter O'Malley once sat. They were an attractive couple—he perhaps more open and friendly; she a trim, stylish, intense-looking woman. He worked the crowd with waves and smiles. Their Boston friends filled the Dodger section, replacing what used to be the O'Malleys' L.A. social set.

Owner Frank McCourt throws out the ball for the first spring exhibition game at Holman Stadium. The administration building stands in the background beyond right field. (Courtesy of Los Angeles Dodgers, Los Angeles, California.)

The Dodgers beat the Mets with Shawn Green, as a neophyte first baseman, backhanding a sharp drive and getting two hits. Rookie James Loney, after a so-so year with Vero, replaced Green at first in the later innings and smacked three hits, including a homer. Forty-three-year-old star reliever John Franco, a 1981 Vero Dodger, made a one-inning appearance for the Mets.[15]

The ax fell on March 5. Dodger president Bob Graziano resigned with little explanation.[16] Executive vice president of business operations (which included marketing) Kris Rone quit over "philosophical differences" with the new owners.[17] Had Kris Rone been responsible for the advertisements on as many spots in Holman Stadium as possible, even the men's room? Over each urinal were Nozzle Nolan ads with "cute" sayings, such as "Its not hemorrhoids, its asteroids."[18] With Graziano's and Rone's departure Frank McCourt assumed the Dodger presidency; wife Jamie took over marketing.

In an exhibition game with the Cardinals, the new owner fielded a bouncing foul ball in the stands and gave it to a fan with a smile and a thumbs up. Everyone applauded. A woman with frizzy hair in a Cardinal sweatshirt, unable to get a picture of Lasorda, sat in section 17 across from the Dodger brass, waiting for the inning to end. She went down the aisle, camera in hand, but Lasorda was talking with manager Jim Tracy. Frank McCourt saw her plight, put an arm around her, and then called Tommy to pose. She went away smiling with pictures of both Tommy and McCourt.[19]

Communications vice president Derrick Hall was the next to depart. It was distressing that the young, ex-Vero Dodger intern, who rose so fast in the organization, would leave. Who was Frank McCourt? The friendly, smiling, relaxed man in the owner's seat or some kind of Jekyll and Hyde? Derrick had stood side by side with McCourt at his first game at Holman Stadium. And now, in less than a month, four top Dodger executives were gone. One of the remaining managerial staff remarked about "the incredible naiveté with which Frank and Jamie McCourt have infected the organization in a short time."[20]

The *Los Angeles Times'* Jason Reid conducted a telephone interview with Jamie McCourt as she and her husband were driving to Dodgertown one evening. She admitted that she and Frank were "learning on the job," but that they expected "an enormous amount of accountability." There was a need to "try and change the culture of the Dodgers." It was "crazy," she said, that the team had missed the play-offs the last seven seasons. "The team should be drawing four million fans, not three million fans, they should be making money, not losing $50 million a year. We want to be winners on and off the field . . . we're going to continue to say that over and over and over again until everybody understands how committed and dedicated we are to that."[21]

The manner in which Jamie McCourt framed her comments was not well received by the organization, the press, or other baseball executives. As a newcomer she was criticizing the establishment. The McCourts were making their mark both bad and good.[22] A story surfaced about a local citrusman having dinner with his lawyer at the Ocean Grill. The lawyer said how much he liked baseball. A round of drinks arrived. The waitress said they came from the new owner of the Dodgers, who had overheard the conversation.[23]

Writer Tony Jackson interviewed Frank and Jamie McCourt and asked them about the story. He wrote: "Vero Beach, Fla. is a small town and it doesn't take long for stories to get around." The McCourts acknowledged that they had bought the round. Jamie McCourt also told Tony, "I wish people could really understand how much we really care about this organization, how much we care about winning a championship on the field, and how much we care about the people in the organization. From that standpoint, we wish people knew us better."[24]

Into the Manager's Office

On March 15, the Dodgers beat the Mets 11–9. After the game, as they always did, the five Dodger beat writers—Steve Megargee of the *Vero Beach Press Journal*, Tony Jackson of the *Los Angeles Daily News*, Bill Plunkett of the *Orange County Register*, Bill Shaikin of the *Los Angeles Times*, and Ken Gumick of Major League Baseball's *MLB.com*—walked over to the clubhouse behind the right field berm.[25] They stood in the middle of the large room, the walls surrounded by lockers and by players in various states of undress. Four players sat at a table playing cards and opening mail. TVs hung from the ceiling, mostly displaying sports shows.

While the writers waited for the signal to go into the manager's office for the after-game interview, they talked with the players and scribbled notes on their pads. Rookie James Loney, with a locker at the far end from the regulars, talked about what he did for fun in Vero that past summer when he was with the Vero Dodgers. He said, "Go to the mall, go to the movies, the beach, but we mostly slept when we weren't playing baseball. Some girls showed us around."[26]

One of the Dodger public relations people ushered the writers through the coaches' locker room, where Tommy Lasorda and Manny Mota were dressing, and into the manager's office. Jim Tracy sat behind a desk. There were six writers, plus a fellow holding a radio mike in the manager's face, crowded into the small room. The writers leaned against the wall or sat on the floor. Jim Tracy talked about the progress of the day, "advancing men from second base"; praised his pitchers; and said that Shawn Green had "passed the test at first base . . . played flawlessly." But he also remarked that the right thing to do would be to keep Shawn in right field: "This is due to the offensive load Shawn Green has to carry with our club and the fact we need him to be 100 percent comfortable."[27] Owner McCourt had waffled on his pledge to get the Dodgers an impact hitter, saying that one more bat would not solve the team's problems.[28]

Jim Tracy had an amazing recall of every detail of every inning of the game. It was said that Walter Alston did too and that after a game he could fill out a scorebook from memory.[29] One of the L.A. writers said of Tracy, "He was steady; he rarely showed frustration."[30] And he had dealt with malcontents Gary Sheffield and Kevin Brown. Perhaps he was indeed a Walter Alston: not as physical, but with more personality.

After the daily interviews, the writers crossed the hallway from the clubhouse to the pressroom to post their stories. (The room is named for Bob Hunter, a former *Los Angeles Herald Examiner* writer and a member of the Baseball Hall of Fame.) The room was sparse despite a huge picture on the wall of Garvey, Lopes, Russell, and Cey standing together at Dodgertown. A counter ran the length of two walls with designated spots for the few newspapers covering the team. The place lacked the friendliness of the lounge-like pressroom in the old barracks where Buzzie Bavasi and Walter O'Malley, at a time when many more writers covered the team, entertained. Before the new administration building, the pressroom was at least located next to the Stadium Club bar in the conference center. No wonder the writers called this new place "the bunker."[31]

The biggest Holman Stadium crowd of the spring and the largest in twelve years—7,800 fans—saw Odalis Perez outduel Curt Schilling of the Red Sox through five innings as the Dodgers won 3–2. Catcher Paul Lo Duca said that with the crowd, "it was more like a regular-season game."[32]

One morning, Jim Tracy, without a shave and wearing a bright sport shirt, arrived with his laundry in hand at the Flamingo laundromat on Route 60 across the canal from Dodgertown. He chatted with a local artist sketching some of the people there. He said, "Doing my laundry is the only time I have peace and quiet. I can sit and read the newspapers and listen to the whir of the machines." He stayed in the villas in Dodgertown during spring training. His wife remained in California with their three sons. Two were in college, and a younger one was in high school. It was nice Vero remained small enough that a person could run into the Dodger manager in a laundromat.[33]

We Will Be Better

The Dodgers were batting .280 for the spring, fourth in the league, but Shawn Green hadn't hit a home run yet. The pitching was bad, giving up almost six earned runs per game, a major reversal from last season when the pitching led the league. The team's spring record stood at 10–15. Did it mean anything?

The Dodgers beat the Mets in the last exhibition of the spring at Holman Stadium. Before the game, Vero residents Steve Mulvey and his Aunt Chickie Mulvey Anderson presented the Mulvey Award to James Loney, the top rookie of the spring. He batted .343 in twenty games, hit one home run, and drove in seven runs. After the game in Tracy's office, one of the writers asked him, "How do you characterize this team versus last year's team?"

"We will be better," he said. "This team has a much better understanding of what needs to be done. Bullpen choices are pretty good. Other teams are aware of this. We'll get a few more hits. . . . Sure we have some concerns. Is there any club that doesn't? I'm encouraged by more good at bats. Better opportunities to score. When guys came to the plate last year, there was no one on base. Shawn Green is getting the barrel on the ball. He has his own time line." Of the pitchers, Tracy said, "Nomo, Ishii, Weaver, the last couple of times [they pitched] have been better. Perez is locked in."[34]

Despite several impressive wins at Holman Stadium, the writers weren't particularly optimistic about the team's prospects. After the Dodgers lost two games to the Angels in the Freeway Series, their spring record stood at 12–22, the first time the Dodgers had lost twenty games in a spring since moving to Los Angeles in 1958.[35]

The day before the season started, an "impact hitter" fell into the Dodgers' lap. The Cleveland Indians traded "bad boy" Milton Bradley, who had chastised his manager once too often, to the Dodgers for their best prospect, the former Vero Dodger, Frank Gutierrez. Shawn Green lived up to his commitment, made during spring training, to move to first if the team found another hitter.[36]

A Stick of Dynamite

As July ended, the Dodgers led the West Division. Dodger first-base coach John Shelby, who had played for the 1988 World Championship team, remarked that the current group reminded him of that team—"just the attitude and the way these guys have bonded together."[37]

On July 31, general manager Paul DePodesta shocked Dodger fans and the baseball world by ripping that bond apart. In four trades in two days involving the Marlins, the Diamondbacks, the Red Sox and the Braves, the Dodgers lost team leader Paul Lo Duca, regular outfielder Juan Encarnacion, reliever Guillermo Mota, base-stealing outfielder Dave Roberts, another reliever Tom Martin, plus an assortment of not particularly critical minor leaguers. The Dodgers received starting pitcher Brad Penny, first baseman Hee-Seop Choi, veteran outfielder Steve Finley, backup catcher Brent Mayne, and some prospects. DePodesta anticipated that further dealings would bring perennial Cy Young pitcher Randy Johnson plus catcher Charlie Johnson to the team, but both had no-trade clauses in their contracts and refused to join the Dodgers.[38]

Paul DePodesta explained his moves. He told his staff that he had to improve the team, in spite of how well it was playing, because with its lack of postseason experience, "it wouldn't last long in October."[39] The net result of DePodesta's handiwork was questionable. Penny developed a sore arm and couldn't pitch. Hee-Seop Choi hit so poorly that Tracy benched him. For the balance of the season, only Steve Finley's hitting provided any help.

While Paul DePodesta had made no mark on the Dodgers' minor league operations, he acknowledged the work of scouting director Logan White and former general manager Dan Evans. DePodesta was impressed with the "studs" in the Dodger minor league system. *Baseball America* had ranked the farm system 28th in 2002, 14th in 2003, and now 4th in 2004.[40] Some of those "studs" led the Vero Beach Dodgers to the best record in the Florida State League play-offs in the second half of the season and to the play-offs at the end of the season. Pitchers Jonathan Broxton and Chad Billingsly, catcher Russell Martin, and reliever Steve Schmoll would be regulars on the big team two years later.

Francis and Jeanne

While the Dodgers struggled to maintain the division lead in September, Vero Beach faced two disasters, Francis and Jeanne. Not since 1949 had Vero been hit by a powerful hurricane. Francis arrived on September 5 with hundred-mile-per-hour winds and, moving slowly, attacked the county for eighteen hours. The winds ripped up beachfront hotels, condominiums, and homes. Wind-driven rain tore through roofs and destroyed houses and businesses. Water rose in the Indian River and flooded elegant homes. Three weeks later, Jeanne, with gusts to 120 miles per hour tried to tear down the little that Francis had missed. A sea of blue tarps, covering roofs, blanketed the area.

Dodgertown director Craig Callan rode out the storms with his family and staff in the major league clubhouse in the administration building. He figured it was the safest place in Vero. When he looked out at Holman Stadium, he saw what looked like a flood. Light poles lay across the field, broken in two or bent. Wind blew the radio booth off the top of the press box and destroyed the scoreboard. An oak tree lay across the third base seats. Dodgertown damage totaled $3.5 million: all eight light towers at Holman Stadium had to be replaced, and every building in the facility except the new clubhouse needed a new roof. "You could hear it all night," Callan said, "like a train coming through. It was like watching a horror movie, and we were in the theater."[41] After the storms passed, the villas and conference center housed city officials, local emergency workers, FEMA personnel, and National Guard troops. The dining room staff fed 150 people a day. Because President Bush might fly into Vero to inspect the hurricane damage, power crews restored electricity quickly to the airport area, including Dodgertown. As it turned out, the president flew into West Palm Beach.[42]

Despite the hurricanes, growth continued in the county. Builders had started 1,600 new homes in 2004, an increase of 30 percent from the previous year. Developers bulldozed orange groves west of Vero, and the area looked like Southern California—new developments everywhere. Speculators began to tear down old homes on the island and replace them with multimillion-dollar mansions. The county's population shot through the 100,000 mark in 2000 and was now approaching 125,000.[43]

The city began a visioning process to determine how the community could remain attractive, given the rampant development. In a town-hall session, the facilitator polled the audience about the benefits of Vero Beach. The crowd mentioned the beach, the small-town atmosphere, the absence of high-rise condos, good medical facilities, cultural activities, et cetera. Finally someone mentioned Dodgertown. The fact that it came up so low on the list indicated how things had changed over the years. As Vero grew, the Dodgers had become less significant within the community, especially after the O'Malley sale. People no longer held the Dodgers in the high esteem of the past.[44]

Proud to Be a Dodger Fan

Jim Tracy managed DePodesta's reconstituted Dodger lineup to the West Division championship, the first since 1995. Steve Finley hit a bases-loaded home run in the bottom of the ninth against the Giants in the next-to-last game of the season to clinch the win.

The Dodgers lost in the play-offs to the Cardinals three games to one. The one win represented the Dodgers' first postseason victory since the

World Championship in 1988. When the Cardinals won the deciding game, Jim Tracy led his team in shaking hands and congratulating the winners, an incredible gesture for major league baseball teams. Dodger Stadium fans applauded.[45]

Dodger fans could be proud. It had been a long time.

26

The Ugly and the Lovely

2005

The Way Baseball Is Today

Spring training approached, and there was not much excitement locally. Pride in the Dodgers had unraveled in the off-season. Winter is, of course, the time when manipulations, transactions, and money overpower the game, and there is no on-the-field baseball activity to counterbalance it.

It started with a month's delay in signing Jim Tracy to a new contract. He wanted to stay with the team, but expected a salary comparable to other managers with his experience and success. He had made $550,000 a year, and it took time to reach a two-year, $750,000 a year, plus incentives, agreement. Jim Tracy finally said that the contract was something he could live with.[1] This was a man who, at least during spring training, did his own laundry.

With his manager signed, Paul DePodesta came up with a new team, his second in less than a year. Add the trades of the past summer and the off-season activity, and shortstop Cesar Izturis ended up the only full-time position player left from the previous spring. Lost, released, or traded over the winter were Adrian Beltre, Shawn Green, Steve Finley, Alex Cora, and Jose Lima—all major contributors to winning the division championship. DePodesta signed free agent second baseman Jeff Kent, a potential Hall of Famer; outfielder J. D. Drew, who came off a good year with Atlanta but was prone to injury; and Red Sox World Series hero, pitcher Derek Lowe, among others. With four years as a Dodger, Eric Gagne became the senior member of the team.

A phone call might have kept free agent Adrian Beltre, who, it was reported, wanted to stay with the Dodgers. With DePodesta handing out

$144 million in contracts for new players, a slightly higher offer for Beltre should not have been a problem. The *New York Times* wrote that Beltre's loss was "part of a weird off season for the Dodgers who undertook a major roster shuffle despite having won their first division championship in nine years." The article quoted Jim Tracy as saying of Beltre: "After a hell of a lot of work over the last six years [to develop Beltre] it's tough to lose him; that's the way baseball is today."[2]

Commenting on yet another shake-up, Frank McCourt said, "I'm 100 percent confident we're heading in the right direction. We're doing this with thought, compassion, great consideration, and a passion to win." He went on to point out, "I want the nice guys, but I also want to win. Let's not forget this team hadn't won a play-off game in sixteen years until last October."[3]

ESPN, the sports TV channel, conducted a survey of the top sport franchises. The Los Angeles Angels finished fifth; the Dodgers ranked eighty-second. This was a change. From the late 1970s through the mid-1990s, the Topps baseball card company had consistently selected the Dodgers under Peter O'Malley as the Organization of the Year. *Fortune* magazine had listed the Dodgers as one of the best companies to work for in the nation.[4] And, of course, *Baseball America* consistently chose Dodgertown as the best spring training site in the major leagues.

While Dodger fans worried about lack of stability, the citizens of Vero Beach suffered a similar fate. A new city manager did an excellent job of getting Vero Beach operating again after the hurricanes but was a bit loose with the city budget. City officials and their families stayed at Dodgertown, enjoying air conditioning and meals at city expense, while their constituents lived in damaged homes, eating peanut-butter sandwiches by candlelight. A divided council forced the city manager's resignation as the community looked on in amazement.[5]

The city council *did* agree on one subject and made an interesting move. They approved a city purchase of the Dodgertown Golf Course property for $10 million from a Dodger joint venture that now included two of the original Dodger Pines investors. The city hoped to finance half the purchase with a state grant.[6] The city was not sure what it would do with the property other than make it a park or leave it as green space. The concept of a mini-town and the additional county taxes that had been part of the original Dodger buyout package was a thing of the past. This sale aroused little local concern except in a *Press Journal* editorial that referred to the buy as "Dumb Dodger Deal II." The author contended that had the city bought the course in 2001, it would have paid far less than the current price. "Dumb Dodger Deal I," the original Dodgertown complex buyout, had turned out well in the writer's view, "as skyrocketing property values have given the county a huge return."[7]

A Beautiful Day in Paradise

No one would know this new team of Paul DePodesta's when it showed up at Dodgertown. It was like 1990, the year Fred Claire turned over the roster, and the only returning position player was Mike Scioscia.

To compound the problem, the names of the Dodger players were no longer on the backs of their uniforms. This might have been all right in the '50s, the '60s, the '70s, and even into the '80s when the Dodger roster was stable and faces were recognizable, but not anymore. Why had the names been taken off the uniforms? There were several answers, none particularly satisfactory. It's not about the individual; it's about team unity. It's about tradition: Dodger players never used to have names on their uniforms, that is, not until thirty-five years ago. And the Yankees and Red Sox don't do it. But those teams had some recognizable players. The Dodgers no longer did. One of the writers said McCourt liked the "Red Sox Nation" and now wanted a "Dodger Nation."

During a game with the Mets, Number 7 for the Dodgers stepped to the plate. Who was he? The roster said J. D. Drew. The name, if not the face, was recognizable. As a hitter, he was supposed to replace Adrian Beltre. Dick Crago announced "J. D. Drew" over the public address system. The crowd gave him a ripple of applause. With a half swing, he blooped a high pitch over the right field fence onto the berm for a home run. The crowd applauded more loudly.[8]

In a game the next day, Drew and the Dodgers' other new star, Jeff Kent, hit consecutive singles. They batted third and fourth, but they didn't seem to acknowledge each other. Drew kept to himself.[9]

Jeff Kent talked through the fence to the fans. Kent encouraged outfielder Milton Bradley, a holdover from last year, to address the team in the clubhouse, pull the group together, and talk about goals.[10] Maybe Kent, who had hit the most home runs ever for a second baseman, would become the new Dodger fan favorite. All the previous favorites were gone.

During the game, Paul DePodesta stood in the back row of the press box, leaning against the wall, eating a piece of pizza, as he viewed all his new players. He looked younger than the Vero Dodger interns who scurried around doing odd jobs.[11]

On a one-day visit to Dodgertown early in the spring, Frank McCourt sat in his office overlooking Holman Stadium and talked with a *Los Angeles Times* writer. He said he wanted to communicate better with the fans. "The first year, I had lots to learn. I had to do a lot of listening. This time here, it feels like I'm coming home." Earlier he spoke to the team at the first full-squad practice, outlining the goals for the season. He talked about the fiftieth anniversary of the 1955 World Series win as an inspiration. "We are stewards of a beloved franchise and a civic treasure," he told the team.[12]

In another change, Emily Christie became the new general manager of the Vero Dodgers. One of her many spring duties included managing the press box during exhibition games. The twenty-eight-year-old Princeton graduate had started as a Vero Dodger intern the previous year and now had replaced the popular Trevor Gooby, who took a position with the Pittsburg Pirate organization. She told the *Los Angeles Times*, "Baseball is a boys' club, to an extent. But in the Dodger organization there are women in very prominent positions so it seems normal to me."[13] To support her point, she referred to Jamie McCourt, now the Dodger president, and to assistant general manager Kim Ng. The Dodger minor league assistant director, the chief financial officer, and the assistant legal counsel were also women.

On a day when the big team played away, Dodgertown was quiet. A security guard named Frank stood by the bridge joining Holman Stadium and the practice fields. The security guards wore yellow shirts and generally were retirees, working at Dodgertown mostly for the fun of it. Frank lived in Rhode Island but spent the winter in Vero. "Been coming down for eighteen years," he said. He remembered walking home from junior high and stopping to watch the Dodgers in the World Series on a storefront TV. Another fellow in a yellow shirt called out, "Another beautiful day in paradise."[14] Dodger historian Mark Langill, handling public relations during spring training, agreed with this assessment, noting that *New York Post* writer Kevin Kiernan in a recent article stated, "Dodgertown is the most beautiful place on earth."[15]

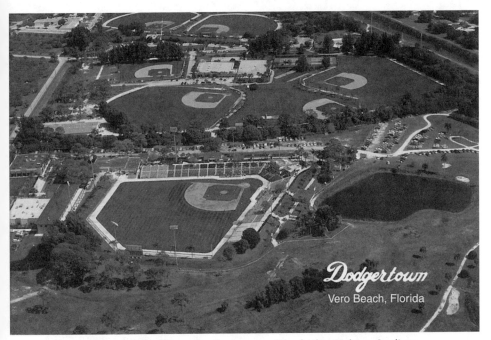

Dodgertown
Vero Beach, Florida

A Dodgertown postcard illustrates the beauty of the facility. Holman Stadium occupies the foreground, with the new administration building to its left. Beyond them, fields #1 and #2, the conference center and villas, and the minor league fields (top) are visible. (Courtesy of Los Angeles Dodgers, Vero Beach, Florida.)

The World Champions Come to Town

The World Series champion Boston Red Sox came to Holman Stadium, bringing an atmosphere of excitement. During batting practice, World Series hero David Ortiz hit ball after ball out to the berm. Red Sox fans already filled the stands and cheered him on. He threw his arms up in the air with joy as he finished batting.

Former baseball commissioner Fay Vincent, who wintered in Vero, sat in a golf cart down the right field line watching the pregame practice. He was known as the "last commissioner" after the owners replaced him with the ineffectual Bud Selig. According to the press, Selig objected to his predecessor being on a major league field, though he was there as a guest of the Dodgers.[16] Fay Vincent had attended the January SABR (Society of American Baseball Research) meeting at Dodgertown. He had said then, "The business of baseball is ugly; the game of baseball is lovely."[17]

In the Dodger section, Jamie and Frank McCourt sat in the traditional owner's spot. Jamie McCourt wore an orange hat with a yellow flower, which she soon took off and hung on the fence behind the players' bench. On that cloudy day, she didn't need a sun hat. The McCourts' Boston friends filled the Dodger section and behaved nicely, not cheering conspicuously for their hometown team.[18]

Unlike the Rickeys, the O'Malleys, and even Bob Daly, the McCourts spent little time in Vero. One of the Dodger beat writers said they had been too busy working to establish long-term bank financing to pay off Fox and strengthen the shaky position under which they had bought the Dodgers.[19]

During the game, Dodger base-stealing and bunting coach Maury Wills sat down in a vacant seat in section 17. He talked about golf. Maury liked to play the local courses at Sand Ridge and Bent Pine. He talked about when he first came to Dodgertown in 1951 and about Vin Scully, Tommy Lasorda, and Billy DeLury, all of whom had been at Dodgertown for over fifty years.[20]

Before 8,135 mostly Red Sox fans and the sixth biggest crowd in Holman Stadium history, the World Champs beat the Dodgers 7–3.[21] The *Press Journal* in a "Thumbs Down" editorial criticized the Red Sox for bringing only three players—David Ortiz, Trot Nixon, and Bronson Arroya—the fans might remember from the World Series. "Paying the high ticket price," the editorial asked, "how much longer will crowds come to see the second, third or fourth string?"[22]

Two season tickets for the sixteen-game spring season cost $480. Compared with the eight-dollar tickets of the early '90s, single game tickets now cost $18, $16 on weekdays.[23] Local resident Chet Hogan, who has been a season-ticket holder since the 1970s, told the *Press Journal*: "There aren't a lot of young faces in the stands. That's got to be cost-related."[24] The Dodgers *did* offer $8 sit-on-the-berm tickets on weekends, for night games, and when reserved seats sold out. In Los Angeles, tickets ranged from $75 in the new Dugout Club area to $6 a seat in the top deck and the center field pavilion. But at Dodger Stadium a person saw the regulars in competitive, major league games.

Entitled Brats

The spring games weren't as much fun to watch as they used to be when the players were more friendly and acted less like prima donnas. A couple of local fellows ran into some of the young-guns on the Dodger pitching staff drinking at the Riverside Cafe. They sat down and talked with them for an hour or so. When asked what kind of guys they were, one of the locals answered, "They acted like punks." An individual close to the team said that these players, with all their money and acclamation, had never grown up: "There isn't a guy on this team I would want to go out and have a beer with."[25] Columnist Bill Plaschke expressed similar sentiments in a column he wrote shortly after spring training: "It is the game we love. It is not the players. Not anymore." They act like "entitled brats . . . coddled from childhood to stardom."[26]

Billy DeLury, who for many years served as the team's traveling secretary, talked about how the players had changed. Billy loved the old barracks and the "huge, huge lobby where everyone would congregate, seven guys here, ten guys there." He said, "You don't see that today. These guys go to their room and watch TV."[27] At the SABR meeting at Dodgertown, former Dodger coach Danny Ozark, talking about how important team chemistry is, mentioned how the team on road trips used to ride together on a bus to the games. Now, he said, the players each take a cab.[28]

The minor leaguers were more fun and more approachable than players who had reached the major league level. Such were Florida State League All-Stars, catcher Russell Martin and second baseman Delwyn Young, who together led the 2004 Vero team to the play-offs and made the major league, forty-man spring roster. Some of the other rookies, who played in the middle and late innings of the spring games, would see an unusual amount of major league action in the coming season. This young group represented a change from previous springs, when the spring roster tended to be filled with older players, past their peak, instead of upcoming prospects.

Jason Repko received the Mulvey Award for best rookie in camp. In a game with the Devil Rays, he made a leaping catch to save a home run from going over the center field fence. In another game, from right field, he threw out a runner going into third. These plays represented the "lovely" aspects of the game. Repko hit .350 for the spring. Because of the big team's injuries and poor performance, Repko would spend the 2005 season in Los Angeles, joined by many of his rookie compatriots.[29]

Wanting an Unselfish Foundation in Place

After the last game of the spring, the writers moved into Jim Tracy's office. Despite a loss that afternoon, the manager was pleased with the team's execution. "The relievers did a terrific job. Repko's throw was fantastic."

Tracy talked about this year's Dodgers: "Each team has its own identity. This is a quieter group. Personalities change. We have a number of new people. It's good to see what's happening the last four or five days. There are two types of teams: On one the guys go out and play 162 games. On the other, the guys play for a championship." He talked about how to play championship baseball and referred to a bunt in a game the previous night. The word "execution" came up again. He wanted an "unselfish foundation in place." He wanted his players to feel comfortable. "The new faces are wondering what we are really about." Jim Tracy concluded by saying, "This is the 2005 version of the Dodgers."[30]

The Dodgers ended the spring with the lowest per-game attendance of any team in the area, despite having the biggest single crowd for the Red Sox game. This included the Cardinals and Marlins at Jupiter, the Mets at Port Saint Lucie, and the Washington Nationals (ex-Expos) at Viera near Melbourne. The Cardinals led the group with an average attendance of 6,324. The Dodgers averaged 4,195, down slightly from the previous spring.[31]

A county commissioner in Sarasota said, "We have matured economically, and I don't think spring training carries the charisma or financial clout that maybe it did twenty years ago."[32] This statement applied to Vero Beach as well. Some people attributed dwindling public interest to there being too much competition from the other nearby teams. And then, the Dodgers hadn't been a winner. But the real problem was the O'Malley sale. Since then, chaos had reigned. The McCourts were nonresident owners, as far as Vero went, and had not yet brought stability to the organization.

Going from Disappointment to Embarrassment

The Dodgers had an awful 2005 season. Injuries limited the playing time of both position players and pitchers. Second baseman Jeff Kent was the only steady player, hitting twenty-nine home runs and batting in 105 runs. Twenty first-year players, most of whom weren't ready for the major leagues, had to be used to get through the season.[33] The team for which Paul DePodesta had committed all those millions for free agents ended the season in fourth place with a 71–91 record.

Making matters worse, Jeff Kent and Milton Bradley had a clubhouse altercation over Bradley's lack of hustle. Owner Frank McCourt had to go into the clubhouse and talk to the team, attempting to defuse the impact of the feud. Afterwards, Frank McCourt described his reaction to the Kent-Bradley affair as going "from disappointment to embarrassment." He said, "No question, the biggest lesson I've learned so far is the importance of character in building a winning baseball team."[34]

Celebrating Young Talent and the 1955 World Series

While the big team collapsed in 2005, two Dodger minor league teams had great seasons. *Baseball America* tagged Class AA Jacksonville as the "Most Talented Team" in Minor League Baseball. Led by manager John Shoemaker and by players like pitchers Chad Billingsly and Jonathan Broxton, their battery mate Russell Martin, and first baseman James Loney—names Los Angeles fans would know the next season—the team won the Southern League Championship with a 79–61 record. Almost matching those numbers, the Vero Beach Dodgers had the best won-lost record in the Florida State League. Third baseman Andy LaRoche hit .333 and had twenty-one homers before moving up to Jacksonville where he hit another nine home runs. Second baseman Tony Abreu also advanced to Jacksonville after winning the Florida State League batting title with a .327 average. Outfielder Matt Kemp hit twenty-seven home runs, a Vero Dodger record.[35]

The Vero Beach Dodgers inaugurated a Hall of Fame in a ceremony on the team's twenty-fifth anniversary in Vero. A committee selected three initial members: all-time winning minor league manager Stan Wasiak; inaugural-year pitcher Butch Wickensheimer; and Rob Slezak, who had a 24–14 career record with the team and who was currently director of the City of Vero Beach's Recreation Department. Butch Wickensheimer had last seen Vero Beach in 1982. Among changes, he noted the Wal-Mart, a mall, the outfield fence at Holman Stadium, and new buildings at Dodgertown. He said, "It's special. This place treats you different from other places. The people are the same and they still treat the players here like they're their kids."[36]

Press Journal sportswriter Steve Megargee, who covered both the Vero Beach Dodgers and the big team during spring training, selected an all-time Vero team. He chose players by position who had performed the best in the major leagues: catcher Mike Piazza; infielders Sid Bream, Steve Sax, Mariano Duncan, and Adrian Beltre; outfielders Karim Garcia,

R. J. Reynolds, and Henry Rodriguez; starting pitchers Sid Fernandez, Ramon Martinez, and Juan Guzman; and relievers John Franco and Eric Gagne.[37]

There was also a celebration in Dodger Stadium—the fiftieth anniversary of the 1955 Brooklyn Dodgers' World Series championship. The thirteen living players from that time attended: Bob Borkowski, Roger Craig, Carl Erskine, Sandy Koufax, Clem Labine, Tommy Lasorda, Billy Loes, Don Newcombe, Johnny Podres, Ed Roebuck, George Shuba, Duke Snider, and Don Zimmer. Owner Frank McCourt, revisiting his own recent lesson on the team value of character, said, "It's important to celebrate not just winning, but a type of winning we can respect. . . . They had that thing called character."[38]

Without a Manager, Without a General Manager

Near season's end, Manager Tracy, with one year left on his contract, requested a contract extension through 2008 so he could rebuild the team and have some security. For the first time he openly stated that, in effect, he and DePodesta had difficulties when it came to roster changes. He said, "If there is any disappointment from my end, it's that several of those components from a year ago were not in the clubhouse at spring training at Vero Beach."[39] He was referring to Adrian Beltre, Shawn Green, Alex Cora, and Steve Findley, plus those players DePodesta traded away at midseason in 2004, like Paul Lo Duca and Dave Roberts.

McCourt and DePodesta did not respond to Tracy's demand for a contract extension. One day after the season ended, Jim Tracy left the Dodgers and became manager of the Pittsburgh Pirates. Paul DePodesta described Tracy's move as "a mutual parting of the ways": "Despite how hard we tried we couldn't get on the same page." At the last home game of the season, Tracy had blamed the front office saying, "The abundance of off-season moves disrupted clubhouse chemistry."[40]

Paul DePodesta began seeking a new manager. Candidates included Dodger farm director and former major league manager Terry Collins, Las Vegas manager Jerry Royster, former Dodger pitcher and now Texas Ranger pitching coach Orel Hershiser, Davey Lopes, and assorted other candidates. It was obvious that the goal was not to hire a big-name manager (as Davey Johnson had been) who would demand a big salary. Another candidate was Bobby Valentine, currently managing in Japan and whose name always came up because he was a Tommy Lasorda favorite and a member of the old Dodger family.

In the midst of the hunt with Terry Collins as the leading choice, Frank McCourt fired Paul DePodesta. The first inkling of trouble surfaced when DePodesta was not part of a dinner where McCourt and Tommy Lasorda interviewed Orel Hershiser. Some thought DePodesta was looking for a friend in a manager—the friend that Jim Tracy was not—and that it could be Terry Collins. A Bobby Valentine or an Orel Hershiser would be a threat to DePodesta.[41]

Paul DePodesta became the eleventh Dodger executive fired in the twenty-month McCourt reign. Owner and chairman Frank McCourt and vice chairman and president Jamie McCourt faced the 2006 season without a general manager, without a manager, and with a team that had achieved the second worst record in Dodger history since 1909.[42]

27

Like Brooklyn, a Fond Memory

2006

Free to Do What Was Needed

The fifty-ninth spring for the Dodgers in Vero Beach began, and again an almost entirely new team arrived. New meant a new general manager, a new manager, new coaches, and more new players.[1] Names still didn't appear on the backs of the uniforms, so a fan's first move was to get a roster at the small concession stand between fields #1 and #2. The main action occurred on a nearby practice infield where a couple of coaches worked with the pitchers, picking runners off first base. A nondescript, gray-haired fellow in uniform leaned against the fence watching, occasionally giving instructions. He wore number nine. This was Grady Little, the new manager. On the field, bullpen coach Dan Warthen put the pitchers through their paces, as if they were little leaguers. Two faces were recognizable: pitching aces Derek Lowe and Brad Penny. Warthen had them hustling.

One new player easily could be recognized: Nomar Garciaparra. The thirty-two-year-old, two-time American League batting champ and five-time All-Star shortstop was taking ground balls at first base under the close watch of batting coach and Hall of Fame first baseman Eddie Murray. The lanky Garciaparra chatted, chuckled, and moved gracefully as he handled the ground balls. For a skeptical Dodger fan, an initial impression of the team seemed encouraging.[2]

On November 16, 2005, eighteen days after firing Paul DePodesta, Frank McCourt hired a new general manager. Ned Colletti had spent eleven years with the Giants, of all teams, as their assistant general manager. McCourt had talked with other candidates but only Colletti had been offered the job. This fifty-one-year-old general manager with

Fans, the media, and players mingle in front of the administration building at the beginning of spring training. (Photograph by author.)

a mustache and bushy hair was far from a young, new-image baseball executive, but he had had extensive experience putting Giant teams together. As one writer put it, Colletti had "quite a mess to clean up."[3]

"It's never a good sign when you are interviewing managerial candidates and you're running from airport to airport, [and] the music is Christmas carols," said Colletti.[4] But Ned Colletti wasted no time. On December 6, he hired Grady Little as manager. Also in his fifties, Little, a grandfatherly North Carolinian, had managed sixteen years in the minors before taking over the Boston Red Sox in 2002 and 2003.[5] There he had been scapegoated, fired for not replacing pitcher Pedro Martinez when the Red Sox lost to the Yankees in the 2003 American League Championship Series.

By early January, Colletti had built a team. He signed shortstop Rafael Furcal, third baseman Bill Mueller, infielder Nomar Garciaparra, catcher Sandy Alomar Jr., outfielder Kenny Lofton, and pitcher Brett Tomko.

He traded the troublesome Milton Bradley to the Oakland A's for Texas League Player of the Year Andre Ethier. In other trades he acquired four pitchers.[6] Told by McCourt that he was "free to do what he thought was needed to do," he had spent $68 million on the six free agents.[7]

Character Surfaces

Grady Little managed his first Dodger game not in Holman Stadium but in Jacksonville, home of the 2005 Minor League Team of the Year. It was an intrasquad game between the former Jacksonville players and other Dodger roster players. Despite home runs by new third baseman Bill Mueller and rookie Andre Ethier, the Jacksonville crew won 8–3. Home runs by Joel Guzman, the top-rated hitter in the minors, and by Delwyn Young and good pitching led by top prospects Jonathan Broxton and Chad Billingsly gave the rookies the win.[8]

Despite the rash of recent player additions by Paul DePodesta and Ned Colletti, both the former and current general manager had resisted giving up these young players in trades. The Dodgers were now considered to have the top prospects in the major leagues. Not since the early 1970s when Steve Garvey, Davey Lopes, Bill Russell, Ron Cey, and others were ready for the big team had there been such a collection of prospects. Chad Billingsly said, "We have a chance to keep this team together for many years." The group was close, having established themselves with a bit of a "swagger" in the rookie end of the clubhouse at Dodgertown.[9]

At the other end of the clubhouse, members of the big team were talking to each other, a vast change from the situation a year earlier. Grady Little had what could be called the "old fashioned ballplayers"—like Jeff Kent, Bill Mueller, Kenny Lofton, Sandy Alomar Jr., and Nomar Garciaparra—giving talks to their teammates. Bill Plaschke described the noise in the clubhouse as "a consistent mixture of language, Spanish matching English, country talk matching city slang, crusty old voices mixing with youthful howls." Grady Little encouraged the players to go to dinner together, a rare thing among today's major leaguers. He even picked up the tab. One night the veterans gathered up the rookies and there were sixteen guys at the same table.[10]

That thing called character that Frank McCourt had recognized and spoken about the previous summer was finally surfacing. Maybe it *was* worthwhile to consider team chemistry, as Ned Colletti apparently had as he assembled the 2006 Dodgers.

Highlights of the spring included Nomar Garciaparra playing first base with spectacular ease. Young players Oscar Robles, Adam LaRoche, Matt Kemp, and Andre Ethier all homered in a rout against the Mets, a play followed by Joel Guzman's hitting a triple and a home run and by Andy LaRoche's hitting another home run in a win over the Orioles. Brett Tomko pitched five shutout innings, and Jeff Kent homered to beat the Astros. Ron Cey, still looking like the Penguin, sat in the Dodger section at a game against the Cardinals. He was a member of the Dodger Speakers Bureau. A proud bunch of Jacksonville Sun team members received Southern League Championship rings before a game. Over 8,000 fans attended what had become the annual Red Sox game at Holman Stadium, but again the crowd was mostly made up of Boston fans. Taiwanese pitcher Hong-Chih Kuo, another member of the 2005 Jacksonville Suns, received the Mulvey Award for top rookie in camp based on his .075 earned run average in ten games.[11]

During a spring in which a mature baseball operations management put together a team with a compatible mixture of veterans and young talent, the McCourts were no longer in the news. Both the ongoing personnel and financial issues that had plagued the owners for two seasons were hopefully settled. The financial structure of the $421 million purchase of the team in 2004 at long last was finalized. The McCourts handed over their twenty-four-acre Boston parking lot property to Fox to liquidate their $145 million loan with the media company. In addition, the McCourts had obtained a twenty-five-year, long-term loan secured by the three-hundred-acre Chavez Ravine property.[12] And as Jamie McCourt had stated in 2005, the team was now profitable.

Whispers in the Dodger Organization

Meanwhile, *Los Angeles Daily News* writer Tony Jackson described the state of the Dodgers' spring training site: "Dodgertown, a sacred cow of the baseball-as-poetry crowd, would seem to have everything going for it: an intimacy between players and fans unmatched in any other spring facility, a rich history dating to 1948 and a pastoral, small-town beauty that is tough to match anywhere else in Florida—much less in the barren Arizona desert some 2,500 miles away." "Yet," he said, "[Dodgertown] by 2006 standards is . . . short on modern amenities, short on creature comforts and woefully short on proximity to the fan base back home." He went on to suggest that "the Dodgers would be much more comfortable in Arizona's Cactus League." He mentioned, "whispers in the Dodger organization that such a move could be coming within the next five years"—despite the twenty-year lease that runs through 2021. Jackson described "the charming relic of a stadium [that] didn't come close to being sold out until the Red Sox nation came to town." He noted that "the bond between the Dodgers and the city clearly isn't what it used to be, whether the result of the threat to vacate or of a changing demographic in a city whose population falls just short of 18,000 and a [growing] county of about 115,000."[13]

Stability may have come to the team, but the issue of a Dodger move from Vero Beach to Arizona hit the headlines again. The cities of Glendale and Goodyear, Arizona, contacted the Dodgers. Indian River County administrator Joe Baird said that Dodger officials (probably Craig Callan) had let him know about the contacts. Goodyear had mailed out invitations to ten teams and was talking about building a ten thousand–seat stadium and a practice facility that could handle two teams. The point was made that a move to Arizona would cut down on travel expenses and improve spring attendance, as the team would be only a six-hour drive from their Los Angeles fan base.[14]

A *Press Journal* editorial reacted to the lure of Arizona by mentioning that the Dodgers would have to pay off the bond issue and other associated costs totaling $17 million (the annual salary of a top player). There would be other teams interested in Vero Beach, but it would be "profoundly sad" if the Dodgers left, the writer argued, because whatever one's "personal loyalties . . . this town bleeds Dodger blue." By contrast, teams today "just follow the money."[15]

Scripps Howard sports columnist Ray McNulty wrote that Vero Beach was "no longer a mostly seasonal, otherwise-obscure small town dominated by hard-core Dodger fans." He said that Indian River County had become more diverse with the population boom and that the franchise's Brooklyn-based following was dying off: "Losing the Dodgers would be tough, especially for longtime residents who've developed an emotional attachment to the team." Of this loss, McNulty nonetheless concluded that "as time went by the Dodgers would become nothing more than a fond memory, just as they are in Brooklyn."[16]

Goodbye Spring

After the last game of the spring the players trotted across the field to the clubhouse, happy to begin the regular season. A couple of rookies

The Dodgers play an exhibition game at Holman Stadium before a capacity crowd on a sunny, spring day. (Courtesy of Los Angeles Dodgers, Los Angeles, California.)

would fly with the team to Los Angeles to play in the majors for the first time; others, disappointed, would stay behind to join a minor league team. The regulars had left the game after the sixth inning and were already dressed and ready for the flight. The old-time season ticket holders had left then as well, leaving vacant seats among the crowd. The remaining fans moved out of the stands slowly as if sorry the afternoon was over. The press box had emptied and the writers, glad to be heading home, were in the clubhouse getting interviews. The visiting team was boarding its bus. Public address announcer Dick Crago had put away his microphone for another season.

The grounds crew came out and tidied up the field, picked up the bases, and smoothed the infield for a minor league game the next day. The sun dropped toward the outfield berm. The palm trees cast long shadows across the outfield.

If Branch Rickey and Walter O'Malley were looking down on Dodgertown they had to be proud. They had disagreed in their time, but their actions had made Dodgertown what it was. The place had changed physically over the years. The barracks were gone, facilities had been modernized, but the atmosphere remained. Memories could not be erased: Roy Campanella mentoring the young players from his wheelchair behind the old barracks; Duke Snider and Carl Erskine in their late seventies returning every year for the fantasy camp; Sandy Koufax dropping by to help the Dodger pitching staff; and Tommy Lasorda, a senior citizen, still wearing his uniform, signing autographs between innings.

Cars moved slowly, one behind the other, on Duke Snider Street, going out the Holman Stadium main entrance as local fans drove home and visitors returned to motels or headed to another training site on their nomadic spring jaunts.

Two blocks away lay the empty field used occasionally by Piper Aircraft for a parking lot. Here, on what was once called Ebbets Field #2, Jackie Robinson hit a home run into the crowd in the first game the Dodgers ever played in Vero. Beyond the field had been the old Naval Air Station control building where Bud Holman, the man who brought the Dodgers to Vero, maintained the Eastern Airlines office.

Another mile or so away, across U.S. 1 and the fairways of the Vero Beach Country Club, the Merrill Barber Bridge rose, connecting the mainland to the beach. It was named after the man who had been mayor and who, with Bud Holman, had done so much to bring the Dodgers to Vero Beach and keep them there. From the crest of the bridge to the west, the view encompassed the downtown and the airport with the protruding light towers of Holman Stadium. To the north and the south spread the glassy surface of the Indian River. To the east lay the island and the ocean. In the sweeping view, water and trees predominated over houses and buildings. Despite the years, the growth, and the changes, Dodgertown and Vero Beach still retained their charm.

The Dodgers might leave, and it would be a shame. But Vero Beach would survive and, perhaps, some other team would come.

Afterword

2007

The shock came—not from the Los Angeles Dodgers but from the Vero Beach Dodgers. At season end an announcement stated that the Vero team, after 27 years, was gone. It would move to San Bernardino in the California League where the players could be more easily overseen from Los Angeles. Gone was this wonderful institution that local fans had enjoyed as they watched future major leaguers like Steve Sax, Ramon Martinez, Mike Piazza, and Eric Gagne pass through to the big team. The Dodgers would run the franchise while a Tampa Bay Devil Rays team played at Holman Stadium temporarily before moving on in 2009 to another Florida location.[1] The Vero Beach Devil Rays—it just didn't sound right. This announcement took place as rumors escalated about a Dodger move to Arizona for spring training.

The loss of the Vero Dodgers snapped the bloom off what had been for local fans a fun season as the Los Angeles team won 17 of 18 games during a streak in August and became the Wild Card entry in the National League playoffs, before losing to the Mets. General Manager Nick Colletti, as spring training foretold, had put together a team with character and one that could win. Manager Grady Little mixed veterans Nomar Garciaparra, Jeff Kent, Rafael Furcal, Kenny Lofton, J. D. Drew, Derek Lowe, Brad Penny, and late season acquisition Greg Maddux with rookies Andre Ethier, Russell Martin, Matt Kemp, James Loney, Jonathan Broxton, and Chad Billingsley to form a cohesive team. Of the rookies all but Ethier had been Vero Dodgers.

In November the Arizona rumors became reality. The Dodgers signed a memo of agreement to move to Glendale, a 230,000-population suburb of Phoenix. The Dodgers would share a $76 million, 12,000-seat facility with the Chicago White Sox. The facility had to be built, so the Dodgers would not move until 2009. Glendale already had a NHL hockey team and a football stadium that was home to the NFL Arizona Cardinals. "It's closer to our fan base . . . and it just makes sense," Dodgertown V.P. Craig Callan told the *Press Journal*.

The Dodgers had a lease with Indian River County, which did not expire until 2021. An option allowed the Dodgers to break the lease if they paid off the remainder of the county's bond issue, estimated at $15 million. Another option gave the Dodgers the right to repurchase Dodgertown at the current market price less what they would have to pay to cover the bonds. In 2000, when this agreement was initiated, no one anticipated the real estate boom that drove up Indian River County property values. The county and the city had paid the Dodgers $10 million for the property; now its value could be as high as $25 million. The county commission had a significantly more valuable piece of property, and they didn't want the property to go to the Dodgers for possible resale as development, preferring to keep the 64 acres with the stadium as green space and recreation. The county commission voted an additional option that would let the Dodgers leave without paying off the bonds. However, there was one stipulation—the state must continue giving the county $500,000 a year as part of the bond payment. That issue remained unresolved. That the Dodgers would be let off the hook caused some consternation in the community. A woman, who had attended the commission meeting, said, "My blood was boiling. . . . They're leaving and getting off scot-free. It's outrageous." Commissioner Sandra Bowden voted for the additional option but said, "We do value the Dodgers. . . . But we don't want to be snookered."[2]

Effort began immediately to seek another major league team to replace the Dodgers. The Baltimore Orioles had some dissatisfaction with Fort Lauderdale. The Cleveland Indians were considering a move from Winter Haven. Both those possibilities disappeared as Fort Lauderdale promised the Orioles stadium improvements and the Indians moved to Arizona. All other teams in Florida had long-term leases with their communities.

What would happen to Dodgertown became the talk of the town. Some suggested a sports complex where amateur teams would come for competition, or a college might want the facility.

To complicate matters the county and the city had another problem. Piper Aircraft, the Dodgertown neighbor at the airport, who had bought its property in 1964 at the same time the Dodgers bought Dodgertown, announced in December they were considering a move. Piper was looking for the best deal across the country where they could expand their work force to 1,500 and start building a small jet. Russ Lemon, a *Press Journal* columnist, noted that the paper's masthead included a Dodger hat, a grapefruit, the beach, and a Piper plane. With the Dodgers and Piper gone and the citrus business in decline, only the beach might be left.

Over the winter more information about Glendale surfaced. The Arizona Sports and Tourist Authority had committed $50 million to the baseball facility. Part of the deal, or sweetener as some might say, included an option for the Dodgers and the White Sox to buy 30 acres of land in Glendale as an investment. The price was fixed at the current market value and was good for ten years. Frank McCourt, in fact, had initiated the discussions with Glendale for this arrangement. However, he said that he wouldn't pack up six decades of memories at storied Dodgertown only for the money. "This is not an economic decision. This is a fan convenience decision," he said.[3]

Spring Training 2007 was fun with the Dodgers having an exciting array of big name players and a talented group of rookies. Though there were some roster additions—pitchers Jason Schmidt and Randy Wolf and outfielders Luis Gonzalez and Juan Pierre—the team was stable, a far cry from past springs. Even the player's names returned to the back of their uniforms. Ironically for a team about to leave the community, attendance at Holman Stadium grew. The national media publicized the Dodger departure and maybe people wanted to see Dodgertown before it was too late. A game with the Red Sox drew a record Holman Stadium crowd of 9,067, a sell out with the fans packing the stands and the berm. Unfortunately, rain ended the game in the second inning, and the attendance didn't officially count. But add that crowd to the total for the 15 other games played in Holman Stadium and the 85,000 number matched the record attendance set in 1992.

During the spring and before a game with the Astros, Frank McCourt sat with a group of writers surrounding him in the Dodgertown pressroom. He talked about Arizona. The move was not 100 percent but was "very likely." "We're still aiming for 2009," he said. The Dodgers and the county had agreed "in principal on a buyout of the lease." ("Buyout" seemed an exaggeration.) He commented on the big crowd at the Red Sox game the day before, noting that Dodger fans were in the minority. "Our fans are better served by having a spring training facility closer to L.A.," he said. In Arizona every effort will be made "to preserve key elements of Dodgertown, which is widely viewed as the most charming and fan-friendly spring-training complex in the major leagues but far from the most modern, the most functional or the best located."[4]

If another major league team came to Vero, would the local fans support it? Declining attendance following the O'Malley sale might raise a question despite the good crowds in 2007. Is another team going to be interested in a site that has such a strong Dodger history? And what would another team demand that would cost the county? Would a team insist that Holman Stadium be expanded and a roof added over the stands? On the other hand, what will be the cost to the county to maintain Dodgertown, something the Dodgers have done beautifully? Would the Dodgers have stayed longer, if they had to pay off the bond issue? Would they have bought the property with its increased value, but at a time when real estate development had slowed?

Dodgertown's Craig Callan, who had been in Vero since 1978 and who had been an active part of the community, saw the move to Arizona as an opportunity to build as he said "the best spring training facility in the history of baseball." He wanted to "define the Dodgertown tradition and lore . . . preserve it as much as possible and take it with us to Glendale."[5] Craig Callan with former Dodgertown directors Spencer Harris, Dick Bird, and Charlie Blaney had already built the best spring training facility in the history of baseball.

In 2008 the Dodgers would return for one last spring, their 61st year in Vero Beach.

Notes

Abbreviations

PJ   *Vero Beach Press Journal*
LAT   *Los Angeles Times*
NYT   *New York Times*

Chapter 1. Brooklyn Dodgers Select Vero

1. Frommer, *Rickey and Robinson*, 3–16. The conversation is based on excerpts from Frommer. The original source is probably Mann's *Branch Rickey*, 220–23. Rickey would have shared the conversation with Arthur Mann, one of his assistants.

2. Vero Beach was incorporated in 1919. The city's name came from the pioneer Henry Gifford family that settled at the turn of the century along Henry Flagler's Florida East Coast Railroad line and opened a post office. The story goes that Sarah Gifford, wife of Henry, selected the name Vero, the Latin word for truth. The citizens of Vero Beach formed Indian River County in 1925. Johnston, *A History of Indian River County*, 33.

3. Rachel Robinson, *Jackie Robinson*, 38.

4. Golenbock, *Bums*, 128.

5. Parrott, *Lords of Baseball*, 260.

6. Based on Frommer's *Rickey and Robinson*, Golenbock's *Bums*, and Rampersad's *Jackie Robinson*.

7. Frommer, *Rickey and Robinson*, 128.

8. Based on Frommer, *Rickey and Robinson*, and Rampersad, *Jackie Robinson*.

9. PJ, January 28, 1948.

10. *2006 Dodger Media Guide*, 365.

11. Joe Hendrickson, "Dodgertown," 9.

12. Hendrickson, "Dodgertown," 9.

13. Bump Holman, interview by author, March 15, 2003.

14. Hendrickson, "Dodgertown," 9.

15. "Dodger History/Dodgertown/Bud Holman's Dilemma," *Walter O'Malley: The Official Website*, http://www.walteromalley.com/hist_dtown_page2.ph.

Chapter 2. The Future of the Brooklyn Baseball Team Is Here

1. Hendrickson, "Dodgertown," 26.

2. Hendrickson, "Dodgertown," 13.

3. Hendrickson, "Dodgertown," 12.

4. *New York Daily News* as quoted in PJ, March 24, 1948.

5. *Life*, April 5, 1948, 117–20.

6. Hendrickson, "Dodgertown," 14.

7. PJ, March 24, 1948.

8. George W. Gross, *U.S. Naval Air Station*, 13.

9. Barbara Tripson told the story to Katharine Johnson, the author's wife. Also see Gross, *U.S. Naval Air Station*, 82.

10. Hendrickson, "Dodgertown," 39.

11. From a picture of Laraine Day in the Dodgertown files.

12. PJ, February 27, 1958.

13. Hendrickson, "Dodgertown," 16.

14. In fact, the biggest crowd up to that point may have been the one that assembled for the opening of the bridge across the Indian River in 1920.

15. Hendrickson, "Dodgertown," 16.

16. Hendrickson, "Dodgertown," 16.

17. PJ, April 8, 1948.

18. The souvenir scorecard is housed in the Dodgertown files.

19. PJ, April 8, 1948.

20. Hendrickson, "Dodgertown," 17.

21. Hendrickson, "Dodgertown," 14.

22. Hendrickson, "Dodgertown," 17.

23. Hendrickson, "Dodgertown," 17.

24. Hendrickson, "Dodgertown," 10.

Chapter 3. Branch Rickey's Kingdom by the Sea

1. PJ, April 1, 1949.

2. Hendrickson, "Dodgertown," 22.

3. Hendrickson, "Dodgertown," 24.

4. Hendrickson, "Dodgertown," 25.

5. Hendrickson, "Dodgertown," 21.

6. Rex Barney, *Rex Barney's Thank Youuuu*, 136.

7. Lasorda and Fisher, *Artful Dodger*, 23.

8. Lasorda and Fisher, *Artful Dodger*, 28.

9. Hendrickson, "Dodgertown," 27.

10. Hendrickson, "Dodgertown," 29.

11. Gifford received its name from tycoon Henry Flagler, who wanted property for his railroad in Vero. The white Gifford family held out for an exaggerated price, so Flagler named the nearby black, railroad-labor camp Gifford.

12. Jackie Robinson, *I Never Had It Made*, 92.

13. Buzzie Bavasi, *Off the Record*, 33.

14. Talks with Helen Barber at various times.

15. Hendrickson, "Dodgertown," 19.

16. Rampersad, *Jackie Robinson*, 215.

17. Hendrickson, "Dodgertown," 19.

18. PJ, March 25/49.

19. Mann, *Branch Rickey*, 277.

Chapter 4. Call Me Walter

1. PJ, January 31, 1950.

2. Hendrickson, "Dodgertown," 40

3. Bump Holman, interview by author, March 15, 2003.

4. Hendrickson, "Dodgertown," 34, 35. Hendrickson quoted Curzon from PJ, date unknown.

5. Erskine, *Tales from the Dodger Dugout*, 5.

6. Hendrickson, "Dodgertown," 102

7. Lasorda and Fisher, *Artful Dodger*, 37.

8. Barney, *Rex Barney's Thank Youuuu*, 49, 146, 149, 192.

9. Kahn, *The Era*, 265, 300. Profits were $1.7 million for the year plus $600,000 made on player sales.

10. Delshon, *True Blue*, 4.

11. Golenbock, *Bums*, 253.

12. Also in 1912, the first ball park was built in Indian River County. The town of Fellsmere raised the money with a picnic.

13. Shapiro, *Last Good Season*, 26.

14. Steve Mulvey, interview by author, November 12, 2003.

15. Sullivan, *The Dodgers Move West*, 29.

16. Mann, *Branch Rickey*, 230.

17. Sullivan, *The Dodgers Move West*, 30.

18. Kahn, *The Era*, 267.

19. Kahn, *The Era*, 267. In a letter to the author, dated May 2, 2007, Brent Shyer wrote that the dollar fine was "more in jest that when someone mentioned Rickey they had to toss a dollar into a fishbowl as if to say let's look forward."

20. Kahn, *The Era*, 262.

21. Kahn, *The Era*, 262

22. Bavasi, *Off the Record*, 25.

23. Bavasi, *Off the Record*, vii.

24. Kahn, *Boys of Summer*, 110.

25. Bavasi, *Off the Record*, 39.

26. Bavasi, *Off the Record*, 46.

27. Hendrickson, "Dodgertown," 32

28. Hendrickson, "Dodgertown," 31, 32.

29. Hendrickson, "Dodgertown," 32.

30. PJ, February 20, 1988.

31. Hendrickson, "Dodgertown," 32, 91.

32. "Dodger History/Dodgertown/21–year Lease Signed," *O'Malley Website*, http://www.walteromalley.com/hist_dtown_page8.php.

33. Andy McCue, "Dodgertown," in *Road Trips*, 10. The original source of the two-dollar-bill anecdote is Bavasi. The story seems improbable, however, given that few

establishments beyond a Dairy Queen, the Rose Garden Tea Room, and the Ocean Grill were available at that time to feed five hundred ballplayers over a weekend.

Chapter 5. Grace and the Boys of Summer

1. Grace Goodermote, interview by author, February 25, 2003. Unless otherwise noted, all subsequent Goodermote observations and remarks are drawn from this interview.

2. Waldo Sexton acquired the table and placed it at McKee Jungle Gardens. When McKee closed in 1976, Peter O'Malley bought it and stored it at Dodgertown. With the McKee Gardens' revival in 2004, O'Malley returned it "on loan." PJ, January 16, 2004.

3. Goodermote interview, above.

4. PJ, article by C. E. Wright, undated clipping, Dodgertown files.

5. Golenbock, *Bums*, 308, 309.

6. Hendrickson, "Dodgertown," 34.

7. PJ, March 13, 1952.

8. McCue, "Dodgertown," 10.

9. PJ, February 18, 1952.

10. The total cost of Holman Stadium is unclear. In "Dodgertown," 42, Hendrickson states that the building permit was for $100,000. The *O'Malley Website*, "Dodger History/Dodgertown," cites $30,000 plus $50,000 for excavation; $12,000 for ticket office, toilets, and clubhouse; and $1,000 for the press box (see "Emil Praeger Design," http://walteromalley.com/hist_dtown_page10.php, and "Holman Stadium Dedication," http://walteromalley.com/hist_dtown_page11.php). Local contractors Harry Osborne, Cy Cruze, and Jesse Swords did the construction. Jack Jennings did the engineering.

11. "Dodger History/Dodgertown/O'Malley, Praeger Team Up," *O'Malley Website*, http://walteromalley.com/hist_dtown_page16.php.

12. Langill, *Dodgertown*, 26.

13. Hendrickson, "Dodgertown," 34.

14. Hendrickson, "Dodgertown," 60, 61

15. Hendrickson, "Dodgertown," 34, 35.

16. Kahn, *The Era*, 299.

17. Hendrickson, "Dodgertown," 43.

18. Hendrickson, "Dodgertown," 44.

19. Golenbock, *Bums*, 361.

20. Kahn, *The Era*, 328, 329.

21. Kahn, *Boys of Summer*, 109.

22. Snider, *Duke of Flatbush*, 103.

23. Alston, *A Year at a Time*, 95.

Chapter 6. Champions of the World

1. Hendrickson, "Dodgertown," 48

2. Kahn, *Boys of Summer*, 387.

3. Alston, *A Year at a Time*, 8, 62.

4. Campanella, *Good to Be Alive*, 183.

5. Bavasi, *Off the Record*, 73.

6. Telephone conversation with Carol Moss, February 23, 2004.

7. *Palm Beach Post-Times*, 1957, Dodgertown files.

8. "Dodger History/Dodgertown/Dodgertown Camp for Boys," *O'Malley Website*, http://walteromalley.com/hist_dtown_page14.php. The Dodgertown boys' camp sign can be seen in a picture of Ebbets Field that appeared in a special Dodger edition of the *New York Daily News*, January 31, 1996.

9. Hendrickson, "Dodgertown," 97–99.

10. "Dodger History/Dodgertown/Dodgertown Camp for Boys," *O'Malley Website*, http://walteromalley.com/hist_dtown_page14.php.

11. Barber and Creamer, *Rhubarb in the Catbird Seat*, 279.

12. Barber and Creamer, *Rhubarb in the Catbird Seat*, 101.

13. PJ, February 17, 1955.

14. PJ, February 24, 1955.

15. Hendrickson, "Dodgertown," 50.

16. Shapiro, *Last Good Season*, 66.

17. *New York Daily News*, the 1955 Brooklyn Dodgers Fortieth Anniversary Collector's Edition, January 31, 1996.

18. Golenbock, *Bums*, 411.

19. Golenbock, *Bums*, 412.

20. Hendrickson, "Dodgertown," 51.

21. Hendrickson, "Dodgertown," 52.

22. Hendrickson, "Dodgertown," 51

23. PJ, March 1955 edition.

24. Waldo Sexton letter, undated, provided by his grandson Sean Sexton.

25. The Philadelphia A's had just moved to Kansas City in 1955. The St. Louis Browns became the Baltimore Orioles in 1954.

26. PJ, February 31, 1955.

27. PJ, March 24, 1955.

28. PJ, March 17, 1955.

29. PJ, March 31, 1955.

30. NYT, October 5, 1955.

31. NYT, October 5, 1955.

32. PJ, October 6, 1955.

Chapter 7. So We're Going

1. PJ, February 1956 (exact date unknown).

2. Drysdale, *Once a Bum*, 40.

3. A picture hangs in the Quail Valley River Club in Vero Beach of President Dwight Eisenhower, Walter O'Malley, and Jim Mulvey together at the opening game at Ebbets Field. Mulvey's grandson, Steve Mulvey, owns the club.

4. Snider, *Duke of Flatbush*, 187.

5. NYT, October 1, 1956.

6. Golenbock, *Bums*, 472.

7. Kahn, *The Era*, 327.

8. Kahn, *The Era*, 353.

9. Jackie Robinson, *I Never Had It Made*, 96.

10. Rachel Robinson, *Intimate Portrait*.

11. NYT, February 22, 1957.

12. In *Off the Record*, 81, Bavasi states that Ebbets Field was sold for $4 million.

13. NYT, February 22, 1957.

14. The delegation represented a county and seventy-seven incorporated communities with a population that had grown from four million in 1950 to six million in 1960.

15. PJ, March 5, 1957. Sullivan, *Dodgers Move West*, 83.

16. Campanella, *Good to Be Alive*, 8.

17. Hendrickson, "Dodgertown," 55, 56.

18. There was a story that Joe DiMaggio and Marilyn Monroe visited the Holman ranch. Bud Holman's oldest son, Tom, said he wasn't aware of it but that "a lot of things went on out there."

19. Sullivan, *Dodgers Move West*, 96.

20. PJ, February 28, 1957.

21. PJ, February 28, 1957.

22. Shapiro, *Last Good Season*, 308.

23. Shapiro, *Last Good Season*, 310.

24. Golenbock, *Bums*, 482.

25. Sullivan, *Dodgers Move West*, 43.

26. Steve Mulvey, interview by author, November 12, 2003.

27. Sullivan, *Dodgers Move West*, 43

28. Shapiro, *Last Good Season*, 33, 34.

29. Shapiro, *Last Good Season*, 38, 71.

30. Shapiro, *Last Good Season*, 72.

31. Shapiro, *Last Good Season*, 314. Brent Shyer's letter, dated May 2, 2007, stated that documents indicate that O'Malley had not made a decision at that point and was still in discussions with Brooklyn and New York officials to stay in Brooklyn.

32. Shapiro, *Last Good Season*, 319.

33. Sullivan, *Dodgers Move West*, 4, 133.

34. Sullivan, *Dodgers Move West*, 132.

35. Barber, *Rhubarb in the Catbird Seat*, 290.

36. Sullivan, *Dodgers Move West*, 104.

37. Sullivan, *Dodgers Move West*, 221.

38. NYT, October 9, 2003.

39. PJ, October 10, 1957.

Chapter 8. Los Angeles Dodgers

1. PJ, February 27, 1958.
2. PJ, March 26, 1959.
3. Billy DeLury, interview by author, March 2, 2004.
4. Campanella, *Good to Be Alive*, 19–22.
5. Roseboro, *Glory Days*, 124.
6. Sullivan, *Dodgers Move West*, 139.
7. Alston, *A Year at a Time*, 127.
8. Sullivan, *Dodgers Move West*, 138.
9. Sullivan, *Dodgers Move West*, 153.
10. Drysdale, *Once a Bum*, 70.
11. Sullivan, *Dodgers Move West*, 159.
12. Sullivan, *Dodgers Move West*, 160.
13. Delshon, *True Blue*, 26.
14. Sullivan, *Dodgers Move West*, 168, 169, 172.
15. Bavasi, *Off the Record*, 115.
16. Sullivan, *Dodgers Move West*, 173
17. Wills and Celizic, *On the Run*, 69.
18. Hendrickson, "Dodgertown," 62.
19. Wills and Celizic, *On the Run*, 71.
20. Roseboro, *Glory Days*, 110, 111.
21. Roseboro, *Glory Days*, 112–14.
22. Wills and Celizic, *On the Run*, 104.
23. Campanella, *Good to Be Alive*, 270.
24. Campanella, *Good to Be Alive*, 271, 272.
25. Campanella, *Good to Be Alive*, 177, 278.
26. Roseboro, *Glory Days*, 108.
27. Hendrickson, "Dodgertown," 63
28. Delshon, *True Blue*, 28.

Chapter 9. Dodgers Not Being Booted

1. PJ, December 4, 1960.
2. PJ, May 19, 1960.
3. PJ, May 5, 1960.
4. PJ, June 23, 1960.
5. PJ, October 27, 1960.
6. Bump Holman, interview by author, March 15, 2003. Bump received an e-mail from Peter O'Malley that day remembering that it was the 50th anniversary of the dedication of Holman Stadium.
7. PJ, October 27, 1960.
8. PJ, December 15, 1960.
9. PJ, February 28, 1960.
10. PJ, February 28, 1960.

11. PJ, July 13, 1961.

12. PJ, March 2, 1961.

13. "Dodger History/Dodgertown/Foreign Visitors Welcomed," *O'Malley Website*, http://www.walteromalley.com/hist_dtown_page17.php.

14. Alston, *A Year at a Time*, 163.

15. Leavy, *Sandy Koufax*, 101.

16. Delshon, *True Blue*, 43.

17. Leavy, *Sandy Koufax*, 102.

18. PJ, January 12, 1961.

19. "Dodger History/Dodgertown/O'Malley, Praeger Team Up," *O'Malley Website*, http://www.walteromalley.com/hist_dtown_page16.php.

20. PJ, February 23, 1961.

21. PJ, March 23, 1961.

22. PJ, April 13, 1961.

23. PJ, November 9, 1961.

24. McCue, "Dodgertown," 11.

25. PJ, March 2, 1961.

26. PJ, February 29, 1962.

27. PJ, August 3, 1961.

28. PJ, November 9, 1961.

29, PJ, November 9, 1961.

30. PJ, November 16, 1961.

31. PJ, November 30, 1961.

32. Hendrickson, "Dodgertown," 65.

33. McCue, "Dodgertown," 11.

34. PJ, November 30, 1961.

35. PJ, December 7, 1961.

36. PJ December 7, 1961.

37. PJ, January 25, 1962.

Chapter 10. The Dodgers and Vero Prevail

1. Hendrickson, "Dodgertown," 67.

2. PJ, December 5, 1963.

3. Hendrickson, "Dodgertown," 67.

4. Davis, *Tales from the Dodger Dugout*, 129.

5. PJ, February 12, 1988.

6. PJ, June 24, 2001.

7. PJ, November 1963.

8. Hendrickson, "Dodgertown," 67.

9. PJ, March 1 and 8, 1962; April 26, 1962.

10. PJ, May 24 and 31, 1962.

11. PJ, June 26, 1962.

12. PJ, August 16, 2002.

13. PJ, September 20, 1963.

14. "Biography/Quotes/Media: Jim Murray," *O'Malley Website*, http://www.walteromalley.com/biog_quotes_murray.php.

15. "Dodger History/Dodgertown/O'Malley, Praeger Team Up," *O'Malley Website*, http://www.walteromalley.com/hist_dtown_page16.php.

16. Bavasi, *Off the Record*, 58.

17. Bavasi, *Off the Record*, 57.

18. PJ, February 28, 1963; September 24, 1964.

19. Hendrickson, "Dodgertown," 69.

20. Wills and Celizic, *On the Run*, 143.

21. Drysdale, *Once a Bum*, 118.

22. Hendrickson, "Dodgertown," 41.

23. PJ, December 19 and 26, 1963.

24. Leavy, *Sandy Koufax*, 150.

25. Hendrickson, "Dodgertown," 70.

26. Hendrickson, "Dodgertown," 69.

27. PJ, September 24, 1964.

28. Hendrickson, "Dodgertown," 69.

29. Hendrickson, "Dodgertown," 99.

30. Hendrickson, "Dodgertown," 69.

31. Hendrickson, "Dodgertown," 71.

32. Hendrickson, "Dodgertown," 71.

33. PJ, September 3, 1964.

Chapter 11. Wins and Losses

1. Drysdale, *Once a Bum*, 110.

2. Alston, *A Year at a Time*, 100.

3. PJ, August 13, 1964.

4. Roseboro, *Glory Days*, 114.

5. Roseboro, *Glory Days*, 115.

6. Roseboro, *Glory Days*, 116.

7. Roseboro, *Glory Days*, 114.

8. PJ, September 3, 1964.

9. PJ, March 10, 2004.

10. PJ, August 15, 1965.

11. PJ, August 15, 1965.

12. Drysdale, *Once a Bum*, 134.

13. Drysdale, *Once a Bum*, 126.

14. Delshon, *True Blue*, 78.

15. Bavasi, *Off the Record*, 104.

16. Wills and Celizic, *On the Run*, 218.

17. Wills and Celizic, *On the Run*, 218.

18. PJ, March 31, 1966.

19. "Biography/Quotes/Former Dodgers: Maury Wills," *O'Malley Website*, http://www.walteromalley.com/biog_quotes_wills.php.

20. Hendrickson, "Dodgertown," 72. PJ, February 22, 1968.

21. Hendrickson, "Dodgertown," 74.

22. Hendrickson, "Dodgertown," 72.

23. PJ, July 22, 1966.

24. Dick Bird, interview by author, April 12, 2004. This interview informs subsequent paragraphs concerning the Bird–O'Malley relationship.

25. PJ, August 22, 1968.

26. Hendrickson, "Dodgertown," 75.

27. PJ, October 6, 1966.

28. Delshon, *True Blue*, 84.

29. PJ, February 23, 1967.

30. Roseboro, *Glory Days*, 218.

31. Leavy, *Sandy Koufax*, 158.

32. Leavy, *Sandy Koufax*, 178.

33. Leavy, *Sandy Koufax*, 255.

Chapter 12. Glad the Sixties Were Over

1. Roseboro, *Glory Days*, 211.

2. Drysdale, *Once a Bum*, 176.

3. PJ, November 28, 1968; February 27, 1969.

4. PJ, June 5, 1959; February 9, 1967; May 30, 1968; March 21, 1968; March 6, 1969; July 10, 1969.

5. Hugh McCrystal, interview by author, April 15, 2005.

6. PJ, March 27, 1969.

7. PJ, May 30, 1968; May 12, 1969; February 13, 1969.

8. PJ, April 18, 1968.

9. LAT, April 15, 2005.

10. PJ, April 11, 1968.

11. PJ, March 15, 1969.

12. PJ, February 26, 1970.

13. Alma Lee Loy, interview by author, January 14, 2004.

Chapter 13. A Team and a Town in Transition

1. Hendrickson, "Dodgertown," 77.

2. Lasorda and Fisher, *Artful Dodger*, 120.

3. Hendrickson, "Dodgertown," 95.

4. PJ, March 19, 1970.

5. PJ, May 7, 1970; July 16, 1970.

6. Hendrickson, "Dodgertown," 85.

7. Hendrickson, "Dodgertown," 41.

8. Hendrickson, "Dodgertown," 80.

9. Hendrickson, "Dodgertown," 79.

10. Burk, *Much More Than a Game*, 170.

11. Miller, *Whole Different Ball Game*, 87.

12. McCue, "Dodgertown," 10.

13. Hendrickson, "Dodgertown," 83.

14. Dick Bird, interview by author, April 12, 2004.

15. Hendrickson, "Dodgertown," 79.

16. Hendrickson, "Dodgertown," 92.

17. Hendrickson, "Dodgertown," 106.

18. Bird interview, above.

19. PJ, February 19, 1970.

20. Bird interview, above.

Chapter 14. A New Era

1. Garvey, *Garvey*, 19.

2. Lasorda and Fisher, *Artful Dodger*, 174.

3. Hendrickson, "Dodgertown," 85.

4. Norris Olson, various conversations with author, winter 2004–spring 2005.

5. Hendrickson, "Dodgertown," 86.

6. Hendrickson, "Dodgertown," 91.

7. Dick Bird, interview by author, April 12, 2004.

8. Hendrickson, "Dodgertown," 84.

9. "Open House at the 'New' Dodgertown," PJ, undated 1973 advertisement, Dodgertown files.

10. Hendrickson, "Dodgertown," 89.

11. Hendrickson, "Dodgertown," 89.

12. Delshon, *True Blue*, 118.

13. Lasorda and Fisher, *Artful Dodger*, 192.

14. Lasorda and Fisher, *Artful Dodger*, 192. Lasorda's togetherness policy with his starters was fun to watch, and it was disappointing when subsequent Dodger managers didn't follow his example.

Chapter 15. Hail to the Chief

1. PJ, undated clipping, Dodgertown files.

2. PJ, March 12, 1978.

3. PJ, March 15, 1978.

4. Garvey, *Garvey*, 148.

5. Garvey, *Garvey*, 101.

6. Hendrickson, "Dodgertown," 93.

7. 2005 *Dodger Media Guide*, 314–17.

8. PJ, January 1, 1977. I saw Lasorda running "the Hill."

9. Bobby McCarthy, interview by author, January 18, 2005.

10. PJ, March 12, 2005.

11. Personal observation. PJ, March 21, 1979.

12. John and John, *The Sally and Tommy John Story*, 202, 224, 226.

13. PJ, undated clipping, Dodgertown files.

14. PJ, February 25, 1979; March 9, 1979.

15. *Line Drives* commemorates the deaths of Walter and Kay O'Malley.

16. *Line Drives*. The Kay O'Malley interview was included as part of this Dodgers publication.

17. Alma Lee Loy, interview by author, January 14, 2004.

18. Hendrickson, "Dodgertown," 99.

19. *Line Drives*. Walter O'Malley had not been voted into the Hall of Fame as of the 2003 vote.

20. *Line Drives*.

21. PJ, August 10, 1979.

22. O'Malley described by publicist Red Patterson in Hendrickson's "Dodgertown," 89.

23. "Dodger and Dodgertown Gold," *Indian River Life Magazine*, 1979 clipping, Dodgertown files.

24. PJ, January 1, 1980.

25. Indian River County historical census data, archives, Indian River County Library, Vero Beach.

26. PJ, January 1, 1980. Hendrickson, "Dodgertown," 111.

27. Hendrickson, "Dodgertown," 107.

28. PJ, January 1, 1980.

Chapter 16. We Love Our Vero Beach Dodgers

1. PJ, April 10, 1980; September 12, 1980. Personal observations

2. PJ, April 9, 1980.

3. PJ, July 2, 1995.

4. *Miami Herald*, September 1, 1980.

5. PJ, July 1, 1995.

6. PJ, August 31, 1988.

7. Quoted in Hendrickson, "Dodgertown," 107.

8. PJ, March 2, 1980.

9. Lasorda and Fisher, *Artful Dodger*, 215.

10. PJ, March 2, 1980.

11. PJ, March 10, 1980.

12. Hendrickson, "Dodgertown," 110.

13. Hendrickson, "Dodgertown," 109.

14. PJ, March 18, 1980.

15. PJ, January 1, 1981.

16. PJ, March 10, 1981.

17. PJ, March 10, 1981.

18. Garvey, *Garvey*, 147.

19. PJ, March 20, 1981.

20. PJ, March 26, 1981.

Chapter 17. Ups and Downs

1. PJ, January 1, 1981.
2. Attendance data, provided by Dodgertown ticket manager, Louise Bossey.
3. PJ, March 2, 1982. 2006 *Dodger Media Guide*, 374.
4. PJ, March 8, 1982.
5. PJ, March 4, 1982.
6. Personal observation. PJ, March 18, 1982.
7. Welch and Vecsey, *Five O'Clock Comes Early*, 84, 85.
8. Dodger historian Mark Langill told me in the spring of 2005 about the Bobby Castillo Bridge.
9. Personal observation.
10. PJ, August 31, 1988.
11. 2006 *Dodger Media Guide*, 437. Ned Hanlon was selected for the Hall of Fame in 1996. Tommy Lasorda joined in 1997.
12. PJ, March 2, 1982.
13. Garvey, *Garvey*, 175, 180, 183.
14. Hugh McCrystal, interview by author, April 15, 2005.
15. PJ, August 31, 1988.
16. PJ, February 18, 1984.
17. 2006 *Dodger Media Guide*, 365.
18. PJ, February 18, 1984.
19. PJ, February 25, 1985.
20. PJ, March 10, 1985.
21. PJ, January 1, 1986.
22. PJ, February 22, 1987.
23. PJ, February 23, 1986.
24. LAT March 24, 1987.
25. PJ, July 1, 1995.
26. PJ, July 1, 1995.
27. 2006 *Dodger Media Guide*, 454.
28. January 28, 1986, letter from Charles Blaney to Dr. James Burns, superintendent of Indian River County schools, proposing an "adopt-a-school" program, Dodgertown files. PJ, February 20, 1988.
29. PJ, March 31, 1987.
30. Delshon, *True Blue*, 180.
31. LAT, April 9, 1987.
32. LAT, April 9, 1987.

Chapter 18. Refuse to Lose

1. LAT, March 13, 1988.
2. Delshon, *True Blue*, 190.
3. LAT, May 7, 1989.
4. Gibson, *Bottom of the Ninth*, 114.

5. Gibson, *Bottom of the Ninth*, 115.

6. Gibson, *Bottom of the Ninth*, 115.

7. Gibson, *Bottom of the Ninth*, 116, 117.

8. Gibson, *Bottom of the Ninth*, 120.

9. PJ, January 21, 1988.

10. PJ, February 20, 1988.

11. Craig Callan, interview by author, May 16, 2005.

12. PJ, March 5, 1989.

13. PJ, January 1, 1990.

14. PJ, February 21, 1989; March 5, 1989.

15. PJ, March 5, 1989.

16. PJ, March 5, 1989.

17. LAT, May 7, 1989.

18. PJ, August 3, 1988.

19. PJ, March 10, 1985.

20. PJ, August 31, 1988.

21. PJ, August 31, 1988.

22. PJ, July 1, 1995.

23. PJ, February 20, 1988.

24. PJ, February 21, 1987.

25. PJ, January 1, 1987; January 1, 1990.

26. PJ, January 1, 1990.

Chapter 19. Not for Sale

1. PJ, undated clipping, Dodgertown files.

2. PJ, March 2, 1990.

3. LAT, March 12, 1991.

4. *Los Angeles Daily News*, April 9, 1990.

5. LAT, June 12, 1991.

6. LAT, March 2, 2005.

7. Jerry Crasnick, "From Last to First," *Minor League Memories*, August 1, 2004, www.attheyard.com/Minor League Memories.

8. Delshon, *True Blue*, 216–17.

9. Craig Callan, interview by author, May 16, 2005.

10. I inherited from Lillian Harnsberger, my Aunt Lil, two seats in row 5, section 17, across from the Dodger section.

11. Hendrickson, "Dodgertown," 99.

12. Delshon, *True Blue*, 217.

13. LAT, April 1, 1993.

14. *Los Angeles Daily News*, March 12, 1993. LAT, May 4, 1993.

15. PJ, January 1, 1991; January 1, 2000.

16. *Vero Beach Sun*, January 1, 1993; October 8, 1993.

17. PJ, September 18, 1993.

18. "What if Dodgers Came to Town?" Letter-to-the-Editor, PJ, undated clipping, Dodgertown files.

19. PJ, September 8, 1993.

20. Hugh McCrystal, interview by author, April 10, 2005.

21 NYT, February 20, 2005.

22. LAT, September 4, 1994.

Chapter 20. Like Leaving Your Spouse after Fifty Years

1. PJ, March 30, 2003.

2. Based on attendance data provided by Dodgertown ticket manager, Louise Bossey.

3. PJ, March 3, 1995.

4. PJ, March 3, 1995.

5. PJ, April 1, 1995; May 6, 1995.

6. PJ, April 6, 1995.

7. Personal observation.

8. LAT, January 7, 1995.

9. LAT, January 18, 2004.

10. Claire, *Fred Claire*, 163.

11. LAT, January 7, 1997.

12. LAT, January 7, 1997.

13. LAT, January 7, 1997.

14. *Orange County Register*, January 17, 1997.

15. PJ, January 7, 1997.

16. PJ, January 7 and 10, 1997.

17. PJ, January 7, 1997.

18. LAT, January 8, 1997.

19. County/city letter, October 29, 1998, Dodger Buyout File, Indian River County Chamber of Commerce, Vero Beach, Fla.

20. LAT, March 15 and 24, 1997.

21. Personal observation.

22. PJ, January 1, 1998.

Chapter 21. The Mystique Is Gone

1. PJ, March 2, 1998.

2. PJ, March 2, 1998.

3. PJ, March 17, 1998.

4. Attendance data provided by Dodgertown ticket manager, Louise Bossey.

5. Claire, *Fred Claire*, 165.

6. PJ, March 20, 1998.

7. PJ, March 20, 1998.

8. PJ, March 20, 1998.

9. Delshon, *True Blue*, 262.

10. PJ, March 20, 1998.

11. PJ, January 1, 1999.

12. Claire, *Fred Claire*, 167.

13. LAT, April 6, 2004.

14. Claire, *Fred Claire*, 2.

15. LAT, June 23, 1998.

16. Delshon, *True Blue*, 269.

17. LAT, June 23, 1998.

18. Delshon, *True Blue*, 249.

19. Delshon, *True Blue*, 119, 273, 276.

20. Delshon, *True Blue*, 280. Stout, *The Dodgers*, 396.

21. PJ, October 1, 1998.

22. LAT, October 12, 1998.

23. LAT, October 12, 1998.

24. PJ, October 1, 1998.

25. PJ, October 25–27, 1998.

26. PJ, October 29, 1998.

27. County/city letter, October 29, 1998, Dodger Buyout File, Indian River County Chamber of Commerce, Vero Beach.

28. County/city letter, cited above.

29. PJ, November 7, 1998.

30. PJ, November 7, 1998.

31. The list of members of the "Keep Our Dodgers Committee" was provided in a May 13, 2005, e-mail from Diane Resch, executive assistant to Bill Curtis.

32. Letter from Milt Thomas to Craig Callan, December 10, 1998, Dodger Buyout File, Indian River County Chamber of Commerce, Vero Beach. The $30 million consisted of direct Dodger expenditures of $6.6 million, which included payroll ($4.2 million), local purchases ($1.2 million), and the balance in taxes and utilities. A state study found that $10.6 million was spent by visitors locally because of the Dodgers. A generally accepted economic factor added another $17 million to the total. In comparison, Piper Aircraft with its much larger payroll had an impact of $100 million on the economy.

33. Milt Thomas, interview by author, April 26, 2004.

34. John Rofe, "Is Dodgertown facing Brooklyn's fate?," *Street and Smith's Sports Business Journal*, October 5, 1998.

35. Delshon, *True Blue*, 264.

Chapter 22. Big, Bad Media Company

1. *1999 Dodger Media Guide*, 1–11.

2. Stout, *The Dodgers*, 391.

3. Delshon, *True Blue*, 280.

4. LAT, February 20, 1999.

5. PJ, February 20, 1999.

6. PJ, February 20, 1999.

7. Personal observations.

8. LAT, August 13, 1999.

9. Dodger Buyout File, Indian River County Chamber of Commerce, Vero Beach.

10. PJ, June 9, 1999.

11. PJ, June 10, 1999.

12. Craig Callan, interview by author, May 16, 2005.

13. PJ, June 9 and 10, 1999.

14. *Los Angeles Daily News*, June 17, 1999.

15. *Arizona Republic*, May 29, 1999.

16. LAT, May 21, 1999.

17. Dodger Buyout File, Indian River County Chamber of Commerce.

18. LAT, June 2, 1999. PJ, June 10, 1999.

19. PJ, July 3, 1999.

20. LAT, August 1, 1999.

21. LAT, August 10, 1999.

22. LAT, September 29, 1999.

23. Callan interview, above.

24. "Playing Good Cop to Rupert Murdoch," *Business Week*, September 6, 2003.

25. Delshon, *True Blue*, 281.

26. LAT, October 28, 1999.

27. PJ, December 3, 1999. LAT, December 3 and 14, 1999.

28. Delshon, *True Blue*, 282.

29. PJ, January 1, 2000.

Chapter 23. We Don't Like 'Em Much Anymore

1. LAT, February 25, 2000.

2. "Dodgers lose fire, act like robots," PJ, guest column by author, March 28, 2000.

3. PJ, March 13, 2000. Carlos Perez, signed by Malone and earning $5 million a year, had such a miserable season in 1999 that manager Davey Johnson demoted him to Albuquerque.

4. PJ, March 18, 2000.

5. LAT, May 9, 2000. PJ May 3, 2000.

6. LAT, July 28, 2000. The other five teams Las Vegas wanted were the Baltimore Orioles, Houston Astros, Tampa Bay Devil Rays, Texas Rangers, and Toronto Blue Jays.

7. Mark Anderson, "Officials deny plan to pay Dodgers to move," *Las Vegas Review-Journal*, June 9, 2000.

8. LAT, March 25, 2000.

9. PJ, June 10, 2000.

10. "Memo of Understanding," June 17, 2000, approved by Indian River County Commission and the Vero Beach City Council.

11. PJ, April 30, 2001.

12. PJ, July 28, 2000.

13. PJ, July 28, 2000.

14. Mark Anderson, "Stars changing from Padres' to Dodgers' club," *Las Vegas Review-Journal*, September 15, 2000.

15. Craig Callan, interview by author, May 16, 2005.

16. Conversation with Art Neuberger and Ruth Stanbridge, April 6, 2005.

17. PJ, July 28, 2000.

18. PJ, July 28, 2000.

19. PJ, June 10, 2000.

20. PJ, February 21, 2001.

21. PJ, September 2, 2000.

22. PJ, October 4, 2000; PJ, November 14, 2000. Because of the closeness of the county commission vote and Florida's problems during the presidential election that year, *60 Minutes II* interviewed Frank Zorc.

23. PJ, October 4, 2000.

24. PJ, November 12, 2000.

25. LAT, November 2, 2000.

26. LAT, November 1, 2000.

27. LAT, April 2, 2001.

28. LAT, November 20, 2000.

29. PJ, January 1 and 7, 2001. The other four communities receiving grants were Clearwater (Phillies), Dunedin (Blue Jays), Lakeland (Tigers), and Osceola County (Astros). The Phillies, the Blue Jays, and the Astros had been pursued by Las Vegas.

30. PJ, January 3, 2001.

31. PJ, January 4, 2001.

32. PJ, May 19, 2001.

33. PJ, April 4, 2001.

34. PJ, April 4, 2001.

35. PJ, April 4, 2001.

36. Attendance data provided by Dodgertown ticket manager, Louise Bossey.

37. PJ, April 8, 2001.

38. Informal conversation with a Vero Beach merchant.

39. LAT, October 2, 2001.

40. PJ, August 5, 2001.

41. PJ, August 12, 2001.

42. PJ, August 8 and 9, 2001. The reduced annual $1.2 million debt service consisted of the $340,000 from the sales tax, $360,000 from the tourist tax, and the $500,000 from the state.

43. PJ, August 29, 2001.

Chapter 24. Fear for the Future

1. PJ, January 10, 2002.

2. PJ, January 16, 2002.

3. PJ, January 17, 2002.

4. Mark Hyman, "If You Build It, They Will Train," *Business Week*, March 24, 2003.

5. *2003 Dodger Media Guide*, 240.

6. PJ, August 7, 2002.

7. PJ, January 1, 2003.

8. PJ, July 6, 2002; September 20, 2002.

9. PJ, April 15, 2004. The owners gave the county nine acres for Holman Stadium parking in order to have the parking easement removed from the balance of their property.

10. PJ, March 18, 2003; January 1, 2004.

11. *2005 Dodger Media Guide*, 328.

12. Craig Callan, talk delivered to the Indian River Historical Society, Vero Beach, Florida, February 24, 2003.

13. PJ, February 24, 2003.

14. PJ, February 12, 2003.

15. PJ, February 15, 2003.

16. PJ, March 8, 2003; April 3, 2003.

17. LAT, March 13, 2004.

18. LAT, February 21, 2004.

19. PJ, February 26, 2003.

20. LAT, October 19, 2003. In his letter to the author, dated May 2, 2007, Brent Shyer noted the following Walter O'Malley accomplishments: he served 28 years on Major League Baseball's Executive Council, the longest tenure ever; under his leadership from 1951–79, the Dodgers won four World Series championships and set numerous attendance records; in December 2009, *The Sporting News* named him the Eleventh Most Powerful Person in Sports over the last century; and *ABC Sports* ranked him in its Top Ten Most Influential People "off the field" in sports history.

21. PJ, March 29, 2003.

22. PJ, March 29, 2003.

23. LAT, December 19, 2001.

24. LAT, April 8, 2003.

25. This synopsis of the bidding activity is based on *Los Angeles Times* articles from 2003: April 5; July 30; August 24; October 6; October 8–14; November 3; November 5; December 13; and December 15.

26. PJ, December 18, 2003.

Chapter 25. What's Up Next, Skip?

1. LAT, January 26, 2004. On March 17, 2005, LAT reported that McCourt had a $145 million loan from Fox secured by his Boston waterfront property. This article put the sale price at $421 million, of which $196 million was seller (Fox) financing.

2. LAT, January 30, 2004.

3. PJ, February 8, 2004.

4. Personal observation.

5. LAT, January 29, 2004.

6. LAT, February 17, 2004.

7. LAT, February 17, 2004.

8. Lewis, *Moneyball, 18*.

9. Mark Hymam, "Putting the Lie to Baseball's Big 'Crisis,'" *Business Week*, April 12, 2004.

10. Personal observation.

11. LAT, February 25, 2004.

12. Personal observation.

13. PJ, March 6, 2004.

14. Conversation with Paul Shuey, March 8, 2004.

15. As observed from section 17.

16. LAT, March 5, 2004.

17. LAT, March 9, 2004.

18. Personal observation.

19. As observed from section 17.

20. LAT, March 14, 2004.

21. LAT, March 16, 2004; September 30, 2005. Jill Leiber of *USA Today* would describe Jamie McCourt as "a 5–2, 100–pound, golden-blond tornado in size-0 designer miniskirts and 3–inch heels." See "McCourt revels in running show," August 23, 2005.

22. Frank and Jamie McCourt met while attending Georgetown University. She had also studied at the Sorbonne in Paris, received a law degree from the University of Maryland, and an MBA from MIT. They were married in 1979 and have three sons. See *2006 Dodger Media Guide*, 5, 6.

23. The story was told to the author by a friend. The citrusman was a mutual friend, Bobby Sexton.

24. *Los Angeles Daily News*, April 3, 2004.

25. Personal observation.

26. Conversation with Jim Loney, spring 2004.

27. *Los Angeles Daily News*, March 16, 2004.

28. Personal observation.

29. Claire, *Fred Claire*, 53.

30. In a conversation with two or three Los Angeles writers, Jim Tracy was mentioned, spring 2004.

31. The term "bunker" was also used in a *Sports Illustrated* article on Dodgertown in February 23, 2004.

32. PJ, March 23, 2004.

33. Conversation with Jim Tracy, March 2004. The artist was Katharine Johnson.

34. Response to a question to Jim Tracy in postgame press conference, March 31, 2004.

35. *2005 Dodger Media Guide*, 331.

36. LAT, April 5, 2004.

37. LAT, July 31, 2004.

38. LAT, August 1, 2004.

39. LAT, August 3, 2004.

40. LAT, February 17, 2004.

41. PJ, January 22, 2005. LAT, February 21, 2005.

42. LAT, November 19, 1994.

43. The U.S. Census Bureau estimated the population of Indian River County as 128,594 in 2005. See http://censtats.census.gov/usa/usa.shtml.

44. Personal observation.

45. LAT, October 11, 2004.

Chapter 26. The Ugly and the Lovely

1. LAT, November 29, 2004.

2. NYT, March 27, 2005.

3. LAT, December 12, 2005.

4. Topps selected the Dodgers once in 1978, four times during the 1980s, and five times in 1990–97. *Fortune* picked the Dodgers in 1984, 1992, and 1997. *1998 Dodgers Media Guide*, 5.

5. PJ, April 21, 2005.

6. PJ, June 22, 2005.

7. PJ, July 10, 2005.

8. Observation from section 17.

9. LAT, February 22, 2005.

10. LAT, March 30, 2005.

11. Personal observation.

12. LAT, February 25, 2005.

13. LAT, January 15, 2005.

14. Conversation with security guards, spring 2005.

15. Conversation with Mark Langill, spring 2005

16. NYT, April 1, 2005.

17. I heard Vincent's remarks during attendance at the January 2005 SABR meeting.

18. As observed from section 17.

19. A request for an interview with Frank McCourt to talk about the McCourts' relationship with Vero Beach was turned down. The Dodger publicity department said he was too busy. The McCourts did make a move to put down some roots locally. They joined the Quail Valley Golf and River Club in Vero.

20. Conversation with Maury Wills, spring 2005.

21. PJ, March 22, 2005.

22. PJ, March 26, 2005.

23. PJ, January 11, 2005.

24. PJ, January 4, 2005.

25. Informal conversations with Vero Beach locals.

26. LAT, May 1, 2005.

27. Billy DeLury, interview by author, March 2, 2004.

28. January 2006, SABR meeting, Dodgertown.

29. Personal observation.

30. Response to a question to Jim Tracy by the author, postgame press conference, March 29, 2005.

31. PJ, April 12, 2005.

32. NYT, January 16, 2005.

33. LAT, October 29, 2005.

34. LAT, August 26, 2005.

35. *2006 Dodger Media Guide*, 396.

36. PJ, June 4 and 5, 2005.

37. PJ, June 4, 2005.

38. LAT, August 28, 2005.

39. LAT, September 30, 2005.

40. LAT, October 4 and 12, 2005. Tracy received a three-year contract worth $3.2 million from the Pirates, a sum considerably higher than his $750,000-a-year Dodger salary.

41. LAT, October 28 and 30, 2005.

42. LAT, October 31, 2005. *2006 Dodger Media Guide*, 276.

Chapter 27. Like Brooklyn, a Fond Memory

1. Three of the coaches were old Dodgers: first base coach, Mariano Duncan; pitching coach, Rick Honeycutt; and Manny Mota in his 27th season as a coach and 37th year in the organization. *2006 Dodger Media Guide*, 28, 29, 31.

2. Personal observation.

3. LAT, November 17, 2005. *2006 Dodger Media Guide*, 9, 10.

4. NYT, January 1, 2006.

5. *2006 Dodger Media Guide*, 26.

6. *2006 Dodger Media Guide*, 10.

7. NYT, January 1, 2006. For the 2005 and 2006 seasons, the Dodgers spent over $200 million on free agent contracts.

8. LAT, March 4, 2006.

9. LAT, March 4, 2006.

10. LAT, March 4, 2006.

11. Scorebook notes as observed from section 17.

12. LAT, January 13, 2006; February 19, 2006.

13. *Los Angeles Daily News*, March 15, 2006, www.dailynews.com/search.

14. PJ, April 20, 2006; LAT, May 12, 2006.

15. PJ, April 23, 2006.

16. PJ, April 21, 2006.

Afterword

1. The price for the Vero franchise in the Florida State League, worth perhaps $3 million to $5 million according to the *Los Angeles Times*, could be sold by the Dodgers to the Devil Rays so they could move their Class A team to their new spring training site at Port Charlotte.

2. PJ, November 22, 2006. Telephone conversation with Vero Beach City Attorney Charles Vitnuac, April 4, 2007. The city council a year earlier, apparently without coordinating with county officials, had changed the master plan for the airport and rezoned the Dodgertown property such that it could be used for multi-family housing, hotels, and motels. There was a question whether this zoning action increased the salability of the property and hindered the ability of the commission to negotiate with the Dodgers. The city, however, stated that it was merely cleaning up the zoning to reflect what was already there (a conference center with, in essence, a motel), and the Dodgers, if they exercised their option, could have bought it and sold it for development anyway.

3. LAT, February 15, 2007.

4. *Los Angeles Daily News*, March 17, 2007. I witnessed the press conference and afterwards talked with Frank McCourt briefly in the stands during the game that followed. He said that Dodgertown was a beautiful facility and would get a team.

5. LAT, February 24, 2007; March 3, 2007.

Bibliographic Essay

In addition to observing Dodgertown from its inception for almost sixty years, my prime source for this book is former *Pasadena Star-News'* sports editor Joe Hendrickson's unpublished manuscript, "Dodgertown." Joe covered the activities and personalities every spring at Dodgertown for twenty years, ending in the 1980s. A draft copy of his manuscript came from the Dodgertown files. Joe granted rights to the document to the Dodgers, who gave me permission to use it. I added page numbers so that endnotes can be referenced.

In addition to Joe Hendrickson's manuscript, I also consulted newspaper articles, clippings, photographs, and miscellaneous items in the Dodgertown files maintained by the Office of the Vice President, Spring Training and Minor League Facilities, Vero Beach.

The *Vero Beach Press Journal*, originally a weekly newspaper that became a daily by the 1990s, covered the Dodgertown community and the team in great detail from 1947 until the Schuman family sold it to Scripps Howard in 1997. That detailed coverage declined as the paper became more regional. I reviewed over fifty years of the *Press Journal* on microfiche in the Indian River County Library in Vero Beach. I also found selected newspaper articles, some undated, in the Dodgertown files.

Peter O'Malley's gift to the memory of his father, *Walter O'Malley: The Official Website*, contains a substantial section on the history of Dodgertown, written by Brent Shyer, which proved a valuable resource. The *Los Angeles Times* with its eclectic cast of sportswriters provided insights into the team's later years, spring training, and ownership changes.

Three baseball encyclopedias contributed background information for my book, including player biographies and data, the Dodger team's year-by-year records, and World Series descriptions: *Baseball: The Biographical Encyclopedia*, edited by David Pietrusza, Mathew Silverman, and Michael Gershman; *The Sports Encyclopedia: Baseball* by David Neft, Richard Cohen, and Michael Neft; and *The Baseball Encyclopedia*, edited by Rick Wolff. My collection of *Dodger Media Guides* dating back to the 1960s also proved useful. Vero Beach Dodger player statistics and team data come from the *Vero Beach Dodgers, All Time Records, 20th Anniversary*

Edition. The team prepared the publication with statistics from Howe Sports Data International and the assistance of Sam Tuz and longtime scorekeeper Randy Phillips.

Historical data on Vero Beach and Indian River County comes from four main sources: *A History of Indian River County* by Sidney P. Johnston; *Florida's Hibiscus City: Vero Beach* by J. Noble Richards; *Florida's Historic Indian River County* by Charlotte Lockwood; and *U.S. Naval Air Station at Vero Beach* by George W. Gross.

Chapter 1. Brooklyn Dodgers Select Vero

The relationship between Branch Rickey and Jackie Robinson and the obstacles Jackie endured during his first two years with the Dodger organization are covered in *Rickey and Robinson* by Harvey Frommer, *Branch Rickey* by Arthur Mann, and *Jackie Robinson* by Arnold Rampersad. Because I grew up in Vero Beach and remember the community at that time, I offer firsthand descriptions of the Dodgers' original home base. Gross' *U.S. Naval Air Station at Vero Beach* details the history of the base where Dodgertown would be located. *Press Journal* articles and Joe Hendrickson's "Dodgertown" provide details of how the Dodgers and Vero Beach got together. *Off the Record* by Buzzie Bavasi describes Bavasi's initial visit to Vero and the air base.

Chapter 2. The Future of the Brooklyn Baseball Team Is Here

Hendrickson's "Dodgertown" and *Press Journal* articles of the period provide details of Dodgertown's first year, Branch Rickey's direction of the camp, and the Dodgers' first game there. These two sources also convey the excitement generated by the arrival of manager Leo Durocher and his movie star wife Laraine Day, as well as by Leo's meeting with baseball commissioner Happy Chandler. I remember going to Dodgertown almost every day and watching with wonder what was happening. I knew Mr. Rickey from meeting him in my father's sporting goods store.

Chapter 3. Branch Rickey's Kingdom by the Sea

The portrait of Dodgertown in this chapter is drawn with quotations from various sportswriters cited in Hendrickson's "Dodgertown." *The Artful Dodger* by Tommy Lasorda and David Fisher describes Lasorda's arrival at Dodgertown as a rookie. Hendrickson's manuscript and *I Never Had It Made* by Jackie Robinson relate stories about Don Newcombe's and Rachel Robinson's bouts with race issues. Details of the hurricane that stuck Vero Beach and Dodgertown come from my personal recollections.

Chapter 4. Call Me Walter

The story of Bud Holman acquiring the DC-3 for Branch Rickey comes from my interview with Bud Holman's son, Bump, and from Hendrickson's "Dodgertown." *Press Journal* articles and Hendrickson's manuscript provided Dodgertown social notes. In *Tales from the Dodger Dugout*, Carl Erskine chronicles Chuck Connors' performances. *The Era* by Roger Kahn, *The Last Good Season* by Michael Shapiro, and *True Blue* by Steve Delshon are sources that describe the Rickey-O'Malley troubles.

Chapter 5. Grace and the Boys of Summer

Grace Goodermote told me about the joys of being the secretary for Dodgertown. In *Bums*, Peter Golenbock describes Ralph Branca's fall in the Dodgertown lobby and relates the Jackie Robinson–Russ Meyer story. Hendrickson's "Dodgertown" cites Vero restaurateur, Bud Emlet, who related Walter O'Malley's cooking abilities. O'Malley's efforts to build Holman Stadium and the first game held there are covered in detail in *Press Journal* articles. Roger Kahn describes Chuck Dressen's demise in *The Era*, and Duke Snider comments on the feisty manager in *Duke of Flatbush*.

Chapter 6. Champions of the World

Hendrickson narrates the arrival of new manager Walter Alston at Dodgertown, while Bavasi in *Off the Record* describes the Dodgers' losing Roberto Clemente to Branch Rickey and the Pirates. Rex Barney's former wife Carol Moss told me about the pitcher moving to Vero after his career collapsed. Hendrickson's manuscript provides material on the Dodgertown boys' camp and teenager Terry O'Malley's adventures during spring training. Hendrickson also writes about three young pitchers—Karl Spooner, Don Drysdale, and Sandy Koufax—who came to Dodgertown in 1955 and about Red Barber's Dodgertown memories. The story of Bill Letchworth—a local boy who pitched in a Dodgertown game against Drysdale and Koufax—comes from the *Press Journal*, as do Walter O'Malley's interview observations about Vero and the Dodgers. The exuberance in Brooklyn as the Dodgers won their first World Series is captured in articles from the *New York Times*.

Chapter 7. So We're Going

In *The Era*, Kahn recounts Jackie Robinson's departure from the Dodgers. The visit by Los Angeles officials to Dodgertown and the meeting at the Holman ranch is covered in the *New York Times*, Hendrickson's "Dodgertown," *The Dodgers Move West* by Neil J. Sullivan, and *It's Good to Be Alive* by Roy Campanella. (I spent a night at the Holman ranch many years later.) Sullivan's *The Dodgers Move West* and Shapiro's *The Last Good Season* narrate the shenanigans between O'Malley and New York politicians and the dealings with Los Angeles. With no more games to be played at Ebbets Field, Red Barber expresses his feelings about the old ball park in *Rhubarb in the Catbird Seat*.

Chapter 8. Los Angeles Dodgers

Press Journal articles of the period cover the Dodgers' arrival in Los Angeles and follow developments in Vero Beach. In *It's Good to Be Alive*, Campanella discusses his automobile injury and his return to Dodgertown a year later. The Dodger's first-year difficulties in Los Angeles are reported in Sullivan's *The Dodgers Move West* and Delshon's *True Blue*. In Don Drysdale's *Once a Bum, Always a Bum* and Buzzie Bavasi's *Off the Record*, the authors express their feelings about the L.A. situation. *On the Run* by Maury Wills and *Glory Days with the Dodgers* by John Roseboro feature the black players' perspectives on being in Vero Beach. Writer Bob Hunter told Joe Hendrickson about the Dodgers' visit with Castro in Cuba. Delshon's *True Blue* includes Buzzie Bavasi's comments on the Dodger turnaround and the team's 1959 World Series win.

Chapter 9. Dodgers Not Being Booted

Press Journal articles detail the conflict involving the Federal Aviation Administration (FAA), Vero Beach, and the Dodgers. *A Year at a Time* by Walter Alston, *Sandy Koufax* by Jane Leavy, and Delshon's *True Blue* tell the story of Sandy Koufax's adventures at Dodgertown that were the beginning of his success.

Chapter 10. The Dodgers and Vero Prevail

In his *Tales from the Dodger Dugout*, Tommy Davis describes how the black players encouraged the integration of Holman Stadium. *Press Journal* articles document efforts to integrate Indian River County, the continuing battle with the FAA, the final airport resolution with O'Malley's purchasing the Dodgertown property, and Bud Holman's funeral. The *Walter O'Malley Website* highlights the new Dodger Stadium. I attended a game there during its initial season.

Chapter 11. Wins and Losses

The black players' plight in Vero Beach is discussed in Roseboro's *Glory Days with the Dodgers*. Of all the Dodger player biographies, this book probably has the most depth. Leavy's *Sandy Koufax* and Delshon's *True Blue* are my primary sources for descriptions of Koufax's successes, his joint holdout with Drysdale, and his retirement with arm trouble. Hendrickson's "Dodgertown" tells of Walter O'Malley's fun with golf at Dodgertown. In an interview, Dick Bird told me about his relationship with Walter O'Malley and their expansion of the Dodgertown golf facilities.

Chapter 12. Glad the Sixties Were Over

In his *Once a Bum, Always a Bum*, Drysdale talks about his final years with the Dodgers. During our interview, Dr. Hugh McCrystal reminisced about growing up in Brooklyn and moving to Vero. *Press Journal* articles of the time track the ups and downs of the 1960s and their impact on Vero Beach, including the resolution of the integration situation.

Chapter 13. A Team and a Town in Transition

Two of this chapter's Dodgertown Lasorda stories come from Hendrickson's "Dodgertown" and Lasorda and Fisher's *The Artful Dodger*. *Press Journal* articles report on Vero Beach's growth problems and a building moratorium that irritated Walter O'Malley. Marvin Miller in his book *A Whole Different Ball Game* describes attending Walter O'Malley's Saint Patrick's Day party. My interview with Dick Bird, Dodgertown director at the time, is the principal source for the story of tearing down the barracks and adding the Safari Pines golf facilities.

Chapter 14. A New Era

In his autobiography *Garvey*, Steve Garvey explains how he was "born to be a Dodger." Hendrickson's "Dodgertown" shares players' training camp remembrances. Details of the New Orleans Saints' training at Dodgertown come primarily from my own observations. Lasorda and Fisher's *The Artful Dodger* and Delshon's *True Blue* follow Lasorda's arrival, and Walter Alston's retirement, as manager.

Chapter 15. Hail to the Chief

Steve Garvey's relationships at Dodgertown and his clubhouse problems are addressed in *Garvey*. *Press Journal* articles of the time follow Vero Beach's ongoing growth hassles. In my interview with Bobby McCarthy, the restaurateur talked about his association with the Dodgers and his friendship with Tommy Lasorda. In their husband-and-wife collaboration, *The Sally and Tommy John Story: Our Life in Baseball*, Tommy and Sally John discuss how "big league" Dodgertown and the Dodgers were. The lives of Walter and Kay O'Malley are memorialized in the Los Angeles Dodgers publication, *Line Drives*.

Chapter 16. We Love Our Vero Beach Dodgers

Details of the Vero Beach Dodgers' first season come from my personal remembrances and from *Press Journal* articles. The *Press Journal* also covered the unusual cold front that struck Dodgertown, the Buffalo Bills' training at Dodgertown before a play-off game, and the neighborly associations among the town, the Dodgers, and the New Orleans Saints. In his autobiography, Steve Garvey writes about Fernando Valenzuela joining the team.

Chapter 17. Ups and Downs

Press Journal articles of the period track Dodgertown doings. Depictions of pitching phenom Sid Fernandez come from personal observation: I got to see him throw a no-hitter for the Vero Dodgers. *Five O'Clock Comes Early* by Bob Welch and George Vecsey addresses Welch's alcohol problem. Steve Garvey talks about leaving the Dodgers in his autobiography. In *True Blue*, Delshon discusses the breakup of the Garvey-Lopes-Russell-Cey infield and Steve Howe's battle with drugs. Baseball commissioner Peter Uberroth's visit to Dodgertown, Al Campanis' philosophy on developing players, Vero Dodger manager Stan Wasiak's career, and the Dodgers' adopting a school in Vero Beach are all reported in *Press Journal* articles. Peter O'Malley's comments on free agency appeared in the *Los Angeles Times*, and Campanis' remarks about black managers are documented in Delshon's *True Blue*.

Chapter 18. Refuse to Lose

At Dodgertown, columnist Jim Murray of the *Los Angeles Times* assessed Peter O'Malley's situation after the Campanis incident. Outfielder Kirk Gibson shares his reaction to the Dodgers' spring training in *Bottom of the*

Ninth. Los Angeles Times and *Press Journal* articles report on the injured Gibson's "impossible" home run and the Dodgers' winning the World Series. Dodgertown director Charlie Blaney's remarks on the probability of a minor leaguer making the majors are reported in the *Press Journal*, also my source for regional events, including a crime wave that threatened Vero Beach during the 1980s.

Chapter 19. Not for Sale

Peter O'Malley's positions on developing the team, on its not being for sale, and on his loss of power among fellow major league owners are covered in interviews in the *Los Angeles Daily News* and the *Los Angeles Times*. Particulars of Mike Piazza's ascension from Vero Dodger to L.A. Dodger come from reports in *Minor League Memories* magazine, as well as from my personal observations. The description of Holman Stadium's section 17 is based on my experience sitting in that section. Many *Press Journal* articles of the time followed the Disney resort's coming to Vero Beach. The story of Tommy Lasorda's Vero Beach speech comes from my interview with local Dodger fan, Hugh McCrystal.

Chapter 20. Like Leaving Your Spouse after Fifty Years

The aftermath of the '94 strike and the use of replacement players during spring '95 are reported in the *Press Journal*. Descriptions of the Rodriguez and Beltre plays come from personal observation: I was at Holman Stadium when Henry Rodriguez hit four home runs and Adrian Beltre hit his long one. Peter O'Malley's decision to sell the Dodgers and reaction in Vero Beach and Los Angeles come from *Press Journal* and *Los Angeles Times* articles. Further insight into O'Malley's decision appears in *Fred Claire, My 30 Years in Dodger Blue* by Fred Claire.

Chapter 21. The Mystique Is Gone

Press Journal articles document the Dodger sale to Rupert Murdoch's Fox Group with emphasis on activities at Dodgertown. Details of the Piazza trade and the "Father's Day massacre," when Bill Russell and Fred Claire were fired, come from *Los Angeles Times* coverage. Fred Claire's book provides an insider's perspective. New Dodger general manager Kevin Malone's antics are highlighted in *Press Journal* and *Los Angeles Times* reports. Delshon's *True Blue* further illuminates these matters, as well as the Tommy Lasorda–Bill Russell falling out. The Indian River County Chamber of Commerce's Dodger Buyout File, plus my interview with chamber development manager, Milt Thomas, are principal sources of information on Vero Beach's efforts to keep the Dodgers.

Chapter 22. Big, Bad Media Company

Management changes under Fox are reviewed in the 1999 *Dodger Media Guide*. Arizona's efforts to get the Dodgers away from Vero Beach and Florida governor Jeb Bush's veto of financial help for Vero are reported in *Press Journal, Los Angeles Times*, and *Arizona Republic* articles. Financial details come from the Indian River County Chamber of Commerce's Dodger Buyout File. Fox's assigning Bob Daly to run the Dodgers is covered in *Los Angeles Times* articles. The 2000 New Year's Day edition of the *Press Journal* summarizes Vero's eventful year. Additional details of this chaotic time come from *The Dodgers* by Glenn Stout and from Delshon's *True Blue*. A Vero merchant used the apt phrase, "We don't like 'em much anymore."

Chapter 23. We Don't Like 'Em Much Anymore

Portrayal of the Dodgers' state during spring training 2000 is based on my March 28 editorial for the *Press Journal*. Discussions of whether the Dodgers would leave Vero Beach are reported in *Press Journal, Los Angeles Times*, and *Las Vegas Review-Journal* articles. The June 2000 "Memo of Understanding," approved by Indian River County and the City of Vero Beach, defines the local government's $19 million offer, which the Dodgers accepted. In our interview, Craig Callan provided insight into negotiations. The *Los Angeles Times* covered the continuing team chaos as the manager was fired and the general manager was forced to resign. The *Press Journal* reported the community's reaction to the Dodger buyout.

Chapter 24. Fear for the Future

Survival of the Dodger buyout agreement despite the developer's breach of contract is reported in the *Press Journal*, which also covered the end of golf at Dodgertown. *Business Week* profiled Florida and Arizona cities at that time building facilities for major league teams. Craig Callan's presentation to the Indian River County Historical Society on Dodgertown history provided details of Dodgertown's new look and its addition of an administration building. Fox's decision to sell the Dodgers to the sole bidder, Boston developer Frank McCourt, is documented in the *Los Angeles Times*.

Chapter 25. What's Up Next, Skip?

Los Angeles Times and *Press Journal* articles report on the new owners, Frank and Jamie McCourt; their selection of a new general manager, Paul DePodesta; and their missteps during spring training as the former Dodger management departed. *Moneyball* by Michael Lewis describes the Billy Beane philosophy, which DePodesta espoused during his time with the Oakland A's. Details of 2004 spring training come from personal experience. With a press pass granting me the privileges of beat writers, I was able to observe spring training far more closely than in the past. I went on the field during batting practice, visited with people in the press box, joined the writers interviewing players in the clubhouse, and asked Jim Tracy questions during postgame meetings in his office. The 2006 *Dodger Media Guide* supplied the statistics for the players on a successful Vero Beach Dodger team. *Los Angeles Times* articles covered DePodesta's player shake-up at midseason, the winning of the West, and the play-off loss. Details of the two hurricanes that damaged Indian River County and Dodgertown come from the *Press Journal* and from personal experience.

Chapter 26. The Ugly and the Lovely

DePodesta's wintertime assembly of an almost entirely new team is covered in *Los Angeles Times* and *New York Times* articles. Fay Vincent's observations come from the former baseball commissioner's talk at a Dodgertown meeting of the Society for American Baseball Research (SABR) and from my chat with him at a later date as he sat in a golf cart on the field before a game. Dodger historian Mark Langill, who was in residence at Dodgertown, offered significant general information about the team. Spring training details come from personal observation: With a press pass for another season, I again viewed activities close-up, particularly the game with the Boston Red Sox. I saw rookie Jason Repko make a great catch. A conversation with Jim Tracy after the last spring game provided specifics about his 2005 team. The *Los Angeles Times* covered the 2005 season, with the *Press Journal* providing Vero Beach–related details.

Chapter 27. Like Brooklyn, a Fond Memory

The 2006 *Dodger Media Guide* provides biographical details on Nick Colletti and Grady Little, as well as information about Colletti's player acquisitions. The *Los Angeles Times* reported on the Jacksonville players, the new atmosphere in the clubhouse, and the McCourts' final financial arrangements. Tidbits about spring training come from notes in my scorebook. Tony Jackson in the *Los Angeles Daily News* wrote of the "whispers" of a possible move by the Dodgers, and the *Press Journal* dealt with the latest overtures from Arizona.

Afterword

The afterword is based on clippings from the *Press Journal*, the *Los Angeles Daily News*, and the *Los Angeles Times*, as well as informal conversations with local officials and personal observation.

References

Archives

Dodgertown files, Office of the Vice President, Spring Training and Minor League Facilities, Vero Beach, Fla.

Vero Beach Press Journal files and Indian River County Historical Society photograph file, Archive and Genealogy Center, Indian River County Library, Vero Beach, Fla.

Books

Alston, Walter, with Jack Tobin. *A Year at a Time.* Waco, Tex.: Word Books, 1976.

Barber, Red, and Robert Creamer. *Rhubarb in the Catbird Seat.* Lincoln, Neb.: University of Nebraska Press, 1979.

Barney, Rex, with Norman Macht. *Rex Barney's Thank Youuuu for 50 Years in Baseball from Brooklyn to Baltimore.* Centerville, Md.: Tidewater, 1993.

Bavasi, Buzzie, with John Strege. *Off the Record.* Chicago: Contemporary Books, 1987.

Burk, Robert. *Much More Than a Game: Players, Owners, & American Baseball Since 1921.* Chapel Hill: University of North Carolina Press, 2001.

Campanella, Roy. *It's Good to Be Alive.* Boston: Little, Brown, 1959.

Claire, Fred, with Steve Springer. *Fred Claire, My 30 Years in Dodger Blue.* Chicago: Sports Publishing, 2004.

Davis, Tommy, with Paul Gutierrez. *Tales from the Dodger Dugout.* Chicago: Sports Publishing, 2005.

Delshon, Steve. *True Blue: The Dramatic History of the Los Angeles Dodgers Told by the Men Who Lived It.* New York: Perennial, 2002.

Dodger Media Guides. Los Angeles: Los Angeles Dodgers, 1999–2006.

Drysdale, Don, with Bob Verdi. *Once a Bum, Always a Bum: My Life in Baseball from Brooklyn to Los Angeles.* New York, 1990.

Erskine, Carl. *Carl Erskine's Tales from the Dodger Dugout.* Champaign, Ill.: Sports Publishing, 2004.

Frommer, Harvey. *Rickey and Robinson: The Men Who Broke Baseball's Color Barrier.* New York: Macmillan, 1982.

Garvey, Steve, with Skip Rosen. *Garvey.* New York: Times Books, 1986.

Gibson, Kirk, with Lynn Henning. *Bottom of the Ninth.* Chelsea, Minn.: Sleeping Bear Press, 1997.

Golenbock, Peter. *Bums: An Oral History of the Brooklyn Dodgers.* Chicago: Contemporary Books, 2000.

Gross, George. *U.S. Naval Air Station at Vero Beach, Florida, During Word War II*. Vero Beach: Florida Historical Society, 2002.

Hendrickson, Joe. "Dodgertown." Unpublished manuscript. 1982. Dodgertown files, Office of the Vice President, Spring Training and Minor League Facilities, Vero Beach, Fla.

John, Sally, and Tommy John. *The Sally and Tommy John Story: Our Life in Baseball*. New York: Macmillan, 1983.

Johnston, Sidney P. *A History of Indian River County*. Vero Beach: Indian River Historical Society, 2000.

Kahn, Roger. *The Boys of Summer*. New York: Harper & Row, 1971.

———. *The Era: 1947–1957, When the Yankees, the Giants, and the Dodgers Ruled the World*. New York: Ticknor & Fields, 1993.

Langill, Mark. *Dodgertown*. Charleston, S.C.: Arcadia, 2004.

Lasorda, Tommy, and David Fisher. *The Artful Dodger*. New York: Arbor House, 1985.

Leavy, Jane. *Sandy Koufax: A Lefty's Legacy*. New York: HarperCollins, 2002.

Lewis, Michael. *Moneyball: The Art of Winning an Unfair Game*. New York: W. W. Norton, 2003.

Line Drives: Official Publication of the Los Angeles Dodgers. Los Angeles: Los Angeles Dodgers, 1979.

Lockwood, Charlotte. *Florida's Historic Indian River County*. Vero Beach: Media Tronics, 1975.

Mann, Arthur. *Branch Rickey: American in Action*. Boston: Houghton Mifflin, 1957.

McCue, Andy. "Dodgertown." *Road Trips: A Trunkload of Great Articles from Two Decades of Convention Journals*. New York: Society for American Baseball Research, 2004.

Miller, Marvin. *A Whole Different Ball Game: The Inside Story of Baseball's New Deal*. New York: Simon and Schuster, 1992.

Neft, David, Richard Cohen, and Michael Neft. *The Sports Encyclopedia: Baseball*. New York: St. Martin's Griffin, 2004.

Oliphant, Thomas. *Praying for Gil Hodges: A Memoir of the 1955 World Series and One Family's Love of the Brooklyn Dodgers*. New York: St. Martin's, 2005.

Parrott, Harold. *The Lords of Baseball: A Wry Look at a Side of the Game the Fan Seldom Sees, the Front Office*. Atlanta: Longstreet, 2001.

Pietrusza, David, Matthew Silverman, and Michael Gershman, eds. *Baseball: The Biographical Encylopedia*. New York: Total Sports, 2000.

Rampersad, Arnold. *Jackie Robinson: A Biography*. New York: Knopf, 1997.

Richards, J. Noble. *Florida's Hibiscus City: Vero Beach*. Melbourne, Fla.: Brevard Graphics, 1968.

Robinson, Jackie, with Alfred Duckett. *I Never Had It Made*. New York: Ecco, 1995.

Robinson, Rachel, with Lee Daniels. *Jackie Robinson, An Intimate Portrait*. New York: Abrams, 1996.

Roseboro, John, with Bill Liddy. *Glory Days with the Dodgers, and Other Days with Others*. New York: Atheneum, 1978.

Shapiro, Michael. *The Last Good Season: Brooklyn, the Dodgers, and Their Final Pennant Race Together*. New York: Doubleday, 2003.

Snider, Duke, with Bill Gilbert. *Duke of Flatbush*. New York: Citadel, 2002.

Stout, Glenn. *The Dodgers: 120 Years of Dodgers Baseball*. Boston: Houghton Mifflin, 2004.

Sullivan, Neil J. *The Dodgers Move West*. New York: Oxford University Press, 1987.

Vero Beach Dodgers, All Time Records, 20th Anniversary Edition. Vero Beach, Fla.: Vero Beach Dodgers, 2000.

Welch, Bob, and George Vecsey. *Five O'Clock Comes Early: A Young Man's Battle with Alcoholism*. New York: Morrow, 1982.

Wills, Maury, and Mike C. Celizic. *On the Run: The Never Dull and Often Shocking Life of Maury Wills*. New York: Carroll & Graf, 1991.

Wolff, Rick, ed. *The Baseball Encyclopedia*. New York: Macmillan, 1993.

Index

McCourt, Jamie, x, 230; description of, 232, 268n21, 268n22; and Dodgertown interview, 220. *See also* McCourt, Frank

McCrystal, Hugh, xiii, 106, 147, 171

McDonald, Mary Beth, 187

McGraw, John, 123, 146

McGwire, Mark, 198

McKee Jungle Gardens (Vero Beach), 4, 16, 40, 252n2

McKeever, Ed, 33, 34, 42, 64, 114, 119

McKeever, Steve, 33, 34, 42, 64, 114, 119

McKenzie, Reggie, 140

McMitchell, Les, 50

McNulty, Ray, 242

McPhail, Larry, 34, 35, 212

Mecom, John, Jr., 120, 141

Megargee, Steve, 221, 235

Melbourne, Fla., 107, 119, 234

Mennenger Clinic, 32

Merrill Barber Bridge (Vero Beach), 7, 41, 169, 179, 244

Merriman, Lester, 82

Mesa, Ariz., 44

Messersmith, Andy, 119

Mets. *See* New York Mets

Mexico, 7, 84, 141, 152

Mexico City, 91, 211

Meyer, Russ, 46, 53

Miami, Fla., 20, 31, 36, 37, 39, 105, 169, 174, 183; spring training at, 8, 22, 26, 55, 160

Miami Dolphins, 120

Miami Herald, 26, 39

Miami Stadium, 26, 55, 56

Miller, Betty, 116

Miller, Lemmie, 142

Miller, Marvin, 114

Miller, Roland, 18, 83

Milwaukee Braves, 46, 58, 64, 65

Minneapolis Millers, 55

Minor League Team of the Year, 240

Missouri City, Tex., 211

Modesti, Kevin, 164

Monday, Rick, ix, 123, 141

Mondesi, Raul, 152, 168, 182, 191, 194

Moneyball, 217

Monroe, Marilyn, 254n18

Montreal Royals, 15, 61; and Jackie Robinson, 3, 6; players at, 32, 36, 49; training at Dodgertown, 10, 20, 21, 46

Moon, Wally, 158, 187

Moorings (Vero Beach), 106, 169, 171

Morgan, Bobby, 23

Morgan, Mrs. Bobby, 54

Morrow, Cole, 96

Moses, Robert, 64, 68, 69

Moss, Carol, 49

Most Valuable Player (MVP) award, 27, 88, 91, 120, 156

Mota, Guillermo, 175, 211, 223

Mota, Manny, 108, 111, 139, 152, 158, 221, 270n1

Mulvey, Ann. *See* Branca, Mrs. Ralph

Mulvey, Jim: and Brooklyn, 64, 106, 253n3; as Dodger director, 33, 34; at Dodgertown, 40, 61, 92

Mulvey, Mrs. Jim (Dearie), 34, 79, 106

Mulvey, Steve, xiii, 33, 223, 253n3

Mulvey Award, 106, 119, 168, 175, 181, 223, 233, 241

Municipal Airport Terminal (Vero Beach), 77, 86

Murdoch, Rupert, x, 177, 181, 188, 193, 211–13, 215, 218. *See also* Fox

Murray, Eddie, 158, 238

Murray, Jim, 104, 154

Myers, Kenny, 81

Nashua, N.H., farm club, 9, 36, 47, 48

Nassau, Bahamas, 144

National Football League, 120, 140, 148, 213, 245

National Guard, 225. *See also* Brooklyn National Guard

National League, 45, 65, 124; in the 1940s and 1950s, 21, 33, 34, 52, 64, 65, 69; in the 1960s and 1970s, 102, 104, 119, 122, 124, 128, 139; in the 1980s, 149, 156; the Dodgers as league champions in the 1940s, 7, 27; in the 1950s, 46, 56, 58, 73; in the 1960s, 91, 96, 102; in the 1970s, 120, 123, 125; in the 1980s, 142, 156–57; and the Dodgers as wild-card winners, 175, 245. *See also* Manager of the Year award; Most Valuable Player award; Rookie of the Year award

National League West Division, 104, 113, 114,

122, 140; and the Dodgers as winners, 125, 147, 149, 156, 171, 174, 223, 225, 226

Naval Air Station. *See* Vero Beach Naval Air Station

NBC (National Broadcasting Corporation), 103, 124

Neuberger, Art, 113, 201, 210

Nevada, 78, 187, 199

Newcombe, Don: as Dodger executive, 68, 144; and integration, 25, 26, 35, 86, 107, 108; as player, 27, 36, 49, 53, 68, 144, 236

New Orleans, La., 8

New Orleans Saints, 120, 131, 140–42, 148, 209

News Corporation, 177, 182, 189

New York City, 4, 34, 35, 41, 47, 60, 140; and the Dodger move to Los Angeles; 59, 64–66, 68, 69, 73, 254n31; and Dodger writers from, 11, 15, 22, 23, 36, 39, 63; on flying to, 9, 10, 52, 53, 56

New York City Board of Estimates, 65, 66

New York Daily News, 15, 47

New York Giants, 21, 43, 60; Dodger rivalry with, 38, 49, 52

New York Herald Tribune, 39

New York Mets, 114, 157, 185, 245; at Dodgertown, 156, 204, 218, 219, 221, 222, 229, 241; players with, 142, 145, 146, 155, 166, 211, 219; at Port Saint Lucie, 103, 160, 187, 211, 234

New York Post, 211, 230

New York State, 8, 20, 44, 50, 64, 134

New York State League, 70

New York Times, 7, 49, 61, 228

New York Yankees, 51, 73, 82, 190, 213, 229, 239; at Dodgertown, 15, 55, 85, 124, 126, 148, 173, 207, 212; players with, 26, 90, 127, 190, 214; and World Series losses, ix, 56, 57, 91, 142; and World Series wins, 7, 34, 47, 58, 102, 124, 125

Ng, Kim, 230

NHL (National Hockey League), 245

Nicaragua, 181

Niedenfuer, Tom, 144

9/11 attacks, 206

Nixon, Trot, 232

No-hit games, 27, 81, 88, 145, 208

Nolan, Dick, 120

Nomo, Hideo, 172–74, 181, 207, 223

Norristown, Pa., 165

Norton, J. B., 157, 159, 160

Oakland A's, 120, 144, 157, 216, 217, 240, 281

Ocean Grill (Vero Beach), 16, 23, 49, 100, 120

Oceanside Business Association (Vero Beach), 188

Offerman, Jose, 152, 159, 168

Offutt, Harry, 78, 83, 84

Oh, Sadaharu, 79, 80, 140

Ohio, 47, 48, 70, 119, 203

Olson, Eric, 119

Olson, Norris, xiii, 119

Olympics, 149, 181

Omaha, Neb., farm team, 96

O'Malley, Kay, 35, 85, 113, 128; in Vero Beach, 18, 37, 92, 98, 112, 128–30

O'Malley, Peter, 60, 119; advancing in the Dodger organization, 93, 106, 112, 113, 120, 121; as Dodger president/CEO, 127, 147, 148, 150, 154, 163, 164, 169, 228; and Dodgertown, 99, 108, 116, 117, 122, 157, 183, 197, 252n2, 255n6; early years at Dodgertown, 18, 50, 79, 83, 90, 92, 99, 124; and major league baseball, 164, 171, 181; and the McCourts' purchase, 213, 214, 218; and the NFL, 175, 213; and racial matters, 60, 85, 153; selling the Dodgers, 131, 175–78, 182, 183, 189, 207

O'Malley, Terry. *See* Seidler, Terry O'Malley

O'Malley, Walter, 85, 86, 109, 113, 147, 253n3; and the 1955 World Championship, 56, 57, 59; and the Baseball Hall of Fame, 130, 211, 212, 267n20; and the battle with the FAA and City of Vero Beach, 77, 78, 82, 83, 93, 166; and Branch Rickey, 19, 33, 35, 243, 251n13; changing and expanding Dodgertown, 35, 37, 38, 44, 49, 115, 131, 201; death of, 128–31; and Dodger ownership, 34, 47, 119; at Dodgertown, 91, 98, 100, 105, 116, 119, 128, 131; and the Dodgertown Saint Patrick's Day party, 40, 101, 112, 114; early years of, 34, 35; golf at Dodgertown, 97–100, 101, 111; leaving Brooklyn, 59, 63–65, 254n31; and Los Angeles, 60, 61, 63, 65–67, 69, 73, 176; and racial matters, 60, 117; and Vero Beach, 18, 30, 44, 46, 52, 55,

Thompson, Fresco, 13, 50; and Dodgertown, 23, 24, 26, 37, 40, 50, 51, 58, 59, 153; as Dodger vice president, 52, 106
Thompson, Jim, 128
Thompson, Mrs. Fresco, 37
Thomson, Bobby, 38, 42, 89
Tokyo Giants, 59, 79, 80, 102, 140, 209
Tomko, Brett, 239, 241
Tommy John Surgery. *See* John, Tommy
Topps Company, 228, 269n4
Torborg, Jeff, ix
Toronto Blue Jays, 194, 216, 265n6
Tracy, Jim: and Paul DePodesta, 218, 225, 227, 236, 237; as Dodger manager, 203, 205, 207, 208, 212, 226, 228; at Dodgertown, 191, 210, 211, 220–22, 233, 234
Trent, Tom, 44
Tripson, Barbara, 16, 167
Truman, Harry, 3

Uberroth, Peter, 149
Union Oil of California, 131

Van Cuyk, Chris, 26
Vero Beach, 21, 23, 27, 48, 55, 60, 103, 104, 130, 141, 143, 202, 216, 220, 230; and community feeling for Dodgers, x–xii, 35, 44, 45, 52, 57, 58, 66, 77, 92, 93, 102, 128, 152, 160, 166, 177, 248; Dodger feelings toward, 15, 16, 18, 26, 27, 32, 37, 39, 42, 52, 63, 67, 78, 79, 100, 141, 167, 168; and the Dodgers arrival, 3, 5, 7–10, 21, 45, 52, 244; first Dodger game at, 17–20; growth and economics of, 7, 8, 22, 42, 55, 106, 113, 126, 131, 132, 149, 150, 157, 169, 172, 178, 179; history of, 3–5, 18, 55, 139, 249n2, 250n14, 252n11; and the impact of Fox sale, 170, 177, 181–83, 185, 187, 188, 190–94, 199, 204; and integration, 37, 85, 87, 95, 114; and the McCourts, 212, 232, 269n19; and move to Glendale, 242, 248; and move to Los Angeles, 61–63, 65, 68; player relationships with, 49, 53, 54, 125, 158, 180, 222; publicity for, 15, 32, 41, 50; turmoil and crimes in, 107, 160, 198. *See also*: Callan, Craig; Hurricanes; Piper Aircraft; Vero Beach Naval Air Station
Vero Beach, City of, 9, 38, 113, 147, 149, 228,

235; Dodger leases with, 42, 55, 56; and Dodger Pines, 99, 121, 205; and the Dodgertown buyout, x, 199, 200, 207, 270n1; and the FAA, 73, 77, 78, 82, 83, 91, 176. *See also* Barber, Merrill; Ebbets Field #2; Offutt, Harry; Sturgis, Jack; Taylor, Rex; Vocelle, L. B. "Buck"
Vero Beach Country Club, 16, 32, 41, 58, 189, 244
Vero Beach Devil Rays, 248
Vero Beach Dodgers, 137, 147, 159, 185, 209; attendance, 136, 141, 143, 191; community support for, 136, 137, 139, 164; and the first season, 131, 132, 135, 138; and FSL playoffs and championships, 147, 148, 151, 164, 166, 178, 224, 235; general managers and managers of, 145, 152, 164, 169, 175, 184, 205, 213; and the move to California, 245, 270n1; and outstanding performances, 146, 164, 159, 178, 213, 235; and players who made the majors, 138, 144, 145, 147, 148, 150, 152, 158, 159, 164, 165, 175, 178, 191, 208, 219, 221, 233, 235, 245. *See also* Florida State League; Holman Stadium; Wasiak, Stan
Vero Beach Exchange Club, 120
Vero Beach High School, 46, 99; and Dodgertown, 17, 18, 45, 46, 52, 141; and integration, 108
Vero Beach Jaycees, 16, 18
Vero Beach Junior High, 128, 230
Vero Beach Junior Women's Club, 124
Vero Beach Naval Air Station: and the Dodgers, 6, 7, 9, 11, 13, 21, 31, 32, 42, 52, 244; during World War II, xii, 4, 5, 16, 19, 46
Vero Beach Police, 24, 187, 198
Vero Beach Press Journal: activities of, 10, 102, 136, 137, 200, 235; columns, 31, 44, 131, 212; editorials, 52, 138, 152, 177, 203, 206, 228, 232, 242; history of, xii, 178; reporters and staff of, 31, 78, 87, 131, 159, 212, 221, 247; reports by, 10, 18, 19, 22, 37, 44, 54, 57, 61, 78, 94, 149, 170, 183, 192, 194, 198, 204, 215, 232, 246; special Dodger features and editions, 83, 122, 180, 181, 185, 202. *See also* Schuman, John (J. J.); Schuman, John, Jr.
Vero Isles, 7

Rody Johnson has followed the Dodgers since their arrival in Vero Beach in 1948 when he was a teenager. After a career in the aerospace industry, he became publisher of the *Vero Beach Sun* and the *Sebastian Sun* community newspapers. He is the author of *Different Battles* and *In Their Footsteps*. He and his artist wife Katharine live in Vero Beach and Lewisburg, West Virginia. When not writing, he kayaks and fly fishes.